Doing Research
with Children

Second edition

Anne Greig
Jayne Taylorand
Tommy MacKay

SAGE Publications
Los Angeles ▪ London ▪ New Delhi ▪ Singapore

This second edition first published 2007
First published 1999, reprinted 1999, 2001, 2002, 2004, 2006

SAGE Publications Ltd
1 Oliver's Yard
55 City Road
London EC1Y 1SP

SAGE Publications Inc.
2455 Teller Road
Thousand Oaks, California 91320

SAGE Publications India Pvt Ltd
B 1/I 1 Mohan Cooperative Industrial Area
Mathura Road, New Delhi 110 044
India

SAGE Publications Asia-Pacific Pte Ltd
33 Pekin Street #02-01
Far East Square
Singapore 048763

British Library Cataloguing in Publication data

A catalogue record for this book is available
from the British Library

ISBN 978 1 4129 1844 2
ISBN 978 1 4129 1845 9 (pbk)

Library of Congress Control Number: 2006931122

Typeset by C&M Digitals (P) Ltd., Chennai, India
Printed and bound in Great Britain by Athenaeum Press, Gateshead
Printed on paper from sustainable resources

This book is dedicated to the memory of our parents

Contents

List of figures

List of boxes

List of tables

Acknowledgements

To Sue and Neil who know what it is like to live with me but are too polite to tell everybody — Tommy

To Gordon who, after living with me for so many years and so many projects, deserves to know that he wonderful — Anne

Part I

The special nature of children in research – theories and approaches

Introduction to research and children: a special relationship

The aims of this chapter are:

- To introduce the nature of research with children and why research with child participants is different from research with adults.
- To explore the training and education issues in the acquisition of research skills.
- To identify major research themes involving children.

Take two biologically similar children and rear them in different environments and they will most certainly differ in terms of their behaviour, their physique, their motivation and their achievements. Take two biologically different children and rear them together, giving them similar opportunities and experiences, and they too will differ. It is these puzzling phenomena that have prompted scholars from the fields of psychology, biology, sociology, health and education to undertake research with child participants in order to understand what makes children behave as they do. The body of knowledge built up over the past hundred years has meant that we have entered the twenty-first century with an amazing amount of insight into the minds and behaviours of the children that many of us work with every day. Those of us working in this era carry a great debt of gratitude to the painstaking work of those scholars who have spent their lives helping us to understand children better so that we may be more effective in our work.

When we wrote the first edition of this book our clear intention was to ensure that the 1990s and beyond was not seen as a stagnant time in terms of research with children. Our intention in writing this second edition remains the same. The body of research that we have shows us that this is not an ill-founded intention. There were many periods throughout the last century where the acquisition of new knowledge seemed to be limited, while at other times knowledge acquisition gained an impetus which was staggering. A brief resumé of some of the major research themes will be discussed later in this chapter. While it is important that we are grateful for the knowledge we have, we must, however, ensure that we are always moving forward, always searching and always pursuing greater understanding.

There are many, many ways of achieving new knowledge, but the key to this achievement, regardless of the field we work in, is training. We acknowledge that few of our readers will go on to make pure research their living, but we also recognise that professional people, both during initial training and after qualifying, need a sound knowledge of how to apply research and how to undertake research. This book is about applying research practically and undertaking research practically. It is essentially a practical book which is specifically designed for professionals who work, or intend to work, with children and who have to undertake research as part of their education or who need to undertake research, even on a very small scale, as part of their professional lives.

This book is also practical in that it recognises the reality of studying child participants in the further pursuit of knowledge. Children do not exist in vacuums and their lives are naturally complex; they have to be if children are to arrive in adulthood with the repertoire of skills and behaviours which are essential for modern living. We have therefore taken an holistic perspective of the child and the child's environment, recognising that research training must be cognisant of the many variables that influence development and behaviour. We have drawn from the fields of psychology, sociology, biology, education and health in our discussions about research and in our considerations of child participants. We are explicit in our acknowledgement that children are special, and that research and research training which involves children must also be special.

Not only are children special but they also hold a very special place in society. While some of the research undertaken in pursuit of gaining understanding of children has been appalling in terms of what children have been expected to do and suffer, the majority of work has been undertaken sensitively and has followed correct ethical principles. We will focus on this theme in Chapter 9 but should give recognition in this opening section to the distinctive position children hold in contemporary society. This has not always been the case, however, or at least that is the impression one is left with when studying historical perspectives of child care. As we will discuss later in the chapter, the child of today has rights which are universally held, widely adhered to and in most Western societies are monitored by legislation.

Children are special

As we have briefly mentioned above, children are very special people. Defining what we mean by special is, however, a complex and difficult task. Perhaps what we mean is that children are different from the adults who control and describe the world as we know it. Perhaps it is because children are necessary for the survival of our species. Perhaps it is because children are an enigma – we don't understand so many things about them and they therefore puzzle us. Perhaps it is none or all of these things. What is evident is that children have, from biblical times to the present day, been singled out to varying extents as being exceptional beings who have been afforded special consideration. Children are seen as an outward celebration of life, as the next generation and as the future of mankind. They also eventually grow and develop into adults, which perhaps gives us further insight into why they are considered special. The famous and infamous names from our history lessons at school were all once children themselves, which leads us to wonder why they developed in the way they did.

Special and very special

It is not the intention of this book to give a potted history of the place of children in society – there are many texts which adequately fulfil that aim. However, because we wish to focus upon doing research with children, we must spend a few moments looking at the child within our society so that we can explore the wider contexts of research.

People have children for a number of reasons, which are not always easy to define. They are seen, by some, as desirable assets, as insurance to provide for them in their old age, as a sign of their fertility. Some religions dictate that the purpose of marriage is for the procreation of children, and indeed in seventeenth century England childlessness was even considered to be a judgement against sin (see Fraser 1984). Whatever the reason, on a macro level any society must ensure that it reproduces itself if it is to survive. On an individual level many cultures hold the expectation that adults will eventually marry and produce children. There are also those who have children because they do not believe in the use of, or do not have access to, reliable contraception.

Whether people have children by accident or by design, once born they have certain rights which are upheld by law. Children have the fundamental right to life, and child murderers can expect and receive the severest of punishment. Children also have the right to protection from harm and from neglect, they have the right to go to school and receive an education among other things. In the UK, the Children Acts of 1989 and 2004 in England and Wales and the parallel legislation in Scotland and Northern Ireland, together with several charters, including the Convention on the Rights of the Child (UNICEF 1989), detail explicitly the rights of children, as we will discuss in following chapters. Rights, however, only lay down the minimum expectations society holds for its children. For the majority of parents and people within society, children are their future and they strive to ensure that the mistakes of one generation do not extend to the next. People generally want for children those things they did not have themselves: they want children to have more opportunities, less hardship, more success and so on.

In order to ensure that children attain what society wishes for them, each generation must be analysed and evaluated and steps taken to rectify past mistakes. We must have understanding of children and how they develop, what factors adversely affect their progress and what factors will best promote their optimum development. Gaining this understanding is the driving force behind past, present and future research with children and crosses all professional boundaries. Geneticists, biologists, psychologists, educationists and sociologists have all striven for this greater understanding of children, albeit with differing philosophies, research traditions and methodologies.

If we accept the special status of all children within society we must also recognise that there are many children who, for a variety of reasons, must be considered to be very special. These children differ from their peers because, for example, they are exceptionally gifted or because of a physical or psychological dysfunction or because they are particularly vulnerable. These children have been, and are, the focus of a great deal of research activity which aims to discover why they are different, and the effects of their difference in terms of their present and future development. What we should emphasise here is that their rights and our responsibilities as researchers and professionals remain at least the same as for all children. In many cases, undertaking research with these very special children requires even greater training, as we will discuss in the following section. A particular challenge for the researcher is that of balancing the need for children's participation and inclusion in research activity with the need to protect very vulnerable children. We discuss this more fully in Chapters 8 and 9.

Special but not new

It is very easy for a new generation to fall into the trap of making assumptions about the past. Professionals will generally, as part of their training, study aspects of the history of their profession and will gasp in horror at how children were treated. Take for example, the past practice of separating sick children from their parents during hospitalisation because it was felt that parents upset children, or the punishment meted out to children in schools for the good of their 'moral' development. The important point to recognise here is that these things happened not because those professionals did not view children as special, but because they did. It is only when common practices are questioned that change occurs, otherwise the status quo will persist endlessly. We should not think ourselves superior in any way, for without doubt our own professional practices will be questioned in years to come. We can only ensure that we do our best to question all our practices and strive, as far as possible, to base our practice on sound research and evidence. This involves two different, but related notions. First, all professionals have a responsibility to ensure that they are aware of current research, can intelligently interpret it and incorporate sound research into practice. This will be discussed fully in Chapter 4. Second, we should all constantly ask questions, and where there is a lack of research we should encourage investigation (see Chapter 2 for further discussion). This may mean undertaking research ourselves or enabling and facilitating others to do so. However, such activity requires training, particularly when the research involves children (as we shall discover during the rest of this book), because, as we have already said many times, children are special.

Training for research

As all the professions move towards *all graduate* status, in the future all profession-als who qualify should have undertaken some research training. This is seen by many as a positive benefit of raising the academic expectation of initial training programmes. There are those, however, who find the notion challenging, and one of the concerns frequently raised is that graduate programmes lead to far too much small scale research being undertaken in practice areas by students. This is only one area of the wider debate which we will focus on in the following section.

A significant proportion of professions, the notable exceptions being teaching and nursing, require that those who enter will undergo generic training before specialising with children. Generic training aims to ensure a broad base of knowledge and in many instances gives the professional a 'taster' of work with a variety of groups, including different age groups. Research training has also tended to be generic, with little consideration given to the differences between undertaking research with child or adult participants. There are, however, very important differences. Children are not miniature adults nor, as we have already stated, do they exist in isolation. The social and emotional relationships of the child are more fluid than at any other time of the lifespan and cannot be ignored. For example, studying the child in a laboratory situation without also studying the child in the naturalistic setting will limit the understanding gained (Dunn 1996; Greene and Hill 2005). We will explore this further later on.

It is also important to differentiate between the study of children in general and the study of those children whom we have defined as very special. All chil-dren, for all sorts of reasons, are vulnerable, and this vulnerability is heightened in some children. These children are already in many ways often singled out because they are different, which is frequently what makes them attractive and interesting research participants. Researchers who study these children do, how-ever, require special skills so as not to accentuate differences overtly to the detri-ment of the particular child. The avoidance of harm necessitates particular skills in terms of understanding the nature of childhood, possessing knowledge about issues such as informed consent and, not least, being sensitive to differences. Schaffer (1998) discusses this point and questions past practices of focusing on negative aspects of differences. The current trend of moving away from investigating the negative effects of difference exhibited by some children and towards a focus upon the resilience of similar children is a welcome development (see also Lewis and Kellett 2005).

Research awareness versus research skills

Research training is a far broader concept than undertaking a small survey or experiment. We mentioned in our introduction that research training also involves applying research to our practice, and this is probably the more important skill. There is little point in belonging to a profession which has a sound research base if current research is not integrated into our practice. If the research is ignored and not acted upon, not only will a great deal of research time and money be wasted, but children and their families will continue to receive care that is less than they deserve.

In many instances, a profession's research base relies on experienced researchers, often located within university departments, undertaking research that produces recommendations which should then be put into place by practitioners. This is explored further in Chapter 4. The point is that both research skills and research awareness are needed, but for most practitioners it is the skill of being able to incorporate research into their practice which becomes paramount. Practice should be evidence-based but the evidence does not need to be derived from personal research but from a wider knowledge of research being undertaken within, and outwith, a profession and how it can inform practice.

Small scale research – how valuable?

As we have mentioned above, there is concern about the volume of small scale research which is being undertaken generally, and for those of us who focus upon children in our professional lives, this is a very important issue. Small scale research that is not communicated to the rest of our profession could lead to the duplication of effort, with the potential for many individuals to investigate similar problems over and over again – the proverbial 'reinventing the wheel'. The continual re-investigation of a particular issue does not broaden a profession's knowledge base nor does it advance practice. There is also the potential for wasting valuable and often scarce resources.

There are times, however, when small scale research is appropriate and indeed where it is both desirable and valuable: for example, where a localised problem is identified or where a previous study has poor external validity (see Chapter 5) but the professional recognises that the findings may be applicable to their own practice. In this case it would certainly be of value to replicate a study to discover whether the findings are similar in a different setting. Recommendations can then be safely incorporated into practice because the evidence supports their incorporation.

There is also debate about what constitutes a small scale study. Traditionally, the 'smallness' related to the size of a particular sample, but in more recent years this view has been challenged. For example, a case study may focus on a single child or family but may be extremely complex in terms of what it proposes and very influential to practice. An early example is Axline's *Dibs: In Search of Self* (1964), which is a published study of one child's personality development through play therapy and provides a wealth of detail which can inform practice. Case studies are of immense value to the professions, particularly when they provide a wealth of detail and when a child perhaps portrays a rare behaviour. They may focus upon a single participant or a small sample but provide an excellent means of understanding complex phenomena (Yin 2003). We will discuss the case study in Chapter 7.

We should always be aware, however, that small scale research cannot generally replace studies conducted on a larger scale designed to lead to generalisable knowledge and recommendations.

Interprofessional research skills

We have mentioned above that training for research with children should be different from training for research with adults. A further complication is that the care of children is rarely a uniprofessional activity and yet there is a wide diversity of what professionals are taught and consequently a diversity of opinion about research. Research traditions tend to exist in most professions, ranging from the positivistic, deductive approaches favoured for example by doctors and pharmacists to the more qualitative, inductive approaches favoured by social scientists, many nurses and some teachers (see Chapter 3). If we are to take a truly holistic approach to caring for children and consequently researching with children, it is important that a more interprofessional approach is adopted. Not only do professionals in contemporary practice need to be aware of their own research traditions, they should also be skilled in recognising and valuing the research traditions of colleagues outwith their profession.

One of the greatest hurdles to overcome here is the rigid and hierarchical perspective which some professions hold in relation to methodologies. Yin (2003) discusses this issue and suggests that a more appropriate view of research methodologies is a pluralistic one. Different research strategies can be employed in different ways and rigidity only serves to hamper innovation. For example, case studies, according to Yin, can utilise exploratory, descriptive and explanatory strategies, just as experiments (traditionally seen as the only way of finding causal relationships) can have an exploratory motive. The important issue here is that where problems arise in practice relating to a child or a group of children, and research is undertaken, the process is, of course, important but so too is the outcome. At a 'grass roots' level it does not matter very much if one method or another is used as long as the process is rigorous and systematic, and the recommendations for changing practice (or not) are based upon sound, reliable and valid data (see Chapter 5 for further discussion).

There is also an issue about respecting the research traditions of particular professional groups, which links back to Yin's pluralistic view (Yin 2003) and which is of extreme importance in terms of moving research forward. Collaboration is something of a 'buzz word', both in contemporary practice and in research, and is seen as desirable in that collaboration facilitates the holistic perspective for which we strive when working with children. Respect is about understanding and accepting that, while differences exist, this does not mean that one view is of a lesser value than another. It is very easy to take an egocentric view of the world and to use our own professional background as a reason for being critical of others.

There is, however, light at the end of the tunnel. More and more educational programmes are incorporating shared learning into the curricula, particularly during initial training programmes but also at Masters level and beyond. Child protection training has been at the forefront of this development. In a number of countries progress has been facilitated by statutory developments. For example, in England and Wales the Area Child Protection Committees and their multidisciplinary training subgroups (replaced by Local Safeguarding Children Boards under the Children Act of 2004), set up under legislation emanating from the Children Act of 1989. This not only promotes respect but also leads to a greater understanding of different perspectives. This type of interprofessional education is about the identification of barriers to collaboration and ways of overcoming such barriers. Such interprofessional education is increasingly evident in research training and is a welcome initiative. It is hoped too that the introduction of Children's Trusts (the vision for Children's Trusts was outlined in the *Every Child Matters* Green Paper published by the Department for Education and Skills in 2003) will promote and facilitate greater interprofessional collaboration in research activity in practice. Local authorities are charged with building services around the needs of children and young people in order to maximise opportunity and minimise risk with five key outcomes: being healthy; staying safe; enjoying and achieving; making a positive contribution; and achieving economic well-being.

Major research themes

As we have already discussed, it is important for members of a profession to undertake research to keep a profession moving forward and to advance practice which is based upon evidence. In some ways the barriers and rivalry which traditionally existed between some professions might well have aided progression, albeit in a covert way. Each profession has its pride and none would wish to be viewed as being backward or accused of halting progress. There has been evidence of where this type of scenario has occurred in the past, and the effects have been notable (see Taylor and Woods 2005), as we will discuss in the next section.

What is evident, however, is that because of the complex nature of childhood it is inevitable that research undertaken by one profession relating to an aspect of childhood will impact upon the practice of another profession, or indeed several other professions. Resistance and closing of the ranks (a response which has been observed in the past) does not help the child, the family or the wider society and ultimately does not help the professionals themselves. It can lead to stagnation within a profession and may be one reason why there have been times in the past when professions have appeared not to increase, or build upon, existing knowledge bases. It is hoped that with a greater emphasis on shared learning and training, and greater collaboration in research and practice, we will not in future observe instances of professional resistance to change, which is detrimental to the child.

At the very beginning of this chapter we referred to perceived peaks and troughs of advancing knowledge in relation to children, and we can only really guess at why this occurred. The professional resistance mentioned above might be one answer. When a profession becomes insular it seldom advances. Inward conflict leads to energies being used to resolve inner conflict and research becomes less of a priority. It is also probably true that when a society becomes insular or experiences conflict the same thing happens. The last century has seen periods of war, economic depression and recession, large scale epidemics and political changes, all of which have certainly influenced the forward momentum of research activity. Without doubt, conflict within a society impacts upon the activities of professions and it becomes difficult to decipher responsibility for stagnation in research, or indeed progression. Suffice to say that research activity appears to mirror the concerns of professions and society, and rightly so. Research is about solving real problems and the major research themes of the last century can be seen to relate to changes which have occurred within society. We explore some of these themes in the next section. Clearly we could not begin to cover all such themes and can only offer a few exemplars to illustrate the preceding discussion. These exemplars focus upon two areas: first, how research is generated by the concerns of a society, and second, how research undertaken by one profession impacts on others.

Learning

One of the major areas of research which has spanned the last century is learning. Researchers have sought to discover, from a variety of perspectives, how children learn, and the knowledge gained from such research has influenced virtually all, if not all, professionals who work with children. Much of the early work on learning was restricted to animal studies: for example, Pavlov's work with dogs, which was instrumental in defining the learning process referred to as *classical conditioning* (Pavlov 1927), Thorndike's work with cats (see Carlson et al. 2004), during which he discovered the *Law of Effect,* and Skinner's work with pigeons and rats (Skinner 1938), which defined the learning process referred to as *operant conditioning.* The application of these theories to human learning, and to learning in children in particular, was notable, and the work of these early researchers formed the basis of further research into human learning and human personality. Albert Bandura (1977), for example, utilised Skinner's theories about behavioural consequences and blended them with his own ideas producing the theory (along with others) of *social learning* (a detailed account of this and other cognitive theories can be found in Chapter 2).

The work undertaken on the psychology of learning has had much wider application and has led to the advancement of practice in other professions concerned with the care of children. Sociologists have borrowed these theories: for example, Eppel and Eppel (1966) looked at the influence of early learning upon later moral behaviour. Educationists have also utilised learning theories (as one would expect) to inform classroom activities (Panton 1945; Child 1997; see Raban et al. 2003; Bruce 2004), and health care professionals, particularly those involved with health promotion activities with children (see Taylor and Muller 1995; Taylor and Thurtle 2005), have borrowed such theories to underpin their work.

Clearly then the impact of one profession's work has had a major impact on the practice of others. What is also interesting is to note that the impetus for much of this work came before, between and after the two World Wars. It is also interesting to speculate as to why learning became, and remains, so high on the research agenda. The lack of evidence in this area leads us to speculation, and we don't pretend to have any or all of the answers. Perhaps the pioneering work in Germany by Froebel (see Woods 2005) led to some action by educationists, perhaps academic comparisons with other developed countries prompted the need to ensure that our children did not fall behind, or perhaps concern about the moral behaviour of adolescents was the prompt. The list of possibilities is endless.

Adolescent deviance, delinquency and morality

The moral values and standards of adolescents has long been a subject which has fascinated researchers, and it is the second major theme upon which we focus. Concern was evident for a very long time before the 1950s and 1960s, but it was during these two decades that it became an explosive subject and the focus of a great deal of research. There was much speculation as to whether deviance and delinquency were attributable to genetic or environmental influences, or a combination of both, and particular emphasis was placed upon increasing understanding of the effect of early environmental variables upon later delinquent behaviour (this is a fine example of what Schaffer (1998) described as focusing upon those who showed abnormal behaviour rather than focusing on those who showed normal behaviour).

Again, because of a lack of evidence we are left to speculate as to why there was such a spurt of activity in this field during these decades. The origins of activity probably lie in the interest in a group of young people who had been born during, or just after, the Second World War and who were in their adolescence during the 'flower power' era with its perceived association with sexual freedom, illicit drug taking and a greater questioning by young people of traditional and cultural practices. What we saw here was perhaps a society trying and needing to find a cause for adolescent behaviour in the 1960s because the behaviour was so alien to them. Or perhaps society needed to find some answers because it wished to be absolved of any guilt on its own part in what was seen as declining adolescent morals. How much more comfortable it feels to be able to blame the birth control pill, or television, or drugs or alcohol, or the 'pop' music scene, than to attribute blame to oneself.

Whatever the reasons, as we have already stated, research into this area acquired an incredible impetus which influenced sociologists, psychologists and educationists, and had a major influence upon professional practice at the time. The publication of many studies in paperback form, and adapted for general reading, also influenced media and public opinion. Notable studies included a study of the moral values and dilemmas of adolescents (Eppel and Eppel 1966), a study called *The Unattached* (Morse 1965), involving three social workers working for three years with young people who had experienced varying degrees of family breakdown, Eysenck's study of *Crime and Personality* (1964), and Storr's exploration of the effects of childhood upon later perverse or deviant sexual behaviour (Storr 1964). There were many, many more.

Children's relationships

A third major research theme which deserves our attention relates to the relationships children have with their parents, in particular, and the effects of 'unusual' relationships upon child development. This theme had been apparent in literature earlier in the last century but became high on the agenda after Bowlby (1951) made his bold claims about the importance of early caring relationships to the ability to love in later life (an account of this and other theories of emotion and relationships can be found in Chapter 2). Bowlby's work was extremely influential and as a result of his work a World Health Organisation Expert Committee (1951) declared that if day nurseries and crèches were allowed to proliferate then permanent damage would be caused to the emotional development of the future generation.

We have, in the previous two sections, hypothesised as to the impetus for research and would wish to do so in this section. It is not very difficult. The economic climate following the Second World War was such that politically it was desirable to encourage women back into the home so that men returning from the war could find employment in jobs which had, during the war years, been undertaken by women.

In the years that followed Bowlby's publication a great deal of research was undertaken which sought either to confirm or to dispute Bowlby's claims. Such works include studies by Ainsworth et al. (1978) into secure and insecure attachment, Newson and Newson's work (1963) into patterns of infant care, Stern's work (1977) on the infant and mother relationship and Robertson's work (see Robertson and Robertson 1989) on separation.

The work in this field did not, however, end there. The nursing profession at first ignored the work undertaken by psychologists which was critical of the practice of separating sick children from their parents. The publication of studies by Douglas (1975) and Hawthorn (1974) highlighted the immediate and potential long term effects of separation, and the inception of the National Association for the Welfare of Sick Children in Hospital (NAWCH which later became Action for Sick Children) led eventually to a structured campaign to change practices within hospitals. It was, however, several years after the publications of these studies that practices changed on a large scale.

Work in this field was also transmuted in the past three decades to focus upon the effects of divorce on children and the effects of living in one-parent families and reconstituted families (according to the 2001 census 22% of children live in a one-parent household (National Statistics Online 2003)). Such studies, including those by Hetherington et al. (1979, 1985, 1999), Kulka and Weingarten (1979), Guidubaldi et al. (1986), Dunn and Deater-Deckard (2001), Dunn (2004) and highlighted important variables which influence how children are affected by different situations and it is difficult to draw generalisable conclusions. Clearly, however, this is another example of how research has mirrored the issues of contemporary society – the divorce rate increase correlates positively with the amount of research activity in the field.

Child health and illness

The last major theme which we will focus on relates to child health and the research which has been undertaken in this field. There has always been concern about the health and well-being of children, and assumptions are wrongly made that in the past people had large families, expecting some of their children to die, and therefore the death of a child did not, somehow, matter. Death and illness did matter very much and the fact that well over 100 children in every thousand still died before their first birthday in the first decade of the twentieth century means that there are still elderly people alive who can attest to the pain caused by the death of a sibling. Infectious diseases, such as tuberculosis, cholera, typhoid and diphtheria were rife at the time and spread through communities, often killing several members of a family within days or weeks of each other.

Over the twentieth century a great deal of progress was made. The discovery of antibiotics and the introduction of wide-scale immunisation, as well as the inception of the National Health Service in 1948, had a huge impact upon mortality and morbidity in childhood. Yet, research in this field is again typical of the concerns of society. While children were dying of infectious diseases the focus of research was on a cure and prevention. In the late 1980s and early 1990s the major cause of infant mortality was sudden infant death, and researchers turned the focus of their attention to this field. As a result of research (see CEMACH 2005) practices of child care have changed, including laying babies on their backs to sleep, placing their feet near the foot of the cot to prevent them sliding down the bed, recommendations about optimum room temperatures and recommendations about not smoking near babies.

A further area of research which can be seen to be a direct response to societal issues in child care relates to children and families with Human

Immunodeficiency Virus (HIV) and Acquired Immunodeficiency Syndrome (AIDS) related conditions. When it first became apparent that children were being infected and affected by HIV, particularly those who had been infected by the receipt of contaminated blood and blood products, research tended to focus upon rates of infections (Husson et al. 1990; Prose 1990). Later research has focused much more on the prevention of infection, and upon therapeutic approaches to infected and affected children (see Stine 1997; Miller et al. 2006). Research has not only been confined to doctors undertaking medical research but has widened its focus to include those from psychology, sociology and education who have added further to the body of knowledge within their own professions and to the professions of others, by studying the effects of HIV and AIDS from a wide variety of stances.

Child health is our last brief example of an area of research activity, and as we stated at the beginning of this section, it is impossible to do justice to all areas of research with children, nor do we attempt to do so. The intention of these examples is to look at how research is steered and to highlight how research is, and should be, reactive to society's problems. We have also set out to give examples of how research in one area will impact upon other areas, leading to a cascade of research which focuses upon a similar topic but has its own peculiar approach and perspective.

Conclusion

Research is, then, vital to the health of a profession and likewise reflects the health of a profession. Professions can stagnate and fail to increase or build upon existing knowledge bases, as we have seen throughout the past few decades. At other times, however, a particular research theme has emerged from society and has captured its imagination. At these times researchers from many professions will, individually or in collaboration, focus on different aspects of the same topic. When this happens real progress is made.

Research is not only vital for the health of a profession but is also essential for the client group the profession serves – in this case children and their families. The rest of this book is about the importance of research for the good of our chosen client group, who are special people and who deserve special consideration.

2

Theory for research and practice with children

The aims of this chapter are:

- To show why theory is important when doing research with children.
- To provide an overview of the main psychological theories and their implications.
- To highlight the importance of *context* as well as *content* in research with children.

- *Situation 1.* A mother, having watched a controversial chat show, asks a nursery teacher if she should withdraw her child from day care and give up work because she now believes that children of working mothers suffer and that a group care setting is not as good as being at home with mother. What should the nursery teacher do and say to this mother?
- *Situation 2.* A nurse is concerned about the possible effects and potential damage to families in which there is a child with a long term illness requiring frequent and intensive separations between the child and the family. Is there anything the nurse can do to understand better the process and at the same time provide support for the families?
- *Situation 3.* Following the publication of a story in a popular women's magazine, the helpline of a fostering and adoption support group is besieged with callers seeking advice on the value of cultivating a relationship between an adopted child and the biological mother. What can these callers reasonably be told?

The child care practitioner or researcher is not alone in the quest for answers on important and complex issues like these. For each practice situation described above, there exists an established knowledge base of related theory and research. This knowledge is there to inform and guide those who work or research in the field of child care and development. For instance, there is a great deal known about child–carer attachments, separation and loss. There is a lot known about the relative contributions of home and day care, or parent and teacher to child education. Some of these questions are not, however, so well represented in theory and research as others. Relatively little is known about fathers compared with the extensive research on mothers, or about factors such as age and gender in resilience to trauma. Not much is known about the costs and benefits of maintaining relationships between an adopted child and the biological mother. This does not mean that there is no role for theory in these cases. On the contrary, existing theories in related areas can be adapted or new theories created and this will guide and generate much needed research in important but neglected areas.

Nevertheless, the mere mention of the word 'theory' can drive terror into the hearts of research students and practitioners alike – the former because of the overwhelming range of possible and often complex theories which they are only beginning to touch upon in lectures, and the latter because they have come to rely upon their practice experience or intuition and may feel threatened that the knowledge they have is no longer valued. For those of us who teach about the role of theory in research and practice, it is apparent that, in the undergraduate population and even beyond into the classrooms, wards and homes, 'theory' can be regarded as a dirty word.

In this chapter it is hoped to show that the nature of theory is, in fact, rather like that of a valuable, important and useful friend. The undergraduate needs to realise that a sound grasp of theory – like all good friendships – needs to be worked on and developed over time. The intuitive practitioner need not feel insecure, because experience creates an advantage in being able to recognise and use theory effectively. We all need to appreciate that theory is not a mystical thing visited upon us by superior beings, but is instead an ordinary part of everyday thinking and being human.

The fact is that theorising is a natural, human compulsion that helps us to organise our perceptions of the world and therefore make it easier to predict and control. For instance, a mother who notices withdrawn behaviour and school refusal in her 8 year old child is confronted by an unpredictable situation which disrupts routine and poses a threat to longer term adjustment and security. Finding the reason for the behaviour, describing it, explaining it, predicting it and controlling it is a matter of survival. Theories have been described as nets cast to catch what we call 'the world', to rationalise, to explain and to master it. In the world of child development, you may have a theory that the 8 year old has a behavioural disorder because of an underlying problem in the child's relationship with the mother. You will then investigate the nature of this relationship to describe what is wrong and to implement changes. Or you may have the theory that the child's behaviour is simply a consequence of an ineffective parental regime of rewards and punishments. You will then describe that regime, explain the problems, predict patterns and bring about changes which will control or alter the behaviour. As both these examples suggest, theory can be viewed as a stage upon which observations and experiments can be conducted and serve an important practical function by guiding research and practice.

Why do people who work with children need theory?

Every individual who deals with children has this very human need to make sense of them. If little Ben is creating mayhem in his reception class, foster placement or medical ward, the urge to observe his behaviour, describe what he is doing and find both explanations and solutions is essential. The explanations generated can help predict not only Ben's behaviour but may also be generalised to other similar children and situations. Ultimately, it should be possible to understand or predict and to devise a means of controlling, preventing or curing such behaviour. These processes of describing, explaining, predicting and controlling are the very essence of theory, and professionals in child education, health and welfare need to do all of these things on a daily basis. In many cases, far reaching decisions about a child's future will have to be made on the basis of such theorising. A sound understanding of theory is therefore of the utmost importance.

There are, however, many different theoretical perspectives in child development, many different ways of 'seeing' the world and, consequently, many different explanations and solutions for any one given situation. For example, a mother seeking advice on the disruptive behaviour of her child could, potentially, receive diverse and incompatible explanations and solutions depending on which professional is consulted. An educational psychologist may theorise that a learning disability is underlying the disruptive behaviour and recommend additional support for learning. A health visitor may theorise that food intolerance often underlies child behaviour disorders and refer the child to a dietician. A social worker may theorise that social hardship and inadequate parenting are the source of the behaviour problem and implement a programme of parenting skills and social support. In more extreme situations theoretical perspectives may influence the approach of professionals at the threshold of important decisions, such as the need to be educated in a special school or to be looked after in a residential setting. Theory therefore could potentially have a massive impact leading to a range of possible futures for a given child, and seeking to improve the ways in which different professional groups can understand the theories and practices of each other and work together in the interests of children is an important goal. Finally, another reason why people who work with children need theory is because much of the policy and legislation that dictate the roles, practices and rights of both practitioner and child are formulated on the basis of various established bodies of theoretical knowledge. According to the Guidance on the Children Act (Department of Health 1990), the implicit child care principles have been developed over a long period and have many roots, including knowledge from child development, psychology, psychiatry and sociology. The importance of understanding the nature of these underlying theories is obvious. It will lead to a better understanding of the nature of the job to be done as well as the nature of children.

Theories for guiding and interpreting research and practice with children

In doing research with children we have a range of theories to choose from. The main theories informing child development and research are drawn from the discipline of psychology. Until shortly after the Second World War psychology was characterised by competing 'schools'. Thereafter the discipline grew and diversified enormously, and the old schools that psychologists adhered to tended to be replaced with a variety of fields of study, each utilising various theoretical perspectives. These perspectives might offer different explanations of the phenomena being studied, and each can be seen as providing possible insights without having to be mutually exclusive. The five different perspectives reviewed here have been chosen to represent the main approaches in contemporary psychology as reflected in key foundational texts for the discipline, such as Davey's *Complete Psychology* (2004). These are physiological, psychodynamic, behaviourist, humanistic and cognitive. The popularity of these theories owes much to their ability to inform us about the child in interaction with the environment either as originally formulated or as they have been revised by subsequent theorists. The classic example of explaining a handshake, as shown in Box 2.1, illustrates the differing emphases of these theories.

Box 2.1   Theoretical perspectives

A group of teenagers arrive at a party and are introduced to some friends. They all shake hands. Why do people engage in this particular behaviour? The handshake can be approached by each of the selected theories in a different way:

- PHYSIOLOGICAL   the handshake might be the result of particular sets of neural and muscular processes, or it might be due to a gene for sociability

(Continued)

- PSYCHODYNAMIC   the handshake could be the result of a desire for physical contact
- BEHAVIOURIST   the handshake could be the result of previous conditioning, having been associated with some reward
- HUMANISTIC   the handshake might be the result of a need for acceptance
- COGNITIVE   the handshake could be the result of purposive mental processes – for example, consciously deciding to show friendship

Although individual theorists will have a preferred approach to finding explanatory frameworks, all of these perspectives may make a contribution to our understanding of child behaviour and development.

Source: Adapted from Davey (2004). Reproduced by permission of Edward Arnold (Publishers) Ltd

Physiological approaches

The physiological approach focuses on the biological basis of behaviour and of psychological functioning. The underlying assumptions are that behaviour is determined by biological factors, and that whatever the contribution of other influences the best explanation of behaviour will be framed in biological terms. The roots of this approach go back to the beginnings of psychology as a discipline in its own right, when there was a preoccupation with the sensory and motor correlates of mental events. In 1860 Gustav Fechner published his *Principles of Psychophysics* and in 1874 Wilhelm Wundt wrote his *Principles of Physiological Psychology*, both in German.

In many respects the rise of psychoanalysis and other psychodynamic theories changed the focus of psychology from biological explanations to an interest in inner mental life as shaped by early childhood experience. Currently, with the decline of the influence of psychodynamic theories (see below) on mainstream psychology and with the developments that have revolutionised technology, the place of biological explanations for behaviour has become much more prominent. Three main fields of interest inform the physiological approach: brain function, biochemistry and heredity.

It is in the field of brain function that the advances in technology have had the most far-reaching impact. The study of brain–behaviour relationships has been revolutionised by these advances. Procedures such as functional magnetic resonance imaging (fMRI), positron emission tomography (PET), computerised tomography (CT or CAT scanning) and regional cerebral blood flow (rCBF) (Gazzaniga et al. 2002, describe these and other procedures) have transformed our knowledge of how the brain works. Some of these methods allow us to study the brain at work in live situations, and to watch the effects of the performance of different tasks both at the level of gross brain structures and in much finer detail. It is also possible to study brain impairments and the impact they have on behaviour. Biochemical studies also inform the investigation of the workings of the brain through the study of *neurotransmitters*, chemicals in the brain that affect behaviour and mood. For example, low levels of serotonin are associated with depression.

The study of heredity capitalises on the vast increase in genetic research in recent years, both in animal and in human studies (Plomin et al. 2002), but studies of genetically pre-programmed behaviour are long established in psychology. They include not only the investigation of individual differences in intelligence and personality but also of universal commonalities, such as nurturing routines and protective responses towards infants. For example, a sudden piercing cry from a babbling child will trigger a parental 'pattern of caring'. Consider how adults readily respond to any child in distress, adopt the young of others, respond to baby features of the young of any species and the way that babies smile, reeling adults in and eliciting positive responses such as baby talk or motherese. One of the consequences of these biologically determined, interdependent chains of stimuli and responses is that the child forms a specific attachment to a particular caregiver, usually the mother. John Bowlby (1907–90) was a psychiatrist who applied psychoanalytic theory to his early writings on the mother–child relationship, particularly the view that the earliest relationships were crucially important for longer term development and adjustment. However, he later concluded that biological principles better explain the nature of the tie between mother and child – that is, the complex, interdependent repertoire of instinctive behaviours in both infant and parent which function to create proximity between the child and caregiver and lead to the creation of a bond. However, as the child has to learn who his mother is and what kind of mother she is, and the mother needs to adapt to her infant, conditions exist in which an infant and mother can fail to bond or bond in a maladaptive way. An attachment is an emotional bond in which the person feels secure and the other person is a safe base from which to explore the world around. There are far-reaching implications for this theory and the ideas and methods are further explored below.

Implications of physiological approaches

Physiological approaches have been criticised as being too reductionist, in reducing behaviour to its basic biological components, and too determinist, in focusing on biological heredity to explain human personality and activity. However, they have provided an explanatory framework for a great deal of psychological functioning. Through systematic investigation of brain–behaviour relationships they have opened the way to a clearer knowledge of how children develop and to understanding the ways in which development sometimes goes wrong. They have provided many procedures for conducting research into child behaviour and development, and have been instrumental in establishing new approaches to addressing a wide range of difficulties both through pharmacological treatments and through specialised therapeutic techniques.

Psychodynamic approaches

The starting point for psychodynamic theories was Freud's psychoanalysis (1901, 1905, 1923), but other well-known psychodynamic approaches are those of Adler (1916), Jung (1921) and Erikson (1950/1963). These theories focus on dynamic, unconscious drives that govern behaviour. Freud trained as a physician, specialising in the study of the nervous system. In treating his patients, he noticed that some had illnesses for which no biological cause could be found, such as the 'mental illnesses' of hysteria, anxiety and phobia. He was inclined to cure these patients by listening to them talking freely and without interruption about their current thoughts, feelings and desires. Freud's aim was to understand the underlying processes of the patient's mind and personality and also to provide a 'talking cure'. As a result he formulated a theory on the origins and development of the personality and its disorders. Freud believed that adult mental illness originated in childhood and that analysing what went wrong would lead to better understanding of the process of normal personality development.

According to psychoanalytic theory, the psychological system and its development is best described in three ways: it is dynamic, structural and sequential. It is *dynamic* in that the human psychological system is driven by *psychic energy* which is biologically based. The most powerful drive is the sexual instinct, maintained by the energy of the *libido*. It is *structural* in that personality is made up of three parts, the *id*, the *ego* and the *superego*, which are in constant conflict. The id seeks instant gratification and has free rein until the child is about 2 years old. The ego develops as a rational mechanism and plays an important role in the resolution of the conflicts that arise between the drive for instant gratification and the reality imposed by caregivers. By the school years the superego has developed, representing parental standards which the child has internalised. It is *sequential* in that development is said to go through five fixed psychosexual stages, each representing the focus of the libido on a different part of the body. These are shown in Box 2.2.

	Box 2.2 Freud's five psychosexual stages
• ORAL (age 0–1½)	At birth the child's neurological pleasure centre is focused on the mouth. Oral behaviours such as sucking and biting are the child's pleasure source.
• ANAL (age 1½–3)	As the child's body develops, neurological awareness of the anus is in place. Elimination and retention of faeces are a source of pleasure at the same time when the child is being toilet trained.
• PHALLIC (age 3–5)	At this time there is increased sensitivity in the genital area, and both sexes are likely to find pleasure in the exploration of this area. It is claimed that children become unconsciously sexually attracted to the parent of the opposite sex. This is called the *Oedipus complex* in boys and the *Electra complex* in girls. These complexes are characterised by the rivalry with the same-sex parent for the sexual attention of the opposite-sex parent, a fear of the same-sex parent and an attempt to deal with the resulting anxiety through the defence mechanism of *identification* with their rival.
• LATENT (age 5 to puberty)	At this time, sexual impulses are not an issue. It is a period of resolution following the anxiety of the pre-school years. Identification with same-sex peers is a feature at this stage, and sexual impulses, in whichever form they have been resolved, will remain latent, hidden until the challenges of puberty.
• GENITAL (puberty onwards)	Sexual impulses resurface with the onslaught of hormonal activity and genital regrowth which accompanies puberty. During adolescence, the child should reach a mature form of heterosexual love.

Implications of psychodynamic approaches

The psychodynamic approach has almost certainly been more absorbed into everyday life than any other theory. Its basic concepts and vocabulary have become familiar and are often viewed in the public mind as representing the essence of psychology. At the same time it must be recognised that its claims are largely untestable and they occupy an uneasy position in relation to modern scientific psychology. Nevertheless the psychodynamic theories have served to highlight the importance of early childhood experiences and relationships, and the sequential nature of the developmental tasks facing children at different ages. They have contributed to many therapeutic situations, such as play therapy with emotionally disturbed children. They emphasise how caregivers need to provide a sensitive and responsive type of provision which takes full account of the individual child's needs for experience and stimulation. Environments and relationships should be secure and provide opportunities for the child to play and explore. When dealing with parents, it may be necessary to explore the nature of their own early childhood experiences.

Behaviourist approaches

Behaviourism 'changed the subject of psychology from mind to behaviour' (Davey 2004: 16). Its basic premise is that behaviour is *learned*, and it turned the focus from inner mental life to the role of the environment in shaping behaviour. It offered a strict scientific method, and for many years it was the dominant force in psychology. Behaviourism continues to play an important role in theory, research and practice, and in relation to children it has many applications in teaching and learning, in behaviour management and in therapeutic approaches. The roots of behaviourism are to be found in the work of the Russian physiologist Ivan Pavlov, who was interested in the way certain biological events become systematically related to changes in the environment.

Conditioning

In his famous experiments, Pavlov noticed that a hungry dog will automatically salivate when given food. Furthermore, if the dog hears a bell every time the food is presented it will learn to salivate when hearing the bell alone and in the absence of food. This process of learning to respond to a previously neutral event is called *classical conditioning*. Salivation is an *unconditioned response*, that is, it is natural and reflexive; food is an *unconditioned stimulus*, that is, it is naturally associated with salivation. The bell becomes a conditioned stimulus, and the salivation upon hearing the bell in the absence of food is a *conditioned response*. A child may have a recurring nightmare at night which will eventually become a fear of darkness. These behaviourist principles were formalised into a general theory by J.B. Watson in a landmark paper entitled 'Psychology as the behaviourist views it' (1913), and then in his classic text *Behaviourism* (1930).

Operant conditioning

A further landmark was B.F. Skinner's book *The Behaviour of Organisms* (1938). His Doctoral studies at Harvard in the early 1930s, in which he trained rats to press levers in exchange for food, led Skinner to propose that behaviour is a function of its consequences, and to add to classical conditioning another main theory of learning, *operant conditioning*. When individuals act spontaneously upon their environment, responses that are rewarding increase the frequency of the behaviour in question while responses that are punishing decrease its frequency. Thus, children learn to repeat behaviours that are rewarded and not to repeat behaviours that are punished. The pleasant or rewarding consequences of behaviour, such as attention, smiling, praise, are known as *positive reinforcement*. A child may be behaving badly to receive attention, and in order to stop the behaviour, the parent, carer, teacher may speak to, distract and otherwise give attention to the child. In effect, the child's behaviour is being reinforced through finding a successful way of getting the attention that is craved. *Punishment* serves to weaken undesirable behaviour either by withdrawing pleasant things or by the enforcement of unpleasant things. Many professionals will be familiar with these *behaviour modification* procedures such as 'shaping', which provide a way of changing behaviour by using schedules of reinforcement.

Social learning

Albert Bandura developed behaviourist principles further with his *social learning theory* (1977). He pointed out that there were other ways of learning apart from direct reinforcement. Children learn a whole range of behaviours through observation, such as how to care for a baby, make tea or hit others. Parents and others serve as models of behaviour, and Bandura called this *observational learning* or *modelling*. Furthermore, children learn not only from positive reinforcements and punishments that they themselves receive but also from those given to their models for their behaviour. In this way, children do not model *all* behaviour they observe, such as stealing. Gradually, Bandura took more interest in the role that thinking or cognition plays in the mediation of social learning. There are several ways in which the child's own thinking intervenes between the observation of the behaviour and its imitation. The child needs to *attend* to the modelled behaviour, to *retain* it, to *retrieve* it and to reproduce it. In addition, the child must want to, or be *motivated* to reproduce the observed behaviour. In effect, cognitive processing of attention, memory and information processing all play a role in observational learning and modelling. Thus, Bandura redefined his theory as *social cognitive theory* (1986).

Implications of behaviourist approaches

Modern critiques of behaviourist theories highlight a number of limitations. They are too mechanistic, they ignore mental processes, they see behaviour as being environmentally determined with insufficient regard to biological factors and they are poor at accounting for complex behaviours such as language. Nevertheless, they have established an extremely important principle: behaviour can be learned and modified through the principles of operant conditioning, based on positive reinforcement and punishment, and children learn through observing, modelling and cognitively processing the behaviour of others. The wider theoretical developments that have focused on the importance of social and cognitive factors have provided a broad range of applications of behaviourist principles to theory and practice.

Humanistic approaches

Humanistic psychology emerged in the 1950s as a reaction to both behaviourism and psychoanalysis. It is concerned with the human dimension in psychology, with the study of the whole person and with a focus on positive strengths and psychological health in contrast to the common emphasis on mental illness and disorder. James Bugental (1964) defined humanistic psychology in terms of five postulates:

1 Human beings cannot be reduced to components.
2 Human beings have in them a uniquely human context.
3 Human consciousness includes an awareness of oneself in the context of other people.
4 Human beings have choices and responsibilities.
5 Human beings are intentional, and purposively seek meaning, value and creativity.

The main names associated with humanistic psychology are Carl Rogers and Abraham Maslow. Both were concerned with the concept of *actualisation*. Rogers (1951) proposed that people are born with an actualising tendency. This drives them towards psychological health, which is achieved when the perceived self (how we see ourselves) is aligned with the ideal self (how we would like to be). It was Maslow, however, who was most closely associated with the establishment of humanistic psychology as a formal development. The new movement was known as the 'third force' in psychology, following Maslow's designation of behaviourism as the 'first force', the second being psychoanalysis. Maslow is best known for his 'hierarchy of needs' (1954), depicted in Figure 2.1. To achieve psychological growth and health we must first satisfy lower needs, ultimately reaching self-actualisation.

The most recent development in psychology within the humanistic theories is the rise of 'positive psychology', a term coined by Maslow and adopted by Martin Seligman (Seligman 2002; Seligman and Csikszentmihalyi 2000). This movement has taken up the humanistic theme of emphasising what is right with people rather than what is wrong with them. Its aim is to enable people to live lives of fulfilment, marked by health, happiness and well-being. Petersen and Seligman (2004) have reacted against the preoccupation of psychology with negative features, such as classifications of psychological disorders like anxiety and depression, by producing their own manual of the strengths and virtues that are found in people who are happy and fulfilled. Their approach to areas such as the assessment of children, providing them with support or conducting research with them, would be to focus on their strengths, skills and potential rather than on their difficulties and weaknesses.

Researchers in positive psychology have developed a theoretical model with three overlapping areas of happiness in life. The *pleasant life* or 'life of enjoyment' focuses on how people experience the positive emotions associated with normal and healthy living. The *good life* or 'life of engagement' examines the beneficial effects that are experienced when people are immersed at optimal level in their

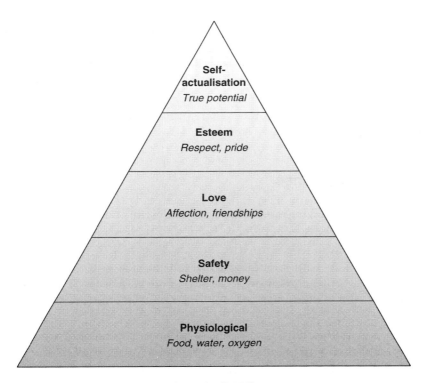

Figure 2.1   Maslow's hierarchy of needs (1954)

primary activities. The *meaningful life* or 'life of affiliation' investigates how people obtain a sense of meaning and purpose from belonging to and contributing to something greater than themselves, such as social groups, organisations or belief systems.

Implications of humanistic approaches

Humanistic psychology has been criticised for lacking a coherent, clearly defined and integrated theory. It has been seen as weak in regard to scientific method, and its overall impact on academic psychology has been limited. Nevertheless, in many ways it has made a significant and increasing contribution, and many of its research efforts and practical applications have been invested in worthwhile areas such as the promotion of international peace and cooperation and the enhancement of social welfare. It also has been responsible for the development of various widely used strategies for providing support and counselling for children and young people, including client-centred therapy, one of the principal therapeutic approaches in psychology.

Humanistic psychology favours qualitative research methods over quantitative ones (see Chapters 3, 6 and 7), viewing the qualitative approach as being most suitable to understanding the whole person and investigating the meaning and purpose of behaviour. It clearly has important implications for research and practice with children. By focusing on children's strengths rather than weaknesses and by taking an interest in the whole child and in the healthy and fulfilling aspects of everyday life it provides a positive approach to doing research with children. In addition, it promotes an approach that is likely to be appealing to all who are concerned with the welfare of the child and in taking forward a positive agenda.

Cognitive approaches

Cognition means thinking, and cognitive theories are about the ways in which children come to think about, know about and understand the world around them. The two main cognitive theorists are Piaget (1929, 1937, 1945) and Vygotsky (1978). As with the other theories mentioned so far, they each regard the child as an active participant in constructing knowledge. They agree that both biology and environment are important, but vary on the emphasis they place on each one.

Jean Piaget (1896–1980) was an influential Swiss psychologist who was also part philosopher and part biologist. As a philosopher he was interested in questions on the acquisition of knowledge, such as what is learning? Are things always the way they appear? As a biologist he was interested in describing and recording systematically the various stages of thought children go through as they develop. In relation to child development he helped to bridge the gap that often exists between philosophy and science, by applying scientific methods to philosophical questions. From studies which began with his own children, he concluded that there are important qualitative differences between a child's understanding of the world and that of adults.

Piagetian structures and processes

Piaget believed that infants are born with mental blueprints called schemas through which they adapt to the environment. Some of the earliest schemas include the sucking and grasping reflexes, which become more complex through the adaptive processes of *assimilation* and *accommodation*. In assimilation, the infant imposes existing schemas upon the environment, for example, in spontaneously sucking anything that might be a nipple. In accommodation, the schema is gradually reorganised to meet the challenges of the environment, for example, the adaptation of sucking to drinking from a cup. Piaget identified four major stages of development:

1 *Sensori-motor stage (0–2 years).* Reflexes gradually become more complex as various schemas coordinate. For example, grasping and looking can combine into a new schema for 'picking up'. Children gradually learn about object permanence, that is, the continued existence of an object that goes out of sight.

2   *Pre-operational stage (2–7 years)*. Thinking is marked by *egocentrism* (seeing the world from one's own point of view) and *centration* (focusing on one aspect of a task and ignoring others). Piaget's classic test for this stage is of *conservation* (of number – see Figure 2.2 – volume, mass, etc.). Children presented with two glasses of water with equal amounts think one has more if it is poured into a taller, thinner glass.
3   *Concrete operations (7–12 years)*. Children who pass conservation tests can now think in relative terms – that things can hurt a little or a lot – and they can grasp concepts such as 'more' and 'less', but they still think in concrete rather than abstract terms.
4   *Formal operations (12 years plus)*. The stage of formal logic and abstract thinking.

As a theoretician, Piaget was more interested in the cognitive processes underlying task performance. He devised a series of tasks which enabled him to describe the development of cognitive processes such as object permanence, perspective taking, conservation and many others. His investigations enabled him to describe the sequence in which children became accomplished in various cognitive tasks. In tasks to assess children's ability to understand *conservation,* the understanding that some property of objects such as number or quantity is not changed by the experimenter's adjustments, is tested. Figure 2.2 illustrates conservation of number, where two rows of coins are arranged so that the two rows are evenly matched in the number of coins and spacing between them. The experimenter then transforms them by pushing the bottom row together and the top row coins apart.

Figure 2. 2   Piaget's counters or coins task

Piaget found that, while pre-school children could correctly answer the pre-transformation question 'Which row has the most coins?', they consistently failed the post-transformation question 'Now which row has the most coins?', believing that, in this example, there were suddenly more coins in the top row. Piaget also wished to test his theory of 'egocentrism' – the proposal that pre-school children are unable to appreciate that other people may view things differently. He devised 'the three mountain task', in which children had to guess whether or not another person looking at the same three mountains as themselves but from a different angle, would see the same thing as them, or different. Although Piaget found evidence to support his view that young children have a problem with perspective taking, subsequent methodological revisions demonstrated greater abilities than Piaget's initial design allowed.

These tasks are interesting to researchers for a number of reasons. They illustrate the elegant simplicity of designing tasks for children of all ages, tasks which reveal information about the inner minds of children. Many other researchers have demonstrated how simpler versions of such tasks can be devised, versions more accessible to even the youngest children, and providing evidence that certain abilities are evident much younger than Piaget supposed. Flavell (1978, 1985, 1988) developed simple tasks which illustrate the perspective taking abilities in 3 year olds. These variations in turn resulted in the emergence of a new socio–cognitive theory, *the theory of mind*, the ability to appreciate the world of mental states such as ideas, beliefs, desires and feelings in self and others and how they may differ (see below). Piaget's tasks have therefore been subject to critical evaluation and methodological revision (e.g. Donaldson 1978; Samuel and Bryant 1984) in elegant demonstrations of how he underestimated the impact of the social and research context and language used on children's perspective taking abilities.

The rediscovery of Vygotsky

The work of the great Russian psychologist Lev Vygotsky (1896–1934) was rediscovered after years of communist censorship. Vygotsky gave much greater importance to the social and cultural origins of thought and the role played by language in its structuring. In *Mind in Society* (1978) he describes how cognitive functioning has its origins in the child's social interactions. A child may reach for an object arbitrarily, an adult intervenes and 'interprets' the child's action and thereby bestows meaning upon the event. In effect, then, every cognitive process appears first on the social plane as part of joint activity and later appears on the psychological plane after it has been 'internalised' by the child. Language is the cultural tool which enables the child to internalise thought originating with others.

An important Vygotskian concept is the zone of proximal development (ZPD). Vygotsky believed conversations between children and adults to be crucial for cognitive development. He found that a child's performance of a task when working with adults or more able peers gave a better indication of cognitive development than independent performance. Thus ZPD is the learning zone in which a child can accomplish a task with the assistance of others. The aim of adults is gradually to remove the support they provide and pass over responsibility for the task to the child. Of course, not all parents, carers or educators are equally skilled in identifying and working within the child's ZPD. For example, depressed parents can be less sensitive to the ZPD (Goldsmith and Rogoff 1995). According to Vygotsky (1978), when children are playing with adults or even older children they are learning how to think. The quality of the interaction taking place should, then, tell us something about the quality of the 'scaffolding' children receive from their elders. Nevertheless, the learning process is not entirely in the hands of adults. Children can or should be able to make their own creative contributions to joint activity.

The Puzzle Task (Wertsch and Hickman 1987) is a nice example of a task that creates a situation which enables the observation of interaction in the ZPD. Pre-school children and their mothers are given two complete identical puzzles. One puzzle is taken apart and the pair asked to reassemble it. Mothers are asked to help their child whenever they feel the child needs help. The quality of the inter-action can then be assessed in terms of helping the child to understand the task, directly and indirectly, referring to the completed puzzle for guidance, the child's contribution to solving the puzzle, for example asking questions, and the mother's ability to encourage the child to 'think' for himself. Two year olds should be able to engage in simple puzzle tasks with a parent, teacher or carer. However, as it is possible to increase the complexity of puzzles, there is poten-tial for similar research on children of all ages. Most recent research continues to find new ways of describing and testing the ZPD (e.g., see Meins and Russell, 1997, for a classic example).

Implications of cognitive approaches

Current work in the cognitive and social cognitive area is not driven by any inte-grating theoretical framework and is very diverse. However, the approach has made a very major contribution to our knowledge of child development and to theory, research and practice with children. It has highlighted that:

- *Children think differently from adults and there are qualitative differences in the way children of different ages understand the world around them.* Whether you are a nurse explaining treatment or pain, a social worker assessing risks, a teacher planning a curriculum or a researcher working with children, attempts must be made to appreciate and respond to these differences.
- *The child's learning, understanding and thinking is influenced by environmental con-ditions, social relationships and cultural conventions.* It is important to find out where the child is at in terms of experience. Is the child from an ethnic minority? Is there a depressed carer? How effectively are the challenges of the world brought to the child?
- *The focus should be on supporting children's potential at the point of development rather than on task performance.* There are implications for people who work with children to recognise and locate the 'zone of proximal development' and to help others involved with the child to do so also. This is important for nurses, teachers, social workers, parents and researchers alike.

Emerging theories

The latter part of the twentieth century saw an explosion in new or emergent theories that began to address the fact that the human mind cannot be reduced to any one of these five main approaches above. This is achieved by looking at the internal and external processes and mechanisms that mediate amongst them. Such theories specifically address the links between the child's outer social world and inner psychological world and are therefore difficult to classify strictly in the five main approaches outlined above. Three important theories of this type are 'theory of mind', 'attachment theory' and the social ecology model of the 'child in context' theory.

Theory of mind

A child possessing a 'theory of mind' has an ability to appreciate the world of mental states, the world of ideas, beliefs, feelings and desires. A task has been developed by Bartsch and Wellman (1989) which demonstrates that 3 year olds have difficulty in understanding the mental states of others. In an everyday situation, if a child is shown a box of chocolates that does not have chocolates inside but instead has marbles in it, she will understand that the box does not contain what she believes it should contain. If the child then sees the box shown to another child who has just arrived, she will believe that the other child, like her, thinks that the box contains marbles. In other words, the 3 year old is unable to attribute a false belief to others. The classic test for children is known as the Sally/Anne test in which Anne secretly removes an object from Sally's basket when she is gone and the child is asked to predict where Sally will look for the object when she returns (see Figure 2.3 for an illustration of this task).

The task described by Bartsch and Wellman entails enacting four scenarios with two dolls, depicting situations similar to the marbles in the chocolate box example above. Practical 2.2 describes in detail how to conduct a false belief or theory of mind task on pre-schoolers. The basic task design has been replicated and adapted in many research studies. Variations of this type of task have been particularly productive as a tool for researching with autism children and for correlating with task performances in other areas of psychosocial functioning such as attachment and with emotion understanding (e.g. Baron-Cohen et al. 1985; Dunn 1995; Fonagy et al. 1997; Meins et al. 1998; Greig and Howe 2001). Theory of mind research has seen staggering levels of growth in the past decade, and as was the case with Piagetian tasks, the method is constantly evolving to include higher levels of task demand such as second-order theory of mind tasks, those that are for older participants and those that use drawings and cartoons rather than concrete props.

Denham and Auerbach (1995) devised a task for assessing the ability of pre-school children to understand emotional states of others. These tasks are similar to the false belief tasks in that they use puppets and other props from the world of children in an effort to assess their ability to assess, in this case, feelings from the perspective of the dolls involved, and, in the case of the *false belief* task, the

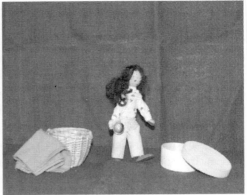

Figure 2.3   A theory of mind task: Where will Sally look for her marble?

intentions and thoughts of others. These authors incorporate a well-known simple method of asking young children to express their own feelings or, in a more complex task, those of others from three faces, made of fabric, wood or paper on which there are three faces drawn, each expressing a different emotion. Even very young children can use these simple prompts to express their own likes or dislikes and the feelings of others. Researchers ask children to point to faces in response to questions on feelings or post them into boxes or attach them to photographs. In this form, especially in expressing likes or dislikes, it is a form of self-report. Denham and Auerbach have successfully employed this task in a more complicated design which involves scenarios evoking the emotions of happiness, sadness, anger and fear and which has been widely used in other studies.

Attachment theory

The most famous accounts of attachment theory are found in the comprehensive works of John Bowlby (1953, 1965, 1979). Since his classic work *Child Care and the*

Growth of Love (1953), there has been an almost unparalleled development in attachment theory and research. The central ethological premise of attachment theory is that the infant is genetically and biologically predisposed to form attachments to caregivers as part of an instinctive mechanism that ensures proximity to adults, safety and, through this, increased likelihood of survival of the species. However, in application to human infants, the theory also draws on constructs from psychodynamic and cognitive information processing approaches. In their classic study, Ainsworth et al. (1978) identified two major patterns of attachment behaviours that are displayed in strange or fearful situations: a secure pattern and an insecure pattern. Insecure patterns can be further classified into avoidant or ambivalent. In practical terms, a secure child is better able to use the parents as a secure zone when exploring new and unfamiliar tasks, while the insecure child will behave in an avoidant/detached manner or in a coercive and threatening manner towards the mother. In later research that included a sample of children who had traumatic experiences of parental care (Crittenden, 1992), insecure classifications became 'defended', 'coercive' or 'defended/coercive or disorganised'. Only the disorganised pattern is viewed as dysfunctional or maladaptive and tends to be characteristic of the most severely traumatised children.

The Attachment Story Completion Task (Bretherton and Ridgeway 1990) is a way of assessing pre-schooler's quality of attachment to their carers. It involves presenting the child with five scenarios, enacted with hand-held, bendy, realistic family dolls and supporting props. The scenes include, first, a training session in which the family celebrate a birthday, and is not assessed. In this scene the tester establishes the nature of 'the game', which is for the tester to start the story and for the child to finish it off. The child is allowed to explore and handle the toys, and the tester can establish an understanding of how to pitch the game and the most effective prompts to use, such as 'and then what happens?' or 'is this story finished now?'. The five scenes include: spilled juice, monster in the bedroom, hurt knee, departure and reunion. Each story is selected as a trigger that is likely to lead the child to represent moments in which a child will be challenged and resort to attachment behaviour patterns.

The issues addressed in story beginnings are: the attachment figure in an authority role; pain as the elicitor of attachment and protective behaviour; fear as an elicitor of attachment and protective behaviour; separation anxiety and coping; and responses to parental return. The child's performance is assessed for security of attachment on all five stories and given an overall classification. Both verbal and non-verbal behaviour is taken into account in terms of appropriateness of content, emotional expression and coherence of story resolution. Box 2.3 describes the procedure and how to classify responses. Figure 2.4 illustrates doll use in the attachment story completion tasks for 'departure' and 'spilled juice'.

Figure 2.4   Attachment story completion scenes for 'Departure' and 'Spilled juice'

Box 2.3   Attachment story completion task

General props

Two sets of family dolls, each comprising mother, father, boy child, girl child. From these sets you need to use one whole family, plus the adult female from the other set as grandmother. Alternate child dolls to suit the sex of the child, i.e. an only boy – use the two male dolls; a girl who has a brother, use one male and one female. For each story begin by saying *'I'll start the story and you finish it.'* Enact your part then say to the child *'Now you show me with the dolls what happens next.'*

Warm-up (a birthday cake to scale of dolls)

Enact a scene in which the mother produces a birthday cake. There may be some exploration of the toys and it may take a while to make sure the child understands the routine.

Spilled juice (table, tablecloth, bottle of juice, cakes)

Enact a scene in which the child leans over the table and spills the juice. Finish by saying *'Then Mummy says "You've spilled the juice" ... show me what happens next.'*

Monster in the bedroom (no additional props)

Enact a scene where Mummy says *'It's getting late. It's time for your bed.'* Show the child going to his/her bedroom, seeing a monster and shouting *'Mummy! There's a monster in the bedroom!'* from the bedroom.

Hurt knee (piece of green felt (grass) and grey sponge (rock))

Enact a scene where the family go for a walk to the park where there is also a high rock. The child sees the rock and says *'Wow! Look, a high, high rock. I'm going to climb that rock.'* The child climbs the rock falls off and cries, sobbing *'I've hurt my knee'.*

Departure (Granny joins the family, a box painted as a car)

Enact a scene in which Granny arrives. Then say *'You know what I think's going to happen? I think Mummy and Daddy are going on a trip.'* The parents say goodbye and *'See you tomorrow'* and leave in the car, which drives away out of sight.

Reunion (same props as Departure)

Enact a scene in which it is the next day. Granny is at the window and says *'Look children, look who's coming back';* the car, with parents in, returns.

Criteria for security/insecurity

- *Very secure:* story issues are resolved fluently, without many prompts, and appropriately.
- *Fairly secure:* slight avoidant or odd responses on one or two stories.
- *Avoidant insecure:* don't know or complete avoidance of the issues over three stories or more, even showing some disorganised responses.
- *Insecure disorganised:* odd or disorganised responses over three or more stories even if displaying some avoidant responses.

Source: Adapted from Bretherton, I. and Ridgeway, D. (1990) 'Story completion tasks to assess young children's internal working models of child and parent in the attachment relationship.' In M.T. Greenberg, D. Cicchetti and E.M. Cummings (eds), *Attachment in the Pre-school Years: Theory, Research and Intervention*, pp. 273–308. Copyright University of Chicago Press, 1990. Reproduced with permission

---

Most recently, Minnis et al. (2006) reviewed some of the latest innovations in research and therapy for assessing attachment relationships with the use of computer software (e.g. West et al. 2003) and go on to describe their own research study using a specially designed computerised story completion assessment: the Computerised McArthur Story Stem Battery (CMSSB). This form of assessment is viewed as advantageous because: children enjoy interacting with computers and are becoming increasingly familiar with their use at work and at play; it can be used to access larger groups of children in community settings; it is less time consuming and can be used consistently. To test the CMSSB, it was administered to two groups for comparison: a group of children in foster care and a group of school children as a control. As anticipated, the vulnerable foster care group showed significantly poorer coherence of story narratives, less intentionality (perspective taking) and greater avoidance than the control group of school children.

The child in context

In considering the various approaches to understanding children it is important to recognise that the child in society is part of a social system. A system, whether biological, economic or psychological, has two basic properties: *wholeness* and *order*. All parts within are related to all other parts, and there must be an adaptive ability to incorporate change. An example might be the birth of a new baby into the family. This event will affect routine, require new routines and have an impact on relationships. In other words, any change in one part of the system brings about changes in other parts of the system.

Bronfenbrenner (1979, 1986, 1992) proposed a 'social ecology' model to describe the progressive, mutual accommodation throughout the life span between a growing human organism and the changing immediate environment. Let us briefly imagine two children. One child has two parents, both working and happy in their jobs. The family lives in an affluent neighbourhood which is well serviced by excellent schools and other community provisions. The parents have a wide network of professionals, family and friends and the child is popular and clever at school, has close friends and attends a number of extra-curricular activities and out-of-school clubs. The family has two cars and takes frequent holidays. The other child has only ever had one parent, his mother. There have been male friends but no real father figure for the child. This mother is unemployed and receiving social security benefits. They struggle financially and do not have a telephone. They live in a rough neighbourhood and never go on holiday. The mother is clinically depressed and finds it difficult to make friends and manage her child's increasingly difficult behaviour. The child is unpopular at school, frequently gets into trouble and is prone to accidents and ill health. As these examples suggest, the child is part of a system or network of social and environmental relationships. There are many players (family, teachers, friends) and many settings (home, play park, school, neighbourhood). Bronfenbrenner proposed four contextual structures within which individuals and places are located: microsystems, mesosystems, exosystems and macrosystems.

The *microsystem* is the immediate setting which contains the child: the garden, the house, the play park. These are examples of physical space/activity. Microsystems also contain people such as parents, teachers, peers and interactions with these people. The *mesosystem* is the relationship between different settings and at different times of development: links between the home and school or hospital. The *exosystem* does not directly contain the child but does have an influence; it includes parental employment and social networks. The *macrosystem* refers to the broader cultural and subcultural settings within which micro-, meso- and exosystems are set, such as poverty, neighbourhood, ethnicity.

Let us consider the model by way of the example of divorce. There are immediate concerns about the individual child. We might wonder how a particular child copes with stress associated with divorce, or if it matters what the age of the child is at the time of the divorce. A specific research question might be: what qualitative differences exist in children at different developmental levels as far as perceptions and interpretation of the divorce process is concerned? At the micro level we may wish to examine the quality of the pre-divorce relationship between parents and child as a predictor of post-divorce adjustment. At the meso level we could examine the impact of divorce on the child's achievement and relationships at school. At the exo level, we may wonder about the availability of the non-resident parent, perhaps by asking: does physical distance from the non-resident parent affect post-divorce adjustment? At the macro level there are marriage settlement issues – for example, were discussions on child support and other concerns settled fairly and via mediation? It is also possible to consider how these various levels work in combination. In asking how post-divorce economic instability affects family relationships, specifically changes in family patterns, we are examining both macro and micro levels. Asking whether kinship and the availability of family members assist the child in post-divorce adjustment combines issues at both the macro and exo levels.

Implications of emerging theories

The human mind and behaviour is wonderfully complex. However, if we are working with or caring for an emotionally distressed child who is struggling with an understanding of self and others and experiencing problematic relationships, perhaps because of a biological impairment or a traumatic early relationships or as a response to social stressors, or, most likely, a complex mixture of these, we are duty bound to develop our understanding of them and to increase our knowledge of the ways in which we can best support them to cope. For further readings that explore these important complex links between the child's inner and outer worlds see the works of Michael Rutter and others on risks and resilience in children (e.g. Rutter et al. 2004) and Robert Hinde on exploring the complexities of interpersonal dynamics (Hinde, 1997). See Greig (2004, 2005a, 2005b) for recent reviews on childhood depression, personal, social and emotional development, and the interaction between play, language and learning.

Context versus content variables in research

When we are doing research with children it is important to take into account not only the whole context of the child but also the whole context of the research itself. Many people conduct research projects and use their findings to develop theoretical approaches without recognising the impact on research of the wider context within which it is carried out. MacKay (2006) has highlighted this by distinguishing between *content variables* and *context variables*. Content variables represent the actual substance or content of the research programme – the factors that have been deliberately built in as the basis of the research. For example, suppose a support teacher wants to find a better method of teaching young children who are having difficulty grasping early reading skills. She decides to introduce the newer 'synthetic phonics' approach instead of the traditional 'analytic phonics' approach that most children have grown up with. She may be using quantitative methods (Chapter 6) and setting up an experimental and a control group, or she may be using qualitative methods (Chapter 7) and investigating the in-depth experience of the children who are using the new method. Either way, the content variable in question is the phonics approach that has been adopted. This is what has been planned as the substance of the research, and if children do better with the new method presumably it is because it is better than the old method. But is it? Or might there be other factors that have brought about the change that have nothing to do with the programme at all?

This is where context variables are important. The children who are doing the old, traditional method just go on doing what they have always done. The children who have the new synthetic method, however, find that it's 'all singing, all dancing'. There is excitement in the air. The teacher has a new interest and enthusiasm, and a belief that her ideas will make a difference. The new method has a lot of interesting, colourful materials, and it involves doing things in a quite different way – everybody doing the actions and shouting out the letters together as they learn them. Clearly there has been a significant change in the teaching *context* and not just in its *content*. So which is the more important factor? Is it the new phonics or is it the unplanned changes that came along with it? The best known example of a context variable is the *Hawthorne effect*. In the late 1920s and early 1930s a series of experiments was carried out at the Hawthorne Works of the Western Electric Company in Chicago with a view to increasing productivity. After varying factors such as level of illumination and timing of rest breaks the researchers found that productivity increased *whatever* the change – including returning to the conditions operating at the outset (Mayo 1933; Roethlisberger and Dickson 1939). The conclusion was that the effect was simply the result of being the focus of interest and attention, resulting in changed levels of expectancy and heightened motivation.

Researchers have two choices when faced with context variables such as the Hawthorne effect. The traditional approach is to view it as a pitfall and take steps to avoid it by finding ways of giving groups the same experiences as much as possible. However, many people reading this book are likely to be practitioners who want an answer to the question, 'How can I carry out research with children that will really make a difference to their lives?'. MacKay (2006) sought to answer this question by taking a quite different approach to context variables. If a factor like the Hawthorne effect can have a positive impact then instead of avoiding it why not celebrate it and build it in deliberately to research interventions? In applying this approach to raising the educational achievement of a whole population he set out to maximise the impact of the context variables, and focused on five key factors: vision, profile, ownership, commitment and declaration. These factors were formally articulated and embraced as part of the research strategy and they became the vehicle for conveying the content of a changed curriculum. The research was presented as being 'visionary' and was given a very high profile. The message to all who participated was that they were involved in something very important. This in turn promoted commitment and ownership. The project belonged to everyone, and all were motivated to play their part in making it succeed. 'Declaration' was also introduced. There were great expectations – and they were declared boldly. In one of the studies children in six of the schools received exactly the same intervention as all others – with one difference. They and their teachers made a bold declaration three times a day that their results were going to improve. The children in these six schools achieved higher levels of improvement than the children in the comparison schools.

These observations should highlight the many factors that influence research outcomes. They represent both a caveat and an opportunity. The caveat is that if you want to carry out some pure research to investigate, for example, whether a new methodology is a better one, then you should be aware of the context variables that may 'contaminate' what you are doing and find ways of controlling these. The opportunity is that if you are charged with 'making things better' and you want to maximise the effects of your innovation, then overall impact will be enhanced if you bring to your project a clear vision and inspire excitement and commitment in those who are participating.

Theory, research and practice: the rise of critical studies

During recent years all aspects of theory, research and practice both in psychology and in other disciplines have been challenged by the rise of the 'critical movement'. This has seen the development of critical psychology (Fox and Prilleltensky 1997), critical social work (Fook 2002), critical teaching (Wink 2004) and critical sociology, with its own international *Journal of Critical Sociology*. The central argument is that science is not and cannot be apolitical and value-free. The debate about values in science is one that challenges the entire research agenda by asking questions about the priorities, aims and methods of research. All of the assumptions on which traditional paradigms for theory, research and intervention are based are called into question, and wider questions are raised about the impact of research and practice in the arena of social justice and human welfare.

The attempt to provide an agreed values framework to underpin the priorities of research is not without significant challenges. In promoting the belief that 'fundamental human needs, values and rights must be met and upheld for a better and more just society to emerge', Prilleltensky and Nelson (1997) propose five core values that may be found generally agreeable among researchers and practitioners working with children. These are: health, caring and compassion, self-determination and participation, human diversity and social justice.

Clearly the agenda of the critical movement could have many implications for how we apply theory and how we conduct research with children. At the very least it should cause us as researchers to pause and think about our aims and methods, and the impact these will have on the children who are our participants. (See also Chapter 9 on the ethics of doing research with children.)

Conclusion

Children are complex beings in a complex world. How, then, do we begin to do research with them? Do we focus on their individual characteristics? Their playful interactions with peers? Their relationships with friends, siblings and caregivers? How can we capture the ways in which children are embraced, supported, punished or isolated by the society and culture in which they live? The remainder of this book is devoted to helping to address questions of this kind.

PRACTICAL 2.1   APPLYING THEORY TO RESEARCH AND PRACTICE

Return to the three situations described at the beginning of this chapter. In groups, discuss each situation and address the following questions:

1   Which theory or theories best describe and explain the issues involved?
2   Why is a particular theory suited and why are others unsuited?
3   To what extent is the chosen theory/theories limited in dealing with each situation?

PRACTICAL 2.2   INVESTIGATING THEORY OF MIND

This practical aims to provide you with experience of conducting a false belief task with children.
To conduct this practical you will need:

- approved access to a pre-school child of 3–5 years of age (see Chapter 8 for guidance on ethics);
- two rag dolls – male or female – which are held easily;
- two boxes of raisins, two boxes of fish food, two boxes of sticking plasters and two boxes of crayons. For each pair of boxes, make sure one has a picture of the presumed contents and paint out the picture on the other box.

Remove contents from the boxes with pictures on them.

Procedure:

1   Sit comfortably with the child at a table.
2   Introduce the child to the dolls, e.g. Sally and Anne/Bill and Ben.

3 Put the dolls aside/under the table to give impression they are 'away'.
4 Put the first pair of boxes on the table in front of the child and say *'Point to the box you think has got raisins/fish food/sticking plasters/crayons in it.'*
5 Let the child have a look to establish that the pictured box is empty and the blank box contains the expected contents.

Stage 1: Prediction (getting the child to predict where the doll will look)
Say *'Look, here comes Sally. Shall we see if she can find the _____?'.* Place the doll, looking from one box to the other as if 'looking', and say *'Where will Sally look for the _____?'.* Note the child's response. Put Sally away.

Stage 2: Explanation (getting the child to explain the doll's intentions)
Say *'Look here comes Anne now.'* This time show the doll going straight to the labelled box and try to open it. Say *'Look, what's Anne doing? What does she think?'* You may need to prompt a bit by saying things like *'She thinks something doesn't she ...?'.* Note the child's response. Put the doll away.

Stage 3: Prediction
Bring out the third doll. Place it in front of boxes as if looking. Say *'Here comes Bill/Ben. Point to the box you think he will look in.'* Note the child's answer. Put the doll away.

Now repeat this procedure for the other three pairs of boxes. The child scores 1 for each correct answer and 0 for incorrect answers.
Questions to explore after the practical:

1 How did your child's performance compare with that of others?
2 What did you learn about controlling the environment, and the sorts of strategies you need to manage the child's spontaneous contributions?
3 How did you feel doing this task?
4 Why do you think the explanation phase is important?
5 What does the literature say about the link between theory of mind (thoughts and intentions) and understanding of feelings of self and others and how has this been addressed methodologically?

3

Theoretical frameworks

The aims of this chapter are:

- To introduce the two major conceptual approaches to thinking about and conducting research with children: *positivism* and *constructivism*.
- To explore the differences and potential overlaps between qualitative and quantitative research designs.
- To provide a practical guide for choosing an appropriate conceptual approach.

Reflect briefly on the many occasions you say 'I have a theory ...' followed by something like 'there is a man whose job it is to coordinate all your bills so that they all arrive on the same day' or 'the middle child develops relationship difficulties in adulthood'. Whether your theories are comic, absurd or revolutionary, they are based on observation. It may be the tenth time this year that you have noticed the sickening thud of all your bills coming through the letterbox at once. It may be the fourth generation in your family where the middle child has never had a successful long term partnership. Some observations and theories are worth testing and some are not. If we do indeed prove that there is a Bill Coordinator, there is not a lot we can do about it. However, establishing a link between adult relationship difficulties and birth order is informative, useful and sets up an intriguing trail of research questions, answers and interventions.

The overwhelming importance of children in our lives makes them, arguably, theorised about more than anything else. When it comes to understanding and helping children, lay theories and casual observations simply will not do. A more cautious, reliable, valid and insightful approach, indeed a 'scientific' approach, is needed when it comes to entering, understanding or predicting the world of children.

Approaching children scientifically

There is a pseudo debate between researchers in the physical sciences (biologists, geologists, chemists, etc.) and the social sciences (psychologists, sociologists, educationists, etc.). This debate rests upon the belief that the theories, methods and explanations one might use in investigating a digestive system, rock, fossil or chemical compound are, of necessity, different from those used when investigating human action, thought and development. Simply and correctly put, a fossil is not a human being. The matter is, however, not that simple at all when we consider how humans are also physical, biological and chemical: for instance, the way in which body chemicals control human characteristics and even how humans both adapt to and alter their physical, geographical and social environments. For researchers interested in the complex problems and the holistic nature of human subjects, the consensus is that one needs to use an eclectic or heuristic approach to the theories, methods and findings in research questions about human subjects.

Research that involves children and childhood needs to be seen from as many angles as possible. It needs to draw upon a wide range of theories and methods from the sciences, social sciences, humanities and arts. As noted by William James:

> Psychology is a science and teaching is an art and sciences never generate directly out of themselves. An intermediary inventive mind must make the application by using its originality. (1899: 3)

Novice researchers, therefore, will do well in taking Robson's (2002) advice to seek out the value of conducting a 'scientific' study, to keep prejudices in check and to clear away some of the common misconceptions about the scientific approach. At the same time, it is important when researching children in the real world to have a broad interpretation of 'science' in order to include a whole range of qualitative and interpretative methods that are nevertheless done with rigour, transparency and open to evaluation by self and others. This is a matter of good research and professional practice. Developmental researchers across disciplines have recognized the limitations of a strict form of 'scientism' and have been actively developing theories (see Chapter 2) and methods (see Chapters 6, 7 and 8) to deal with it. The revision of what is meant by 'science' here is a result of two recent challenges: a social science paradigm shift and new legislation on children. The need for a paradigm shift has been recognized within the social sciences for some time now and calls for the inclusion of a broader range of qualitative and interpretative methods. This is in order to better address the fact that children are in a dialectical relationship with other people and also with cultural and historical contexts. The Children Act 2004 enforces a range of regulations relating to the rights of children to be consulted about matters that affect them. Consequently, creative researchers have been inventing new methods to ensure reliable and valid consultation with children. We now have to think carefully about our research in terms of being 'on', 'with', 'about' and even 'alongside' children, where the latter refers to children as researchers themselves!

In the next section, we will address the traditionally distinct approaches to theory and research and go on to address their similarities, differences and overlaps.

The science of positivism and constructivism

The radical progress in scientific discoveries and new technologies characteristic of the industrial revolution, resulted from an approach to theory and research known as *positivism*. The positivist assumption about the nature of children is that they are accessible to the same scientific procedures one would use on a rock, fossil or chemical. Children are natural, physical beings and are subject to the same laws and principles which govern the structure of the universe. Children are determined, knowable, objective, measurable. As a research method, positivism is a process whereby the researcher seeks to establish the truth or falsity of a theoretical statement such as 'little girls who wear red shoes run faster than little girls who wear black shoes'. Such statements are also known as *hypotheses,* the truth value of which is tested through methods of observation or experiment. This method also requires systematic, controlled procedures to aid verification processes, the aim of which is to discover universal order, to create generalisations together with theories and laws that allow predictions across settings and individuals. The collection and analysis of numerical data is favoured, and the method is also known as *quantitative*. An often cited example of a good positivistic theory is the Law of Gravity. This theory explains falling apples, the behaviour of roller coasters and the position and movement of planets in the solar system. With very few statements about the mutual attraction of bodies, this theory explains a large number of events which can be observed or experimentally tested.

Historically, the advent of schools to prepare children for a technologically literate society, coincides with the need to better understand how their minds work and develop. Child study researchers with a positivist approach assume that law–like relationships can be drawn amongst constructs they identify, operationalize and measure. Hence, children are studied in controlled settings, variables isolated, measured and correlated with other variables, and predictions are made to populations represented by the samples being studied. For instance, a study on one pre-school may be generalised to all pre-schools in that area.

Theories of child development derive from psychology, a social science in favour of positivist methodology. Hence theories on the nature of attachment relationships between a mother and her child, based on observations of bonding instincts and behaviour in geese, can be used to explain much of, if not all of human social behaviour and development. This could be construed as research 'on' children. It is an approach that seeks explanation.

Figure 3.1

The trouble with doing research with human subjects – as opposed to forces, fossils and feathered animals – is that both the researcher and research participant have a conceptualisation of the research situation and what is expected to happen. The cartoon in Figure 3.1 makes the methodological point that the control of a positivist investigation is seriously undermined by the possibility of a human, subjective conceptualisation of the research situation on the part of both researcher and participant. Not only does the researcher need to contend with how the participant perceives and responds to the research situation, he is also dealing with a personality who could, unintentionally or otherwise, sabotage the entire exercise.

It is the human capacity for language, thought and action which poses a challenge for positivist methodology. Buchanan (1994) discusses how the natural processes of the physical sciences are independent of the language used to describe them, but human practices are not. For instance, a single human gesture can have several different meanings depending on the person and the context. Consider the meaning of a raised hand in the following contexts: a child in class when the teacher asks a question; a child playing in the park at football; a child waving to his mother as she leaves him behind; in a group of children who have been asked to vote on indoor or outdoor activities. Furthermore, should we wish to define the construct of 'well-being' for a child, which definition is right – diet and exercise, normal growth and development of physical and psychological functions, or courage, wisdom and modest living? Consider how a young boy may be disturbed and angry by his father's absences yet, once a parent himself, becomes appreciative of his father's sacrifice. These examples illustrate how complex the business of interpreting and defining human behaviour is and how it is bound to the context, time and what it actually means to the people involved. Dealing with children adds further complications for positivist research. The child's capacity for language, action and self-reflection is not only qualitatively different from that of adults but these capacities are also qualitatively different for different age groups of children.

There is, however, an alternative conceptualisation of the nature of children and of the theory and research methods which should be applied to them. This alternative approach is called *constructivism*. Constructivist researchers perceive the child as a subjective, contextual, self-determining and dynamic being. Children and their caretakers are social, relational beings who are engaged in joint action. As they interact they construct joint meanings within a given context. In this way, meaning is constructed symbolically in interaction with others. Children and their caretakers are inextricably part of the worlds they study. They are both the observed and the observer. Children and their relationships are dynamic across individuals, context and time. Furthermore, the meanings constructed and actions taking place in everyday situations are also located within specific cultural and historical practices and time. This could be construed as research 'with', 'about' and 'alongside' children. It is an approach that seeks understanding.

Constructivists argue that, in a subjective world, where understanding and knowledge are symbolically constructed and held in convention and social unity with others, it is inappropriate to seek samples, control and isolate variables, quantify behaviour and generalise to a larger population of people. Instead the constructivist researcher makes an effort to understand how the worlds of children operate, by somehow entering those worlds, describing and analysing the contextualised social phenomena found there. The constructivist view that actions, thoughts, intentions and meanings cannot be conveyed in an analogous way with numbers, but need a more qualitative handling of data, has lead to the approach also being described as *qualitative*.

> Instead of control, constructivists want naturally occurring social behaviour, in place of isolated variables, they seek a contextualised holistic examination of participants' perspectives, instead of measuring, correlating and predicting, constructivists describe and interpret. (Hatch 1995: 122)

Table 3.1 summarises the two principal theoretical frameworks for doing research with children.

Table 3.1 Theoretical frameworks for scientific research with children

Positivism (explanatory research *on*)	Constructivism (understanding research *with*)
The nature of the child is objective, knowable and determined. The child can be observed, controlled, measured and quantified. However, there is only a similarity between the child and natural/ physical processes, and theories are inexact, cannot be proven, and are only probable	The nature of the child is subjective, not objectively knowable or measurable. The child has her/his own perspective, but is also socially determined and theories are inextricable from context and culture

Theoretical frameworks for scientific research with children

Doing research with children could be described as a systematic and scientific search for information which aims to improve our knowledge on children. This definition begs two further questions: what is meant by knowledge and what is meant by scientific? The answers to these questions rest upon which framework – quantitative and/or qualitative – the researcher has chosen to work with. In the next section we address the differing conception of knowledge and science in each framework. As a starting point, let us consider some of the sources of knowledge about children as more or less scientific, where scientific is taken to mean impartial, reliable, valid and controlled. The ways in which we come to 'know' about children include *authority*. We are told what the nature of children is by parents, so-called experts and politicians. Thus, knowing that 'children should be seen and not heard' because this is what some higher authority has told us, is not 'scientific'. Another way of knowing about children is through personal belief or conviction. So, for instance, you may be convinced that children are incapable of knowing and expressing what their needs are despite evidence which contradicts it. This kind of *tenacity* is not scientific and can be tantamount to prejudice. Knowledge which passes itself off as a logical inevitability or a priori knowledge which 'goes without saying' is not scientific. For example, if you define intelligence as 'an innate permanent ability to adapt to the environment and solve problems' then it is a matter of logical necessity that measures of intelligence should be correlated across infancy, childhood and adulthood. A scientific test of this type of knowledge about children is likely to be disconfirmed because it fails to take into account 'other factors' which potentially affect the phenomenon in question.

Deduction and induction

There are two principal methods of scientific activity: *deduction* and *induction*. Deduction in science emphasises theories (ideas and explanations) from which we can 'deduce' likely outcomes. An example which is often given for this is that you may never have seen an omelette fly into an electric fan but you could make an excellent prediction of the likely outcome. Induction in science emphasises data (measures, numbers, observations). In gathering data together, patterns and relationships among the numbers become obvious: if the numbers are 2, 4 … you might predict the next number as 6 or 8 or 16 but you do not have enough figures to predict which one should be next. If you obtain another figure which is 16 you can now predict the next number as 256 because each number is multiplied by itself in order to obtain the next number. It is apparent from this example that the larger amount of numbers available, the easier it will be to reliably discern such patterns and relationships.

As a concrete example of deduction, you may start out with a theory that working mothers have poorer relationships with their children than non-working mothers. In order to test this theory, you simply challenge it by predicting the outcome in the opposite direction – that working mothers will have a better relationship with their children than non-working mothers *or* the hypothesis can be nullified to 'there will be no difference between working mothers and non-working mothers in their relationships with their children'. You then set up an experiment which will clarify the relationship between the two variables A (the number of hours worked) and B (quality of the relationship). However, in order to test this hypothesised relationship, it is necessary to define concept A and B to provide a measure of each variable. These measures can then be observed in two groups of mothers: those with little or no work (group 1) and those with a lot of work (group 2). The type of knowledge this test reveals is considered scientific because it is empirical, impartial, reliable, valid and controlled. It is also open to verification and correction, as it can be replicated, modified and improved by other researchers. If you do indeed find the answer which supports your theory, this will be a powerful scientific finding.

As a concrete example of induction, you may not have a particular theory to deduce from but prefer instead to observe, measure and examine potential patterns amongst the data produced. You may simply observe some mothers and children, noting the frequencies of things indicative of a good quality relationship, such as involvement, positive affect, etc. These patterns may, in themselves, create a theory or suggest the application of an existing one. If you do come to some conclusion, it is still scientific but not as powerful as it would be if you had made an actual prediction about what you would find.

An often cited analogy of the different ways of using deduction and induction is that of building a house. In deduction you start at the top with the roof, the overarching bit at the top and work your way down to the ground. Here you are most interested in predicting, depending on what a given roof looks like, what the house underneath should look like. In induction you start at the bottom with the ground and work your way up and stick the overarching roof on at the end in a way that explains what you happened to have built below. However, to take the analogy further, most research involving children could be described as a functional combination of both, with a bit of roof or foundation to start, maybe a wall, another bit of roof and so on.

The quantitative framework for doing research with children

The quantitative research framework is based on assumptions about the objective nature of children, knowledge and research methods. Such an approach is based on the scientific activity of deduction – the procedure for testing existing theory. The notion that theory pre-exists in a law-like form is consistent with the view that the child is objective in nature and that his or her behaviour, understanding, knowledge or meanings are structured, determined and universal. Hence, the quantitative framework entails a methodology in which theory exists and is tested empirically to be proven or not proven. In the house construction analogy it is a top–down procedure (see Figure 3.2). The basic methodological tool for conducting quantitative research is experimentation.

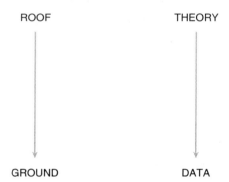

Figure 3.2   **A top-down view of theory and data**

According to McCall (1994) scientific research on children entails two conceptual levels: theoretical and empirical. The theoretical level (deduction) is about general concepts, principles, laws and hypothesised relationships. The empirical level (induction) is about defining the concepts into observable, measurable variables and conducting observations that describe the hypothesised relation. McCall points out that in his simple model of a 'scientific study' (see Figure 3.3) we should be aware of the working assumptions of researchers which operate at each level. Each one of these working assumptions exists because researchers and their child participants are not forces or fossils and because human science is not a perfect science.

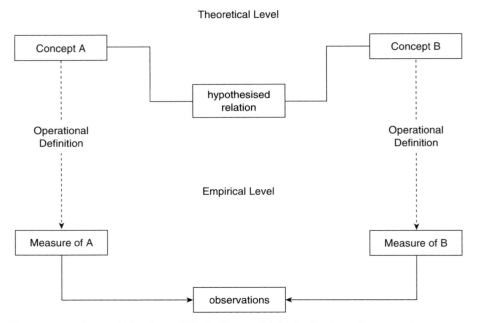

Figure 3.3   A simplification of McCall's model for behavioural research

Source: Adapted from McCall, R.B. (1994) Commentary, paper in *Human Development*, 37: 293–8. Copyright, 1994. Reproduced with permission of S. Karger AG, Basel

At the theoretical level, the reality of the basic concepts can be challenged. For instance, a researcher may be working on the assumption that intelligence is an innate, permanent ability to adapt to the environment and solve problems and is therefore stable across infancy, childhood and adulthood. In fact, when intelligence is tested over time, this does not appear to be the case. Whilst this could be due to a problem with measures, it could also be because the researcher is working on the wrong assumption about the stability of intelligence.

Also at the theoretical level, the hypothesised relationship between variables A and B may not be a valid one. For instance, you may hypothesise that, all other things being equal, mothers who work longer hours will be more tired and therefore spend less quality time with their children than mothers who do not work long hours. An empirical test of this hypothesis is likely to fail because, in the case of research with human participants, it is not easy to hold 'all other things equal'. Things like guilt, overcompensation and fluctuations in energy levels could easily apply in this example.

Another example could be of a hypothesis which is not sufficiently specific or comprehensive. So, for instance, the rather ambiguous and ill-defined hypothesis that 'children who spend more time with their mothers get better school grades' is much better written as 'children who spend one hour each evening with their mothers will get better grades on SATs (standardised achievement tests) than children who spend 15 minutes with their mothers each evening'. The second hypothesis is more specific about measures and implies a particular empirical relationship.

Working assumptions also penetrate at the level of measurement, influencing the quality, validity and reliability of our measures. When a test of some hypothesised relationship between A and B fails, we could simply be measuring it wrongly but it could also be because the concept we are trying to measure is much more complex than we have assumed. The example given by McCall is that infant behaviours are remarkably unreliable even across short–term observation intervals. Where, he asks, does unreliability end and lack of stability begin? Researcher assumptions can also disrupt observational control. For instance, how does one deal with findings from separate studies which compromise each other? One study, for example, might report that children who watch more television are also more aggressive, while in another study the finding might be that aggressive children watch more television.

In deciding what to observe, it is impossible to do so with complete objectivity for, as Goethe noted, 'we see what we know'. Can we ever be certain that what we see is all there is? Or what we see or know is right?

Having described McCall's analysis of a quantitative framework for research in child behaviour and development, it is tempting to reject the model entirely in favour of something more qualitative. This would be foolish, however, as McCall goes on to argue:

> Suppose one defines a better football team to be one that has a better win–loss record and a poorer football team to be one that has a poorer win–loss record. Better teams beat poorer teams, everything else being equal. But if this were so obvious, no-one would play the game. The fact is that everything else is not typically equal. Poorer teams beat better teams on occasion which is why professional football fans often assert that any pro-team can beat any other pro-team 'on a given day'. The implication is that many hypotheses are not all-or-none, but are probabilistic. Even if they appear to be a priori in nature, our empiricism helps to define that probability, that degree of relationship, that extent of influence, recognising the portion not accounted for is due to other factors (which we conveniently call 'error' but which nevertheless consists of potentially identifiable causes). (1994: 297)

The fact is that scientific enquiry is rarely tidy, and researchers need to think more about the conceptualising of variables, specifying theoretical relation or hypothesis and ensuring reliability of measures. Even when measurement problems arise, they are still informative if only because they challenge the working assumptions of the researcher.

A qualitative framework for doing research with children

The qualitative research framework is based on assumptions about the subjective nature of children, knowledge and research methods. The qualitative approach is based on the scientific activity of induction – the procedure for generating new theories and in which theory emerges from the data. The notion that theory is created from or emerges from data is consistent with the view that the child is subjective in nature and that his or her understanding, knowledge and meanings are subjective, and emerge in interaction with others in a given context. Hence, the qualitative framework entails a methodology in which theory is 'grounded' in data such as observations, interviews, conversations, written reports, texts and their interpretations. In the house construction analogy, it is a bottom–up procedure (see Figure 3.4) and the basic methodological tool is interpretation.

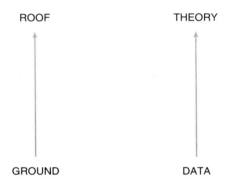

ROOF   THEORY

GROUND   DATA

Figure 3.4   A bottom-up view of theory and data

Interpretivist scientists seek to understand the social world from the point of view of the child living in it. By way of constructs and explanations, interpretivists attempt to make sense of how children understand their experiences and how this affects the way they feel towards others. Interpretivism has roots in those branches of psychology and sociology which acknowledge the need to understand and capture subjective experiences and meanings. Humanistic psychology, for instance, begins with a view of the child as his own psychologist, creating meanings for himself out of his experiences and interactions. When a child encounters problems, the belief is that the child should be enabled to look within himself for both the problem and the solutions. Interpretative sociology encourages entering the child's world and meanings to get the child's perspective from the inside out. This is necessary because situations, meanings and problems are defined in interaction with others. The concept of labelling is a good example of how a child might be socially defined as a problem and ultimately become one.

Framework of working assumptions

How would McCall's simple model of quantitative research on children work on qualitative research at the theoretical and empirical levels, and what are the working assumptions of qualitative researchers at each level? This is depicted in Figure 3.5.

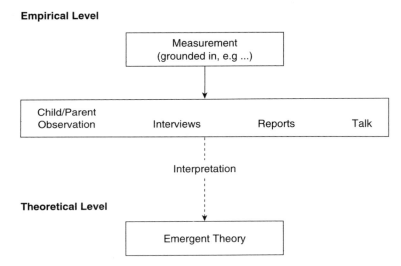

Figure 3.5   A qualitative version of McCall's two conceptual levels of research

Source: Adapted from McCall, R.B. (1994) Commentary, paper in *Human Development*, 37: 293–8. Copyright, 1994. Reproduced with permission of S. Karger AG, Basel

This inductive variation could also be analysed in terms of working assumptions held by qualitative researchers at each level. At the empirical level, the assumption is that it is possible to engage in methods such as observation, interviews, report or text analysis in a theoretical vacuum, with no guiding definitions, concepts or constructs. So, for instance, if your aim is to explore the quality of the relationship between a working mother and her child, it is virtually impossible to do so without some guiding perspective or sensitising concepts on what to look for, why and how.

Also at the level of interpreting the research, there is the qualitative aim of discovering or entering the subjective experience and perspective of the child. Given that the researcher and participant are simultaneously both the observer and the observed, the research experience itself is mediated on several levels by the intersubjective relationship between researcher and participant. Participants have their own tacit and declared understandings; researchers have their own perspectives and interpretations. The relationship is also mediated at a cultural level by conventional meaning systems and power relations which are interpreted within social and institutional contexts.

In essence then, the subjective nature of both researcher and participant is just as problematic for the scientific, qualitative interpretivists as it is for quantitative experimentalists.

Henwood and Pidgeon (1995) propose what they call a 'constructivist version of grounded/inductive theory' for dealing with the impossibility of a theoretical research, and they express it in a procedural framework. Qualitative researchers, they argue, *must* have a perspective from which to build their analyses and recommend a functional relationship between the data and its interpretation. In this way, researchers' perspectives can guide the questions asked and provide a balance between possessing a grounding in the discipline and pushing it further.

At the empirical and interpretive level, in dealing with the problems of inter-subjective understanding and meanings, Hatch (1995) proposes a theoretical framework based on Activity Theory. According to this theory, the goal of inter-pretive research is to understand the meaning that children construct in their everyday action, situated in a cultural, historical setting and in mutually interact-ing intentional states of the participants. This entails a method which goes beyond simply detailing what people are doing and into an exploration of the meanings and intentions which underlie these activities. The required unit of analysis includes both the individuals and the culturally defined environment which is grounded in a set of assumptions about roles, goals and means used by the participants in the activity setting.

In applying this framework to doing research with children, Graue and Walsh (1996), cited in Hatch, advise:

> motivation/intention is central. Individuals are motivated to do some things and not others … need to pay careful attention to young children's actions and ideas. … To get a sense of motives, it is important to watch children's interactions closely, to listen to their explanations of actions and to be respectful of their voices. It requires basic methods of interpretive research, plus attention to the connections between the local context and the broader culture and history. (1995: 148)

In summary then, qualitative research attempts to capture the ways in which our child research participants make sense of the research events under investigation. In an important sense, then, qualitative research enables the voice of the participant to be heard. It is perhaps not surprising then that qualitative methods which specifi-cally deal with the child's perspective have only recently begun to be addressed. As we have discussed elsewhere, the assumption has long been held that children are either unable or not entitled to have a point of view. Obviously, the younger the child, the less likely the child is to be heard in research. The dominance of the experimental method in developmental psychology has meant that the value of creating valid methods of obtaining the child's perspective in research has simply been overlooked. Attempts to address this are now proving fruitful, particularly in the field of child and family social work research, and in the new sociology of childhood. Some of these techniques are reviewed in Chapter 8.

Practitioner research

The reality is that most people who do research with children are practitioners who need to study children and young people as part of their job. This type of 'action' research takes place with people outside of laboratories, in the real world of hospitals, clinics, schools, nurseries, homes and the community. Real world research is not only about people but also takes full account of the advantages arising from the enquirers and participants being people themselves. According to MacKay (cited in Greig 2001):

> Research is basically 'enquiry': but enquiry which is carried out systematically and with the rigour of those who basically adopt the scientific method. I don't really go in for a 'researcher/practitioner-researcher' distinction, any more than I go in for an 'academic/applied' distinction. I simply view research as occurring at various levels and as being of various kinds. What we have in mind with 'practitioner-research' is what is done in messy, real-world situations rather than in laboratories, often (but not only) using a qualitative rather than a quantitative paradigm, often using small samples in single establishments, which don't always lend themselves to RCTs (random control trials), frequently answering questions and priorities that originate with service users rather than the researcher, and often done not for its own sake alone but as a more systematic and enhanced approach to service delivery. (77)

In consequence, the methods used in practitioner research tend to be mainly qualitative, but also quantitative and require a broad interpretation of what is meant by 'scientific'. These topics are covered in more detail in Chapters 6 and 7.

Choosing an approach

As we discussed above, quantitative research demonstrates results in terms of numbers (it quantifies or measures) and usually employs statistics. For instance, measuring the effect of unfamiliar or strange situations on the heart rate and saliva samples of 4 year old children. Qualitative research is concerned with unique situations and phenomena and would describe in detail and interpret with a view to explaining the object of study: for example, a case study of one boy's disruptive behaviour at a playgroup, with interviews of both parents and teachers about his wider social environment; or detailed, intensive long term observations of one child referred to social services. It is generally accepted in research that, in choosing either or a mixed approach, it is best to be guided by the nature of research questions, the participants, the sort of findings you require and what you intend to do with them. This topic is covered in detail in Chapter 5. The relationship between qualitative and quantitative research can be exclusive, but the two aproaches have remarkable potential for overlap in practice. Multiple overlaps can be manifested in eclectic studies: for instance, an experiment on the self-esteem amongst poor readers could include some in-depth case studies of one or two children. Or a child with behavioural difficulties could be studied as a case, observed intensely over a long period of time and in a variety of social contexts, all supplemented by health and education records and interviews of parents and professionals who know the child. At the same time, the child might be assessed using questionnaires or tests on the extent of the behavioural disorder and the child's mental age, both of which are standardised and 'quantitative'. Interpretative tasks could also be included, such as measuring the child's attachment to parents through projective tests or using a technique of story completion in playing with family dolls. It may also be possible to undertake an experimental regime of 'interventions' assessing the child before and after treatment.

Nevertheless, there are clear boundaries, notably in distinguishing the approaches as experimental and non-experimental. Conceptualised strictly in this way, the approaches become polarised. Qualitative becomes non-experimental research which is subjective, insider, holistic, naturalistic, valid, inductive, exploratory, ungeneralisable and discovery oriented. Quantitative becomes experimental research which is objective, outsider, particularistic, controlled, reliable, deductive, outcome-oriented, generalisable and verifiable. This distinction between qualitative and quantitative approaches to research is more useful for the purposes of description and argument than it is a reality, because many psychologists and sociologists engage in a principled mixture of the two. It is a fallacy to assume, for instance, that theoreticians always behave or think like positivist or 'hard' scientists. Freud is a good example for, despite his background as a biologist and clinician whose ideas about human behaviour and development were essentially reductionist – that is, all behaviour can be explained by simple biological processes – his approach to theory, research and practice has been much criticised as 'unscientific' (e.g. Eysenck 1952). Similarly, Piaget, also by training a biologist, intent on a taxonomy of human knowledge and acquisition, and who conducted actual experiments with children, has been accused of less than vigorous scientific methods (e.g. Donaldson 1978). It is also a mistake to assume all psychologists aspire to 'hard' science. Even early in the twentieth century, Vygotsky – a contemporary of Piaget – condemned the misuse of 'positivist' approaches to child behaviour and development – such as standardised tests. These, he argued, did not address the child's individual motives, talent, potential for development or the important effects of the historical, cultural and social context upon the research situation.

Researchers are now addressing the potential similarities or shared goals in conducting qualitative and quantitative research which is 'scientific'. There is a very good argument that any scientific research needs to have a standard of rigour which adheres to issues of reliability and validity. Both approaches can attempt to make the research in question replicable. This is a controversial issue regarding qualitative research, but a consensus is now emerging that, by documenting the decision trail in qualitative research, a process synonymous with specifying methodological details in quantitative reports is achieved (Yin 2003). In this way, it becomes more a matter of making more sense, to other researchers, of the methods used and conclusions drawn, rather than replicability. In both cases, it is essential to gather appropriate evidence so that a judgement can be made about the significance of the findings. Harding, cited in Henwood and Pidgeon,

> makes the important distinction between 'weak' and 'strong' objectivity in science: weak objectivity occurs when the inevitable layers of subjectivity are overwritten or obscured. In moving towards strong objectivity, the researcher makes public the full range of interpretative processes involved in knowledge production. Research that seeks to reveal rather than obscure the hand of the researcher and social bases for knowledge, by this account, has some claim to providing more adequate knowledge. (Hatch 1995: 118)

Figure 3.6 and Practical 3.1 provide a procedural framework for choosing an approach to doing research with children.

Conclusion

In this chapter we have sought to introduce novice researchers to the different existing and evolving frameworks or paradigms which guide research and also to the debates which surround them. We believe that it is possible, depending on the nature of your research aims, to use either the qualitative or quantitative framework in doing research with children. Furthermore, because we acknowledge the complex nature of children, we actively encourage the consideration of research designs which use both frameworks. Psychologists and sociologists, ethnographers, practitioner–researchers such as teachers, nurses and social workers, those who study trends in social structures via official documentation or records, and children who do research of their own, are all individuals researching in the real world of children and childhood. We now turn our attention to the various ways in which they can best go about planning and conducting their research activities.

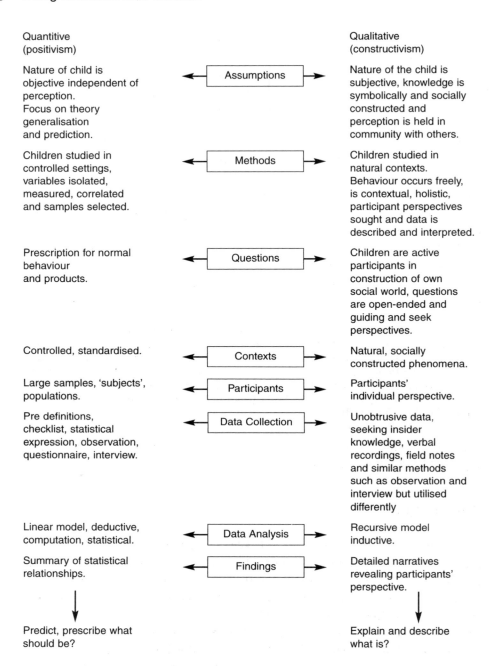

Figure 3.6 A comparison of quantitative and qualitative frameworks for research with children

Source: Based on Hatch, J.A. (ed.) (1995) *Qualitative Research in Early Childhood Settings*. Copyright J. Amos Hatch, Praeger Publishers, 1995. Adapted with permission

PRACTICAL 3.1 DECIDING TO GO QUALITATIVE OR QUANTATIVE

This practical is to demonstrate your ability to choose a basic theoretical framework for approaching various types of research issues.

Below is a list of various projects a researcher might have in mind:
Potential research projects

1 You are curious about the self-esteem of poor readers.
2 You are concerned about the body image of children receiving surgery.
3 You wonder how the birth of a new baby affects the behaviour of pre-schoolers.
4 You are interested in the effects on pre-school children of adoption from abroad.
5 You wonder how children feel about their parents' divorce and subsequent contact arrangements.
6 You are interested in the child-rearing practices of different British cultures.

Either alone or in groups, consider these potential projects with respect to the series of questions below which help you to decide the nature of the enquiry.

1 What is the underlying philosophical system – objective, intuitive/subjective, multiple?
2 What is the purpose of the enquiry – describing everyday reality, finding causes or explanations?
3 What is the nature of your research question/s?
4 What is the nature of the phenomenon being studied?
5 What do you think of advice from colleagues who hold opposing views on this?
6 What are your personal ideas?
7 Is there a way to use both? In everyday practice, multiple methods would be needed to explore the richness of reality.

Part II

Doing research with children – reviewing, designing and conducting research with children

Evaluating research with children

The aims of this chapter are:

- To introduce sources of evidence and how to access evidence.
- To provide a step-by-step guide to evaluating published research.

Learning to be able to analyse critically the research of others is an important skill for the discerning professional. On the one hand, researchers themselves need to be knowledgeable about what has gone on before in their particular field so that they make informed judgements about how they should proceed with their own research. As we discussed in Chapter 1, it is important that research adds to the body of knowledge of the profession, and whilst the replication of research can be useful, it is generally desirable that research should be cumulative and build upon previous work to discover new facts or relationships. The researcher then needs the skills of critical evaluation to identify research problems which have been studied before, to explore methods and approaches which have been taken and, not least, to discover what previous researchers have found through investigation. As we discuss in Chapters 3 and 5, important decisions have to be made when undertaking research about how to design appropriate research strategies. A sound analysis of the work of others in the field will provide a sound foundation for further study by equipping the researcher with the knowledge to make informed, evidence-based judgements.

On the other hand, it is recognised that excellent practice is not only about undertaking research and pushing forwards the boundaries of knowledge, but it is also about being aware of what is going on in our own, and related, professional fields and applying knowledge to our own practices. We must, as professionals, ensure that we are up-to-date and one of the main ways of aspiring to this aim is to access and read professional journals and scholarly works. We must, however, be discerning in what we choose to apply to practice, because to apply all that we read could and probably would lead to much confusion. New and emerging theories are often reported in journals. These theories, generated through inductive processes, are largely untested, so their wholesale incorporation into practice is premature at this stage (see Chapter 3 for further discussion). However, reporting these theories is important so that debate is stimulated around a particular problem and further research in that area is triggered. It is only by accumulating evidence in a field of knowledge that a consensus view of a particular issue can be formed and tentative conclusions drawn.

It therefore becomes very important that the professional practitioner is aware of the whole, emerging debate and not just part of it. A good example over the past 10 years has been the debate about the effects of the mumps, measles and rubella (MMR) vaccination on children and the potential links to autism. Clearly, a professional who had only read one side of the debate without investigating the subject more fully might inappropriately change practice and be open to professional criticism. It is important that the reader can understand the status of a piece of research, be able to evaluate it critically and intelligently utilise the data. In the early stages of an academic debate this may mean doing nothing more than to follow the developments of the debate. Taking parts of an ongoing research debate 'off the shelf' and using bits of it without awareness or analysis of applicability is unacceptable in contemporary practice.

This chapter will follow through the process of accessing and critically evaluating the literature, whilst stressing the necessity of always placing research within a wider theoretical or conceptual frame. Two key contrasting studies, one which broadly fits within a *qualitative* framework and the other within a *quantitative* framework, will be used as exemplars of this process to give a practical focus and to act as case studies for future critical analysis.

Accessing the literature

There is an ever-increasing and wide range of sources for accessing information in a particular field. In some areas the amount of research and literature available can be daunting, making it important that you narrow down your field of enquiry. If you do not do this you may find yourself swamped with the volume of information. The process of refining your search can be difficult, and it may be necessary to undertake some general reading first so that you can identify what are referred to as *keywords*. This general reading can usually be achieved by accessing an academic library such as those found in most universities and colleges, or by accessing research on the Internet.

After you have identified your keywords, there is a range of sources you can use to identify literature. Increased use of information technology has made this task very much easier. Computer databases, compact discs with read only memory (CD-ROM), on-line terminals linked to external databases and the Internet have revolutionised the process, and the arduous task of sifting through cards and bibliographies in the library has become a thing of the past. The skill now is to become familiar with the technology, and most librarians will be only too happy to help. There are also some good texts that will help you with this process (see Ó Dochartaigh 2002; Taylor 2003).

After you have identified a range of references, judgments are required as to which are going to be appropriate for your requirements. Some information sources will provide you only with a title, whilst others will provide an abstract. Some journals are fully available on the Internet so that you have access to the whole article. The next stage is to gather your literature in a manageable, paper-based form so that you can begin the process of critical analysis. This may lead to further searching as, for example, in the case of key research articles which may reference other pieces of work you may also need to access. If a key article appears in a particular journal and you believe the article will stimulate debate, you should access that particular journal on a regular basis so that you do not miss the developing discussion. In some professional fields there are specific and pertinent journals in which such debate will occur whilst in other professions there are literally hundreds of journals relating to a particular field. If, however, a discussion and debate article appears in a particular journal, it is normal practice for the debate to continue in the same journal.

Evaluating research

The most usual and appropriate way of analysing research is the use of the research process as a model for evaluation. However, many students, when analysing research, fall into the trap of using the research process as an inflexible model. Research should always be rigorous and scientific in its enquiry, but different approaches to research inevitably require that researchers place differing emphasis upon the various stages of the process. A *carte blanche* approach will result in confusion for readers as they attempt to fit square pegs into round holes. The reader may make unfounded criticism of the research and the researcher. The following section gives a balanced view of how to approach the evaluation of research, by focusing on two widely available studies which adopt different research approaches so that the need for flexibility and contexualisation can be fully appreciated.

The two studies which have been analysed are:

Hendriks, T., de Hoog, M., Lequin, M.H., Devos, A.S. and Merkus, P.J.F.M. (2005) 'DNase and atelectasis in non–cystic fibrosis pediatric patients'. *Critical Care*, 9: 351–6.
Available online http://ccforum.com/content/9/4/R351

Martin, D., Sweeney, J. and Cooke, J. (2005) 'Views of teenage parents on their support housing needs'. *Community Practitioner*, 78 (11): 392–6

General considerations

The first stage of evaluation is almost an intuitive one and involves reading the whole piece of research at least once and reflecting on your first impressions. It is important to undertake this activity before you begin to engage in the fine detail of the study, when it can sometimes become difficult to interpret the whole (colloquially known as being unable to see the wood for the trees!). You become so enmeshed and engrossed that your objectivity can be compromised.

So what are you looking for at this stage? There is not, unfortunately, an easy answer, but one useful simile is to consider research as a journey. Good research can be likened to a well-planned expedition. The purpose of the journey is well defined and you know what mode of transport you must take. Your route is planned, you have an up-to-date map and you have checked the feasibility of undertaking each part of the journey in the specified time. You have done your homework and know what potential problems lie in your way. You allow extra time for these eventualities. Once you have started you do not deviate from your chosen route, and if you unexpectedly have to take a diversion or you get lost you immediately consult your map and get back on your pathway as soon as possible. You definitely don't 'follow your nose' and head in the general direction of where you believe your original path lies. When you have completed your journey you might make recommendations to other people who wish to go in a similar direction, but your recommendations only relate to the those parts of your journey which you have undertaken and which you therefore have direct experience of. You do not speculate about what you have not seen or heard.

When reading your chosen piece of research you should almost feel a sense of 'completeness' about the research. A good study should have a sense of 'flow'. The research approach should stem from the previous study in this field, the aims should be to expand the knowledge base, the methods should be justified and logical and the data should relate to the aims. You should be able to identify the sources of any conclusions and recommendations from the data. Although intuition is hardly a scientific or rigorous concept, when you become experienced at reading research you will know that when you feel uncomfortable about a piece of research, further detailed analysis will usually show you were right. If you read the piece of research by Hendriks et al. (2005), you will find there is a logical flow to the study. The piece of research by Martin et al. (2005) is less complete, and the reader is left with a number of unanswered questions. For example, the study places great emphasis on describing the research team and the need for developing multi-agency partnerships which were not linked to the aims of the study. The reader is left questioning the relevance of some of the statements within the conclusion to the actual study.

After you have taken a global view of the piece of research it is time to start looking at the study in finer detail, and we have included in the following sections a step-by-step guide to this process using examples of real studies. Prior to doing this there are other questions you should ask yourself before you become engrossed in detail. The first relates to the researcher or researchers: who they are, what job they do and why they are undertaking the research. On reflection this is not such a strange thing to do. You are studying the piece of research in order to establish a base for your own study or in order potentially to change practice. Both will probably cost time and ultimately money. Therefore you should apply a similar logic as you would if you were employing someone to take up work for you and ask if they have the right qualifications for the job and what is their motivation for doing the work. This is particularly important when looking at research involving children, as we have discussed in Chapter 1. Both our studies give the job titles and places of work of the research team. In the Martin et al. (2005) study one of the team is an academic working in a research unit, suggesting that research expertise was at hand.

The second general point relates to the title of the work and whether it is an accurate reflection of the study itself. One of the duties of researchers is to communicate the results of their efforts, and in order to do so the piece of research, if published, should be accessible. In an age where technology is so important and the use of databases is commonplace the use of keywords to access literature has become very important, as we have already discussed. You should therefore ask yourself whether the title of the work contained keywords and gave you an insight into the nature of the study. Short, snappy titles might be clever but are unimpressive when you are searching databases and wading through hundreds of titles. The study by Hendriks et al. (2005) contains key words *DNase*, *atelectasis* and *pediatric* but it does not provide detail of what the study is actually about. The study by Martin et al. (2005) is more comprehensive. Although the title is quite short, you think you instantly know what it is you are going to be reading about. In addition keywords are actually provided – *teenage parents, homelessness, support housing needs, research capacity building* – making the study easy to access. Once you have read the study by Martin et al. (2005) you might, however, question whether the title reflects all that you will read. A substantial part of the study describes why teenage parents need support housing rather than what their view of the support housing is. Neither study makes it clear from the title that the article is primary research, which is important for many students who are required to analyse original research rather than secondary articles, reviews and reports.

Introduction and the problem studied

Researchers, like most other writers, will usually set the scene of the research by formally introducing what they have studied and why. This may or may not be preceded by an *abstract* which is a brief summary of the completed research. In our two studies, Hendriks et al. (2005) give a full abstract which includes an introduction, methods, results and conclusions drawn. The study by Martin et al. (2005) also provides an abstract which is adequate in terms of its detail.

The introduction to the problem being studied is crucial, not only in terms of what follows but also in determining whether you feel it is worth reading the rest! Many busy people will only read the abstract and the first paragraph and discard pieces of work which don't come up to scratch, even though we all know that introductions are notoriously difficult to write and probably do not reflect with accuracy what follows. Abstracts and introductions are the gateway to the rest and should encourage the reader to feel impelled to enter to see what else is on offer.

The opening paragraph of the introduction to the study by Hendriks et al. (2005) places their study within the context of the problems of atelectasis in children – *at least 8% of children on mechanical ventilation develop pulmonary atelectasis* (p. 351) – and the lack of large scale research previously undertaken in the field. By introducing the study in this way the extent of the problem is identifiable and the need to identify treatment is placed in the context of reducing morbidity and length of stay in hospital This is important because research should address 'real' problems which are important and of genuine concern. The study by Martin et al. (2005) also includes an introduction which places the study within a context and introduces an element of familiarity in relation to the accommodation needs of lone teenage parents on the birth of a child. This study also then addresses a real problem which is of significance to many professionals working with children.

Literature review

The review of literature is a vital component of a research study, and with the exception of certain approaches to research undertaken within a qualitative framework (where the related literature is studied at a later point), it is usual to include a literature review after the introduction so that the reader can grasp what has been undertaken in this field before, thus setting the background to the study. We have referred before to the importance of research adding to the body of a profession's knowledge, and this should be demonstrated so that it becomes clear as to how *this* research will contribute to the profession by building upon what has gone before.

There are few hard and fast rules about what literature should be included, and this is largely dependent on the field of study. For example, in relation to the age of the literature used, a study looking at current pharmacological interventions for children who are HIV positive is likely to refer to very recent literature whereas a study looking at the long term effects of institutionalisation on adults who were in care as children is likely to use a much broader scope of literature dating back over several years. Regardless of the topic it is usual to refer to 'classic' literature and 'seminal works' even if they are dated. Each discipline has its own repertoire of such research: for example, in nursing there is Hawthorn's (1974) study *Nurse, I Want My Mummy*, in psychology there are the Isle of Wight studies by Rutter, Graham and Yule (1970) and so on.

All literature should, however, clearly relate to the topic under study, and the researcher should give a balanced view, particularly where there is debate. The strengths and weaknesses of each piece of literature should be discussed and then compared and contrasted with other literature. The literature review should also provide a link between the problem and how it is investigated (we refer back to the notion of a good study which will 'flow'). If there is only a very limited literature review it might be that the particular journal puts constraints upon the researcher who is preparing work for publication or it might be that there is a very limited amount of relevant literature available because of a lack of previous research in the field. In the case of the latter, the researcher should tell you that this is so.

Turning now to our two studies, the literature review in the study by Hendriks et al. (2005), while brief, is very pertinent to the field of study, although for a study about the efficacy of medication one-third of the references are in excess of 10 years old, one-third are between five and 10 years old and only one-third of citations are less than five years old. The literature is not compared and contrasted but is simply described and the strengths and weaknesses of each piece of literature are not analysed. The second study by Martin et al. (2005) uses a range of literature in age (including seminal works in the field). As with Hendriks et al.'s study, the literature is described rather than analysed, making it difficult for the reader to make judgements about what is the existing research base in the field.

Research questions, aims, objectives and hypotheses

From the literature review there should logically follow clear statements about the purpose of the research, usually expressed in terms of aims, research questions, objectives or hypotheses or a combination of these depending on the type of research. In Chapter 5 we discuss the importance of research questions and in Chapter 3 we further discussed the use of hypotheses within a quantitative framework. Within qualitative frameworks formal hypotheses are inappropriate because they test existing theory and, as we have previously discussed, qualitative research uses inductive processes to build theory.

Aims, questions, objectives and hypotheses are pivotal to the research process which the study should address through investigation. When evaluating research the reader should seek to make judgements about the relevance of aims, questions, objectives and hypotheses and should refer back to them when evaluating later parts of the study to ensure that they have not become lost in the debate. This is all part of the completeness of the study. In the study by Hendriks et al. (2005) the study aim is never clearly stated and the authors do not make explicit what they are seeking to test. The reader has the task of making the assumption that the statement *the present study analysed the resolution of atelectasis following treatment with DNase in a large series of hospitalized children who were refractory to conventional treatment* is the aim of the study and it is only possible to make this assumption after you have read the complete article. The study also tests a number of the effects of DNase on a number of variables but the reader is never given a hypothesis for these tests. The study by Martin et al. (2005) makes specific reference to three study aims, although these are fairly well hidden half-way down the third page of a five-page publication.

The sample

In our experience students undertaking research often become confused over the meanings of samples and populations, and yet understanding is important if the reader is to make sound judgements about the accuracy of data analysis, reliability and validity. Samples are drawn from, and aim to be characteristic and representative of, a population. Sampling strategies are designed to achieve that aim. If sampling is poor it can be disastrous (see also Chapters 5 and 6 for further discussion). Researchers should be absolutely clear about who or what provided them with their data and justify how they selected their sample. Within a quantitative framework the ideal is to utilise *probability* sampling where each member of a population has an equal chance of being included in the sample. In practice this is rarely possible and certainly much of the research within the caring professions utilises convenience sampling (selecting convenient participants) or some form of pseudo–random sample drawn from a convenience sample. Within a qualitative framework samples tend to be smaller, convenient and therefore *non-probable*, with each member of the population having an unequal chance of being selected. Qualitative researchers do, however, employ strategies for trying to ensure that their chosen sample has characteristics which are largely similar to the population from which it is drawn. One type of qualitative sampling is *purposive* or *judgemental,* where the researcher selects participants who could not be identified through other sampling strategies, employing judgement to ensure that the sample is selected on the basis of the information required (a sort of hand picking of people who you know will have the knowledge or experiences you require).

The sample in the study by Hendriks et al. (2005) was simply constituted but was also complex because the children were not an homogenous group. All children who received DNase treatment for atelectasis between 1998 and 2002 were included unless they had cystic fibrosis, in which case they were excluded. The authors presented a simple and clear table in the text giving demographic details of the 30 children included in the study. However, on reading this table the reader can see that, for example, the age range was 14 days to 12 years and the duration of disease before the onset of the atelectasis ranged from 2 to 365 days. The implications of these variables are not fully explored within the study.

The study by Martin et al. (2005) gives brief details of the sample and states that the 25 teenage parents who took part in the study were recruited through existing service networks – health visiting services, Young Children's Centres and social services networks. Inclusion criteria were given – for example, became parents before the age of 18 years, could speak English, were able to understand and give informed consent and that there were no child protection issues. The study states that *practitioners were asked to identify relevant young parents and refer them to the project*. There is no information about the possible numbers of teenage parents in the city where the study took place so the reader is left not knowing what the extent of the problem is. Nor does the reader know if 25 was the total number of young parents who were referred to the project or whether there were more and the sample was drawn from these. The study then goes on to state that the sample was *purposively* selected to ensure that a range of views would be captured. It would have been useful if the researchers had stated this before giving the reader the impression that professionals had referred all of those who met the inclusion criteria. There are further issues with the sampling in this study. The authors provide a table which takes up the majority of a page of the article giving a description of the sample. This table provides details of the age of participants when interviewed, sex, age of children, mother's age at last child's birth, planned pregnancy or not, whether the mother lives with the father and contact with the father. The gender of one of the sample is missing and in two cases the sex is 'M' and 'F'. The reader assumes that in these two cases the interviewees were a couple. However, there were three other males and the reader has no way of knowing whether the children lived alone with the fathers, whether the mothers lived in the same household but did not take part in the study or what the situation was. The column *lives with father* has a 'yes' recorded for two of the males but a 'no' for one of them so the reader does not know if this column refers to whether the mother lives with the father or whether it means the children live with the father. The reader is left will the following questions:

- How many young parents were referred by professionals to the project?
- If it was more than 25 how were these selected from the overall referrals?
- How did the purposive sampling strategy work?
- What is the status of the males in the sample?

Ethical implications

In Chapter 9 we discuss fully the ethical implications of undertaking research involving children and what measures researchers should take to ensure that their research is *ethical*. When evaluating research it is important that the reader evaluates whether or not the researchers have followed correct ethical procedures, such as gaining permission, obtaining informed consent and so on (see Chapter 9 for a full discussion). In our two studies, Hendriks et al. (2005) made scant mention of the ethical implications of their study or how they addressed potential ethical issues, stating only that because the DNase was administered as part of patient care and not a medical trial formal approval from an ethics board was not required by their hospital. However, as you will read in Chapter 9 this would certainly not be the case in the UK and ethical approval for any study involving the records of patients (as in the case of this study) would be required. The study by Martin et al. (2005), on the other hand, makes clear statements about gaining ethical approval and the rights of the parents in terms of confidentiality. Linking back to an earlier point, however, the reader is left wondering whether this study did uphold confidentiality, particularly as the scope of the potential population is not known. For example, one of the sample was a female with 9 month old twins who gave birth at 17 years, and four of the sample had two children by the age of 16 years. It might be that there were hundreds of young parents with housing support needs who fit these descriptions but the point is that the reader simply does not know.

As you will read in Chapter 9, following correct ethical principles is a vital stage of the research process, and researchers who do not give adequate acknowledgement to this should expect to receive criticism in relation to their omission.

Data collection

In Chapters 5, 6 and 7 we explore research techniques and ways of collecting data from children. When evaluating research it is important to identify precisely what the participants within the sample had to do in order to give the researcher the information required, what tools the researcher used to collect and/or measure the response and whether these were appropriate. Data collection tools (or instruments) include such things as interview schedules, rating scales, questionnaires and observation schedules and frequently will incorporate more than one instrument within one piece of research. Clearly when collecting data from children the choice of an instrument will be influenced by a number of factors, including the developmental stage of the child.

Returning for a moment to our completeness theme, when evaluating the research the data collection tools should appear logical and should be directed towards meeting the aims, research questions, objectives or hypotheses. In complex studies it is a useful exercise to take each part of the study and map through how each area of data collection will work. This will also highlight any assumptions on the part of the researcher and obsolete data. It is not unusual for researchers to use an array of tools to collect data that do not apparently relate to the stated purpose of the study.

The reliability and validity of the research tool are a very important part of the research process, which should be addressed by the researcher and which are rather like an internal quality assurance system (for further detail see Chapter 5). Within a quantitative framework issues of reliability and validity are addressed in a different way from that for research which is undertaken within a qualitative framework. In quantitative research the researcher is concerned that objectivity is achieved and bias is eliminated, that the study methods can be accurately replicated and that findings can be generalised across populations. The qualitative researcher should not ignore reliability and validity, but these are viewed differently. Replication is not generally sought, and reliability is established through verification by or with the participants.

If we look at our two studies the contrast is evident between the two research paradigms. In the study by Hendriks et al. (2005) data were collected from children's notes and the physiological parameters were measured two hours after the administration of the DNase. Chest X-rays were coded, blinded and interpreted randomly by two independent radiologists and comparisons were made using Cohen's kappa (a measurement of agreement of observations). On the other hand, the study by Martin et al. (2005) refers only to increasing the validity of the study by feeding back the results to the steering group, which included young people. This type of confirmation of the likelihood of results is known as 'member checking' – that is, checking with informants that the interpretation by the researchers matches the respondents' understanding of what was said.

Data analysis and results

When evaluating research it is important that the reader gains an understanding as to how data are analysed so that an accurate link can be made between the gathered data and the results. This might be as simple as a researcher describing the use of percentages or tables and graphs, or more complicated as in the use of inferential statistics. In qualitative research, data analysis may involve defining categories, employing varying levels of content analysis, coding and so on. Quantitative and qualitative frameworks may also differ in terms of the separation of actual results from discussion arising from the results. Quantitative research will usually report results in what is defined as a *value-free* way, which simply means presenting results without interpreting them in a wider context. There usually follows a distinct discussion which will provide interpretation within the context of the theoretical framework, previous work and the aims, questions or hypotheses. In qualitative research the results may be structured in a similar way, but not always. For example, as we have described previously, a grounded theory approach will describe the data generated through a particular investigation and will seek to verify emerging categories through comparison with other studies. When you evaluate data analysis and results you should attempt to make informed judgements about whether the correct techniques have been used in an appropriate way. For example, if the researcher has used a particular statistical test, is the test appropriate for the type of data analysed? If a parametric test is used are the data normally distributed, was the sample random and of sufficient size, were the measurements used at least interval and so on? (Chapters 5, 6 and 7 deal with some of these issues.) Don't worry if these questions seem daunting and alien to you. The important point here is that you should be aware that there are questions you *must* ask, even though you might need help in identifying what those questions are.

In our two studies there is a contrast in approach to reporting results. The study by Hendriks et al. (2005) has a separate results section which is followed by a separate discussion section. The Wilcoxon matched pairs signed rank sum test was used to identify differences in the parameters before and after the administration of the DNase. This is a non-parametric analysis and was suitable for the type of data being analysed. The study by Martin et al. (2005) incorporates elements of discussion with the results followed by a combined discussion/conclusion section. The first study analyses and describes the data using a range of descriptive and inferential statistics, whereas the study by Martin et al. (2005) describes themes and sub-themes using *verbatim* data from the interview and focus group transcripts to illustrate meaning and illustrate response.

Conclusion, recommendations and limitations

The final aspect of the evaluation is about tying up all the loose ends and moving forwards. As with any academic piece of work, the research should be concluded, and because research is about the discovery of new facts or relationships these should be defined in terms of application to practice, future research and other recommendations. These should be made within the context of any limitations of the research: for example, a study which used a convenience sample may refer to the inappropriateness of generalisation across a population and suggest that further study using a different sampling strategy be undertaken.

The conclusion is also about 'closing the loop' and emphasising the completeness of the work. We used the simile of a well-planned journey at the beginning of the chapter, so it may be useful to view the conclusion as arrival at your destination when you sit down to relax, reflect, plan what you are going to do now that you have arrived, and look forward to your next journey.

Turning for a final time to our two studies, Hendriks et al. (2005) conclude their study by summarising what they had found through their investigation and by referring to how their study added to the existing body of knowledge in the field, making suggestions for further research relating to their particular findings. The study by Martin et al. (2005) highlights the major themes explored, including lack of money, isolation and support. The study then goes on at some length to discuss how multi-agency working would be beneficial to the young people in the study although this was not actually an aim of the research and did not appear to be explored during the data collection. Both studies are explicit in recognising the limitations of their work in terms of not being able to generalise findings.

Conclusion

Evaluating the research of others is important for two reasons. First, in order to be informed about the knowledge base within your own profession you must be aware of research which has been and is being undertaken and be able to analyse that research. Second, if you wish to undertake research yourself you must be able intelligently to use previous research to guide you. The process of evaluating research is not difficult but does involve practice and a level of knowledge about the research process. In this chapter we have taken two contrasting research papers and highlighted briefly some of the areas that are important in evaluating research as an example of the considerations that should be given when reading research.

PRACTICAL 4.1   SEARCHING FOR INFORMATION

This practical is to enable you to practise searching thoroughly in a narrow area to help you improve your skills of accessing information.

During the process of this practical, keep a note of problems encountered, help received and from whom or where, solutions to problems and any other information which may be helpful in the future.

Think of an area you might like to know more about which relates to children – if you cannot think of anything look at the research hunches in Practical 3.1 (see p. 61) for an idea. Then:

- Go to the library and find one general article or book relating to the topic and from there identify two *keywords.*
- Find out what databases are available.
- Ask the librarian to show you how to use one of the databases.
- Using your keywords, search the database.
- Find out which sources of information are available in the library.

If you have access to an Internet connection, using your keywords search the Web to see what information you can find.

PRACTICAL 4.2   CRITICAL EVALUATION OF A KEY STUDY

This practical aims to give you experience of critical evaluation.

- Access and look at the two studies evaluated within this chapter.
- Then select a different study, which might be one which you have identified in Practical 3.1.
- Follow through the process described in this chapter, keeping a note of any difficulties you experience.

5

Designing and doing research with children: the importance of questions

The aims of this chapter are:

- To consider the role of questions in designing and doing research with children: discriminating between *hypotheses* and research *questions*.
- To introduce core research principles of reliability and validity.
- To provide a practical guide for formulating and asking reliable and valid questions in doing research with children.

A small child who is asked the question 'What is a Prime Minister?' may offer the correct answer, an inventive one, such as 'somebody who marries people', or a comic one which has no logical relation to the question, like 'a blue thing you put into the oven'. The inability to predict the answer a child will give is a fact which, in addition to providing entertainment for adults, demonstrates that children's minds are special. The relationship between children and questions is special in several ways: the questions you need to ask yourself when designing research with children; questioning the assumptions behind your research questions on children; and questioning children themselves. You may wish, for example, to explore the nature of children's relationship with their mother and to know, in particular, how children feel when their mother has to leave them. The way in which you will go about this investigation needs to be *designed* and this entails asking yourself the following questions: What is the basic research issue? What do I want to do? With whom do I want to do it? When do I want to do it? Are my intended methods reliable and valid?

Many basic research designs flounder because the research issue lacks a clear rationale which conveys a sense of the importance of doing the research in the first place. Thus, the following questions prove helpful: Why is this important? Who will be interested in the results? Having set up a basic design and addressed the rationale, it is wise still to challenge the theoretical and popular assumptions which may underlie it. The rationale behind this particular research issue could be based on the assumption that a secure mother–child relationship is essential for normal development. The researcher needs to consider the sources of evidence for this. Is it based on research data or clinical evidence? Is it based on popular wisdom, personal conviction or a political or professional ideal? Finally, we return to questioning children themselves. In order to determine how children feel when their mother leaves him, each child could be asked directly, 'How did you feel when your Mum left you in the hospital?' Even when put to a primary school child, the usefulness of the answer will depend upon the age of the child and also on the child's verbal abilities. Younger children are usually unable to cope and, in the case of pre-school children, require the researcher to enter the world with which the child is familiar – the world of stories, dolls, puppets, sand and drawing.

Clearly, asking questions in designing and doing research with children is a skill which needs to be cultivated, and an effective training programme will deal thoroughly with the issue at all levels of research. In the following sections, we will cover these topics in more detail.

The question of research design

The research tutor has just handed you the Guidelines for Research. How do you feel? Your heart may flutter in excitement, anticipation and adventure at this new challenge and opportunity systematically to investigate a topic close to your heart. Or your heart may sink in panic and dread at the prospect of coming up with a topic and coping with new research skills. The best studies usually come from researchers who have a 'hunch', and those who start from this point are likely to feel positive about the ensuing challenges. The hunch may be something the researcher has observed about children when working in a school, hospital, home, or from the researcher's own experiences as a parent or child. Whatever the source of the hunch, it will be something which interests the researcher and consequently will be a source of intrigue and passion. It has been well said that the challenges of doing research are such that only researchers who 'fall in love' with their subjects to the point of total immersion will succeed! Deciding on the right questions and approaches will make the difference between an interesting study and a mundane one. Equally important is knowing why the question needs to be asked in the first place and how to do it. Therefore, before attempting to design and investigate the proposed question, researchers need to ask themselves questions like: *Why is it important to ask this question about children? To whom will the answers matter and what can be done with them? What kind of question is it – one which can be objectively tested, a subjective enquiry or an exploratory problem?*

Why is it important to ask questions about children?

At the general level *any* question on children is important if only because of their importance in our lives. Furthermore, the climate for doing research with children has never been better, with new policies encouraging easier access to children and cooperation between individuals and agencies in order better to understand and support the developmental needs of children. Over the past generation technological advances such as video cameras and recorders have transformed the opportunities we have for investigating a wider range of research questions effectively. Subtle qualities of relationships and split-second gestures are the sorts of behaviours which can be captured on camera, played and replayed and rigorously analysed on our computers which further increase our power in doing research. Figure 5.1 shows some video footage of live research, the quality of which allows a detailed investigation of children's behaviour and relationships either in naturalistic or free-flow settings or in experimenter led, controlled tasks. Researchers are now well placed to ask previously inaccessible questions in greater quantities, better and quicker. Given the current climate of research conditions for researching children it is more a case of why not than why do such a study! Other good general reasons for asking research questions on children include: the fact that their rapid growth enables us to observe developmental changes and monitor intervention outcomes within a fairly short time span; finding out about children informs us about adults; research on children can help practitioners learn more about and improve their practice; and finally, child studies often help to support or disprove some theory about the nature and development of children. More recently, advances in methods for consulting with children on their perspectives as well as actively involving them as participant researchers, means that we are becoming more able to listen to their voices and to empower them. The relation between research, theory and practice is explored further in Chapter 2. The question may also be of personal importance to the researcher. Indeed, the *raison d'être* of the research question may be a direct result of a childhood experience of illness, abuse, adoption, emotional behavioural disorders, school experience or relationship difficulties. Finally, and perhaps most importantly, is that the research question should be important for children themselves and lead to an improvement for them and the worlds in which they live. In fact, a research question *should* be important in all the ways described.

When a research question is not a question

People wishing to do research with children come from many professional backgrounds – child health, social care and education being prominent examples.

Figure 5.1   Video footage of live research which enables detailed behavioural analysis

Associated academic disciplines of psychology, biology and sociology each have preferred approaches to asking research questions. In considering the nature of an attachment relationship, for example, a biologist might ask: do stress indicators in saliva increase during separations between mother and child? A developmental psychologist might ask: do insecurely attached children perform less well than securely attached children in tests of psychosocial functioning? A social worker would perhaps ask: what is the social history of this child who is insecurely attached to his adoptive parents? Clearly all of these are viable research questions but there are some important differences. The first two questions imply an objective test or experiment of some kind together with the use of specific tests and equipment. In research these sorts of questions are referred to as *hypotheses* which propose a relationship between two variables. An example could be attachment security and the child's performance on a test assessing understanding of emotion. The nature of the proposed relationships will be based on theory, in this case attachment theory, which allows predictions to be made about the relationship and to be tested in an experimental and controlled setting. Generally, a prediction is a statement that a change in one thing (the independent variable) will produce an effect in another thing (the dependent variable). Thus, a change in security of attachment is predicted to produce a change in performance of the emotion test. The aim of this type of research is to explain *why* children behave as they do as opposed to merely describing their behaviour, and findings, being based on assessment of many children, are relevant to all.

The question posed by the social worker requires a different interpretation. Here we are concerned with an individual child with a unique history. It is a matter of asking questions rather than hypotheses, and these questions are subjective and aimed at describing *what* is going on with this child. While questions can be highly generalised, as in 'what is this child's social history?', they can also reflect an intention to use a particular theory: in this case, where does attachment theory inform our understanding of this child and how can we help him? The main difference in the two approaches is between seeking explanation and seeking understanding.

Table 5.1 illustrates the differences between research hypotheses and research questions, and Box 5.1 illustrates the evolution of a research question.

Box 5.1   The evolution of a research question

Julie is on a teacher training course and wishes to work in reception classes. As an experienced classroom assistant she has noticed that very young children tend to have more behavioural disturbances than older children in reception. In addition, she has been concerned about recent government legislation which means that children can now join formal education classes as young as 4 years of age. She watches television debates and reads the national press. She is annoyed that nobody appears to be considering the long term developmental effects of the new legislation on very young children who are, she believes, at a most critical stage in their development. She decides that this will be a good research topic and begins to formulate a number of research questions to discuss with her supervisor.

(Continued)

Julie must first of all question her assumptions and those of established authorities. The assumption underlying her point of view is that younger children are disadvantaged in some way. Can she say that this is true of all the younger children or are some individuals doing at least as well as the older reception children? At this point all she has is an opinion based on limited personal experience and a belief based on a theory that children go through critical phases of development. She needs to question these opinions and beliefs and find 'scientific' evidence to back up her views. Julie consults a number of research journals to find out what is known about the adaptation of very young children to formal education. She finds that there has not yet been a systematic study of this kind, so 'scientific' evidence is unavailable. This is the rationale and importance of her study. Policy decisions are being made with the potential to damage the development of very young children while no investigations appear to be taking place to justify decisions. The answers to her question will have the potential to inform policy makers and practitioners who wish to minimise any potential threats to the children involved. This means that she has indeed found a topic worthy of further investigation but also that her study will be exploratory rather than adding proof to an established body of scientific research. This is the difference between asking the general question 'what are the effects, if any, of entry to reception classes on the behaviour of very young children?' and predicting a very specific outcome such as the hypothesis that 'younger children in reception class will manifest more behavioural and emotional difficulties than older children in reception class'.

Table 5.1   Examples of research questions which are best posed as either hypotheses or as exploratory questions

Pose as hypotheses (Seeking explanation)	Pose as questions (Seeking understanding)
What parenting strategies *determine* emotional and behavioural difficulties in children?	What are the feelings and thoughts of children and parents *themselves* about how they get on together?
What are the social and environmental variables that *predict* child abuse?	What are the definitions of the parents and children themselves of *experiences* of child abuse?
What is the *relationship* between family disruption and child characteristics of age, gender and temperament?	What are the *perceptions* of children from broken homes about conflict and divorce?
Emphasis is on determinants, predictions and statistical relationships. These questions seek explanations for WHY children behave and develop as they do.	Emphasis *is* on description and interpretation of the participants' perspective. These questions lead to an understanding of WHAT is going on in the child's world, and the child guides the research.

Source: Adapted from Hatch (ed.) (1995) *Qualitative Research in Early Childhood Settings*. Copyright J. Amos Hatch, Praeger Publishers, 1995. Adapted with permission

Research design: the basic questions

Once the research questions or hypotheses have been formulated and deemed important, the researcher has to come up with a basic design which addresses *who* are to be the participants, *what* exactly is to be done, and *when?*

Who? Given the nature of the purpose of the study and the research question or hypotheses, who should the participants be? Babies, toddlers, pre-schoolers, school-aged children, adolescents, pairs of mothers and children, whole families or children from several age groups? Perhaps the study requires the participation of a particular group or a range of different child educare professionals such as social workers, child-minders, mediators, nurses, teachers, doctors, psychiatrists and service managers. Should the study include only boys or also girls? Is it about fathers rather than mothers or are both equally important? Another crucial question is *how many* participants to include. If you ask only 10 children to complete a questionnaire on personality and relate it to their academic performance, you would not be very confident that your conclusions are accurate. If, however, you do the same thing with thousands of children, you would be much more confident. Another requirement is to ensure that the sample is representative of the general population – in this case, to include a range of child abilities and cultures. The above example is appropriate for testing a hypothesis, the purpose of which is to make generalisations with the results and make predictions. However, large numbers are not so important when the purpose of the study is to describe what is going on in the world of a particular child or relationship.

What? What is to be done to or with the research participants? The purpose of the research may be to find out what happens when you subject them to particular treatments or conditions. If the aim is to test whether children perform better in achievement tests after a schedule of self-esteem enhancement then an *experimental* design is required. If the aim is simply to observe or measure the relation between actual self-esteem and achievement tests then a *correlational* design is needed. On the other hand, the study may focus on one particular child with reading difficulties, the aim of which is to obtain rich descriptions of both the teacher's and the child's view of her reading ability, supplemented by other school, medical and social records, and an exploration of teacher strategies which do and do not work for this child. If this is the purpose of the study then a *case study* design is needed. Each of these designs and others are described in detail in Chapters 6 and 7 and the theoretical frameworks which support them in Chapter 3.

When? Do you need to assess the participants only once or more than once? A study addressing the relationship between current self-esteem and test performance need only be done once. A study comparing a child's performance on tests after intervention requires at least two assessments: before the intervention and after the intervention. Some studies which aim to say more about developmental pathways will entail continuous assessment throughout childhood:

measures at 18 months, a presumed critical stage for longer term outcomes, can be related to a variety of other measures at the pre-school stage, primary school stage, adolescence and beyond. These studies, which look at the same child or group of children over a long period of time, are known as *longitudinal designs*. An alternative, less time consuming, approach is to study the same measures in children at different developmental stages. Thus self-esteem and achievement scores in a group of primary school children can be compared with self-esteem and achievement scores in a group of adolescents. This is known as a *cross-sectional design* which is efficient but unable to map the developmental pathways of individuals.

Table 5.2 summarises basic research designs for studying children. These designs are more commonly associated with large samples of children, but most can apply to individual case studies also. An individual child can be studied longitudinally, receive experimental interventions and correlations between a variety of measures, say school achievement, social hardship, health, attachment security and self-esteem.

The question of reliability and validity

Continuing with our hypothetical examination of self-esteem, let us suppose that you wish to assess self-esteem in children who are disabled or who have been disfigured as a result of an accident. All existing measures, you think, are not specific enough about certain issues that you feel are particularly important, so you create a new version. How can you be certain that the instrument you have designed is accurate and truly assesses what you want it to do? How can you tell how good any instrument is at assessing what it is supposed to do? In order to be confident about your instrument's accuracy, you need to determine its *reliability* and *validity*.

Reliability

A reliable instrument will give a consistent measure of the behaviour or construct in question – in this case, self-esteem. If we have children complete the same questionnaire on several different occasions and the outcome varies each time from low to high self-esteem then we cannot be certain than it does indeed measure self-esteem or that self-esteem is a consistent construct in itself. Likewise an instrument supposedly assessing IQ does not tell us much about a child's intelligence if it varies dramatically between tests every Monday morning for a month. Another way of ensuring reliability is *inter-observer reliability*. This is a procedure in which two independent assessors agree on the behavioural codes being observed or the score obtained in a particular instrument. The greater the correlation or agreement between the results obtained by the two independent 'observers' the greater the reliability of the behavioural codes or instruments. If

Table 5.2   A summary of basic research designs for doing research with children

Design	Features	Aim	Advantage/disadvantage
Cross-sectional	Children from different age groups assessed at the same time	To describe developmental age norms	Quick, efficient, economic/Not about individual development
Longitudinal	Same children assessed periodically as they grow up	To describe developmental changes for particular groups or individual children	Addresses continuity of development/ drop outs, and participants know the test
Correlational	Various child assessments are taken at the same time and correlated	To examine the relation between two or more child scores and tentative explanations	Easy to implement/cannot imply cause and other potential variables
Experimental	An experimenter controls an independent variable or intervention	To test hypotheses which explain children's behaviour and development	Valuable for providing strong evidence of cause and effect in child development

the aim is to assess, by observation, the extent of a child's solitary play, an inter-observer test would look as shown in Figure 5.2.

It can be seen, at a glance, that there is a perfect correlation or agreement in this case. However, it is acceptable to have merely good or high levels of agreement or correlation because human behaviour always entails an element of subjectivity and inconsistency (random error). In addition, where many behaviours are being assessed or there are many participants, it is necessary to run an appropriate statistical test (see Chapter 6). Yet another measure of reliability is the *internal consistency* of instruments such as a self-esteem questionnaire. If the instrument has 10 items assessing body image, you would expect children who score high on self-esteem generally to score high also on most of the other items. In effect, an instrument is internally consistent when all items yield similar scores. Establishing the reliability of a research tool can be a complicated and lengthy affair, so novice researchers are advised to use instruments which are already accepted as reliable by the research community.

Validity

As a researcher you need to ask yet another series of questions about your data. Once the self-esteem or behavioural scores are in you must ask 'Do my data

Child	frequency of solidarity play	
	Observer A	Observer B
1	5	5
2	2	2
3	6	6

Figure 5.2   Example of an inter-observer test

make sense? Does this measure what it's supposed to measure?'. If you had interviewed a group of professionals on their strategies for dealing with low self-esteem in children and they spoke at length about what they do, in principle, because you know they seldom have the time to implement their strategies, then your method does not do what it is supposed to do. It does not have *face validity*. Similarly, if the group of confident children all score equally badly on your measure of self-esteem, then you need to question the face validity of your instrument and its general usefulness as an index of self-esteem. It has been argued that controlled, experimental laboratory-based research studies do not reflect the properties of the real world and real relationships in which the child lives. This type of research is said to be low in ecological validity and researchers need to be interpreting their findings from this research for real life situations. Controlled, experimental research has high internal validity, however, because confounding variables are systematically controlled for. There is quite a lot of psychological child and family research done in quasi–naturalistic research settings such as the one depicted in Figure 5.3. This shows a laboratory set-up which mimics a real domestic setting and has an observation and recording facility built in. What do you suppose are the advantages and disadvantages of this type of research setting?

Ecological validity can be enhanced by doing more naturalistic research, in natural settings such as homes, schools, playgrounds, hospitals and neighbourhoods, and using familiar people such as parents, peers and professionals in the research design. In some cases, researchers become 'participants' themselves, perhaps by assuming a teacher, nurse or carer role.

Reliability and validity of methods may never be perfect. It is certainly possible for a highly reliable instrument to lack validity. Although it is more difficult to assess validity than reliability, by obtaining similar scores on a variety of instruments and measures which supposedly measure the same construct and assessing whether various scores relate in meaningful ways, it is possible to improve the validity of your research. This method is used most by researchers using a deductive

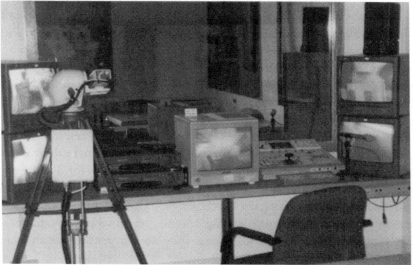

Figure 5.3 **A laboratory domestic setting with observation mirror and record-ing facilities built in**

model – that is, one which is theory driven and requires hypothesis testing. An equivalent method called *triangulation* is used by researchers using an inductive model – that is, one which is driven by exploratory, subjective questions and the participants' perspectives (deductive and inductive models are fully explained in Chapter 3). Triangulation enables researchers to capture, to some extent, the shifting realities of their participants. Case study triangulation entails obtaining more than one, usually three, perspectives on a given phenomenon. Research into agency thresholds in dealing with children in need could include similar interviews addressed to field workers, service managers and parents. Triangulation also occurs by using more than one researcher or a mixture of all of these.

The questioning of assumptions

It is ironic that a researcher, who has once been a child, needs seriously to consider questions such as: What is it like to be a child? How does a child think and feel? How can I find out? The feeling and thinking of childhood are lost to the adult, at least in a direct sense, for all we have are memories of varying degrees of reliability and validity. Nonetheless, until the researcher has attempted to answer these sorts of questions, there is little point in researching children at all. The best place to begin is to challenge the assumptions we typically have about children and childhood. The researcher's own view of childhood will be affected by personal experience as a child or parent, by professional training, identity and experience, by cultural views and by current trends or fashions. Caring professions, such as nursing and social work, naturally see the child as an object of concern. A child needs to be assessed and protected, and decisions will have to be made about the future of the child. Honourable as this is, the downside is the disempowerment of the child and the oversight of the child's own perspective. The assumption has long been held that children are not able to contribute reliably towards discussions on their feelings, needs and future. This, in turn, has clearly affected the nature of the research questions which have been posed and a delay in the development of methods for speaking directly to children and eliciting their views. Certainly researchers within the academic discipline of psychology have had assumptions about children. Hill et al. (1996) describes the psychologist's view of children as 'objects of study'. This means that they too have largely ignored the child's point of view, subjective opinions and the methods which need to be used to obtain them. In effect, psychological research is done *on* children rather than *with* children. Theories and hypotheses are generated by adults, standardised tests are done on the children or controlled experiments, and the data are statistically analysed. Such psychological research has achieved a great deal in improving techniques for studying children (see Chapter 6) and should continue to do so in the future, for, as we will presently discuss, some questions need to be tackled in a controlled fashion. Professional assumptions can also influence our views of children. Teachers are likely to see them as objects of learning and development. In addition, historical or cultural trends come into play. For instance, a teacher trained in the 'child-centred' 1960s would have perceived the child as an active player in the development of knowledge, requiring only the provision of an appropriate environment and the biological readiness to learn. Compare this with the early twentieth century view of children as passive recipients of reading, writing and arithmetic. Practitioner researchers, then, should critically consider how their professional identities and assumptions of children may colour their research questions and methods. The child is always so much more than it is professionally convenient to believe.

Schaffer (1998) gives specific examples of the fashions influencing our views of children and their development. Child-rearing methods, working mothers, separation from parents, divorce and fathers as competent carers are all child development issues which have been known to vary in emphasis over time and across cultures. Schaffer also warns of the danger of forming beliefs about children based on the wisdom of established authorities. It often is the case that such wisdom is derived from a mixture of personal opinion, guesswork, folklore, work with clinical cases and experiences of rearing their own children. Indeed, this is true, to some extent, of some of the most influential developmental theorists, including Darwin, Freud and Piaget!

Questioning adults about children and childhood

In some types of research it may be necessary to question an adult on the child's behalf. This is likely to be the case when the child is too young or unable to speak. It could also be that it has been deemed unethical to raise particular types of questions with children directly or that the researcher has a particular interest in the parent's or carer's relationship with the child or the perspective of the child. Another approach is to assess the parent's own experiences of childhood and perhaps relate them to how they perceive and relate to their own children. All of these approaches are important and relevant for anyone doing research with children. Regardless of the focus of the main research question, a questionnaire or an interview with an adult or parent who knows the child well can add a new dimension to the research. The techniques for interviewing parents and adults who care for or work with children are discussed in detail in Chapters 7 and 8.

Questioning children themselves

The novice researcher about to question children for the first time will have to deal with a number of myths which surround the whole process. Typically these include assumptions about the child's capabilities. Notions that young children cannot be asked direct questions or chatted to are common, as are beliefs that they should not be seen alone or for any length of time. Nonetheless, in the context of the child's age, there are important issues which do need to be taken into account. Very young children or pre-schoolers do have limited communicative abilities relative to school-aged children and also to teenagers. On the other hand, they are also surprisingly competent in ways not usually appreciated by researchers. The issues primarily concern the cognitive abilities of the children, the validity of their statements and researchers' interpretations of their statements.

While reliability is important for specific measures, it is mainly validity that matters when verbally engaging with children. The accuracy of children's responses largely depends on their developmental capacities, including their ability to manage the demands of the research tasks used to pose the questions, to cope with one-to-one interviews or group interviews, and their understanding of the reason for the interview. The questioning of children takes place in a variety of social contexts, such as clinics, classrooms, playgrounds, or the family home, which in themselves may have a direct effect on the validity of the child's response. Every effort should be made by the researcher to choose the context wisely, to understand the child's developmental and individual abilities in the design of questions and supporting materials, to explain to the child why he or she is there and what will happen. Researchers should present themselves in a friendly and reassuring manner and the child should be allowed time to become familiar with a strange environment or new pieces of equipment or toys that are part of the research. Let us consider some kinds of questions a researcher might want to put to a child.

Who? What? Where? Very young children are able to identify people, objects and places either verbally or by pointing to them. They can distinguish self from others. Very young children, however, are prone to errors of classification: all male adults could be labelled 'daddy'.

Why? When? How? Even though 2 year olds can make simple inferences about cause and effect and understand the permanence of objects, it is not until reaching school age that children are consistently able to respond to questions requiring explanations such as 'Why?', 'When?' or 'How?'.

The past, present and future Pre-schoolers are able to talk about present and past experience, but their concept of time is not fully developed. Order of recall and use of past tense is not always easy for them. At around 4 years of age they are using past and future tenses but their notions of time are still associated with routines such as meals or television programmes. Their concept of time improves gradually once at school and they become able to deal with clocks and calendars.

Questions relying on memory A related issue is the memory capacity of children. Like adults, a child's memory can be affected by other factors such as the circumstances around the event in question and associated emotional arousal. Children will not be comparable to adults until the end of the primary school years. Consequently, young children often need support in remembering, and this can be improved by using familiar toys and allowing the child to play or enact past events with the help of toys. This enables a researcher to clarify who or what the children are talking about.

Sensitive questions   The child's ability to distinguish fact from fantasy is important in questioning a child about a traumatic event, as is the researcher's ability to interpret what the child says and does. Even quite young children do not create a false picture. Three year olds are able to tell the difference between pretend play with materials and its real nature, and 4 year olds understand the difference between truth and lies and that telling lies is wrong.

Reporting on knowledge and beliefs   When using open questions or statements, nursery and early primary stage children tend to agree with the questioner, even if they do not know what is meant. They are capable of invention and can be distractible and literal.

Questioning adolescents   Problems can be anticipated in questioning adolescents due to over- and under-estimation of their abilities to respond appropriately and poor attention to impact of gender and ethnicity on responses. Adolescent research does not often enough differentiate between stages of adolescence, namely early (10–14), mid (15–17) and late (18–20), and this can introduce intervening variables that can compromise the integrity of the research findings. For example, early adolescence is characterised by greater pubertal conflicts (Dashiff 2001). Questioning adolescents in the real world is affected equally by all of the above issues. Research in clinics, homes and schools all present potentially high levels of distraction due to the imposition of regular routines (holidays, appointments, exams and associated increase in stress and study leave, lack of a regular private space free from intrusions, holiday periods, absences, poorly controlled classes, collaboration with professionals regarding the time allowed to work with adolescents). Obviously it would be wise to plan to meet these eventualities in so far as it is reasonably possible. In health, social welfare and education research, youngsters may be concerned that their responses can be accessed by those who have power over them and consequently may expect to receive poorer care, support and understanding. Thus, attempts must also be made in the designing of adolescent research to provide privacy of responses.

In general, a model of good practice for questioning children would entail: preparation and the use of clear, unambiguous instructions; the creative use of ability-appropriate materials such as visual aids to memory; careful choice of context; attention to impression management in one-to-one or group interview situations; skilled interviewing; avoidance of leading questions; obtaining views of others for comparisons; and making it fun.

Interpretation of child's response

Problems in interpreting children's responses are related to social and cognitive factors. The fact that children are social beings, engaging with researchers and co-constructing the meanings of events, means that they are just as vulnerable to the social demands of the research situation as adults. Children's self reports are vulnerable to suggestibility and denial and are therefore influenced by the status of the interviewer as well as the context. Thus, children interviewed in school are already in a power relation with teachers and have various rote responses in that context. As Donaldson demonstrated, children's abilities in learning tasks have been underestimated because of social presentation. For example, most children will assume their first answer is wrong if a question is repeated in a power relation. If they are interviewed at home, children may be unlikely to be open about sensitive matters. For example, does the child feel safe at home right now? In disclosing painful experiences, children may experience anxiety which either prevents them from speaking about it or causes them to deny it or change their minds. Fears of losing loved ones, punishment of self and others and rejection are common. It is generally believed, however, that events which are important to the child are fairly resistant to such distortion. Children can respond differently to questions depending on whether or not they are asked in a one-to-one or peer group situation. There are advantages and disadvantages to each and these will depend on the child and the issues being discussed. Younger children tend to engage more easily if questioned in small groups or pairs. Groups are good for generating ideas, for finding key areas to follow up individually and for increasing confidence – and they can be more fun. However, gender composition can affect participation and the nature of the question is important, especially when it is more meaningful to some of the group than others (for example, having a looked after child in a group of pupils being asked questions about family life). Some children can dominate the group discussion. Individual interviews can be good where specific questions can be followed up in more detail and where there are any sensitive questions.

Problems of interpretation relating to cognitive factors are due to the over- and under-estimation of the child's ability based on performance. Even standardised tools can fail to take account of an individual's actual ability. All questioning of children involves the use of the cognitive abilities of language, thought and memory. If the task is oral then verbal skills are important. If the task is written then literacy skills are important. Therefore, whether written or oral, account will need to be taken of the complexity of the language used and the demands placed on the child. Chapters 7, 8 and 9 describe various designs used by a number of researchers in attempting to overcome these problems and the ethics of engagement and interpretation with children in research.

Children's drawings

Drawing is fun. Most children enjoy it and the activity is a good form of initial engagement for getting to know a child. There is robust evidence, however, that drawings can be a reliable indicator of cognitive development. Spontaneous drawings of a man or woman reveal conceptual abilities in terms of which body parts are depicted and where they are located and these have been standardised on a developmental scale – for example, the Goodenough–Harris Drawing Test (Goodenough and Harris 1963). Children's drawings are also believed to reveal the child's inner mind. The clues are believed to lie in the child's alterations of line

Figure 5.4   A comparison between a neglected child and a normal child on the 'draw a person/tree/house' task

quality, disguising of shapes and use of unusual signs or symbols. One of the easiest and most common drawing tasks for children is the 'draw a person, draw a tree, draw a house' task. This is depicted in Figure 5.4 together with a case outline of the two children who drew the respective pictures. Child A's drawings are depicted on the left. He is seven years old and has been physically abused. His parents have a history of mental ill-health. He is rejected and bullied at school. Child B's drawings are depicted on the right. He is a happy, normal, 7 year old. One is immediately struck by the impoverished work of child A in terms of size, detail and imagination.

There are a number of other possible indicators in drawings. Anxiety is believed to be represented through intensity of line pressure, excessive shading, smallness of the figure and rigidity of the drawing process and abused children may include sexualised body parts or shaded over body parts and sad or expressionless figures. Heavily scratched areas and repeatedly overworked lines across the body or torn hands may indicate physical abuse. Of course, drawings are particularly susceptible to false interpretations by the questioner and to be mediated by fine motor abilities and the conceptual development of the child. It is therefore crucial for such drawings only to be used by trained professionals and correlated with a variety of other sources of information. It is important to operate in an open, exploratory manner with children and their drawings. See Box 5.2 for guidelines on questioning children and interpreting their answers.

Box 5.2   Improving the validity of questioning and interpretation of answers

Improving validity: questioning

- Break complete events or issues into simple, manageable units for pre-schoolers who are unable to keep two concepts in mind at once. Use simple yes/no questions followed by more open-ended ones. Use familiar toys to clarify identities and demonstrate events.
- School-aged children can be expected gradually to understand and use more complex sentences.
- Children occasionally tell stories which parents know did not happen. In taking their capability to distinguish fact and fantasy and the possibility of denial into account, be prepared to accept an unclear conclusion.
- Ask the child if particular fears are affecting what he or she say.
- Take individual differences into account. Some children may be learning disabled or may prefer to reveal information slowly over longer periods of time.

Improving validity: interpretation

Children's reports are more likely to be valid:

- where the child uses age-related language;
- where the account is relatively detailed for the child's age;
- where the child displays appropriate emotional behaviour;
- where younger children express emotional feelings behaviourally rather than in a detailed verbal account;
- where a child's report is consistent over time;
- where hesitancy is evident during traumatic disclosures.

Source: Adapted from Reder, P. and Lucey, C. (1995) *Assessment of Parenting.* Copyright Routledge, 1995. Reproduced with permission of Taylor & Francis Ltd

The child's perspective and involving young researchers

Listening to the voices and views of children themselves is one of the most neglected aspects of child developmental research. It has been too long assumed that children have little to add to research that is valid and also that the whole business of the child expressing a point of view or desires is too distressing for the child and therefore is ethically unsound. Nonetheless, the Children Act 1989 and the more recent Children Act 2004 in England and Wales and their counterparts in other countries have set up a legal requirement to consult the wishes and feelings of children when assessing their physical, emotional and educational needs. These Acts have not only had a direct impact on the decision makers, agencies and educarers who deal with children on a daily basis, but also kindled the interest of researchers, especially practitioner researchers, in designing and improving the reliability and validity of techniques of obtaining the child's perspective in the light of what we do know about the child's age and understanding. This topic is developed fully in Chapter 8.

A particularly encouraging development is the realisation that we can and should invite children directly into the world of research by supporting them to become co-researchers or researchers themselves. This may mean recognising the impact of their perspectives on altering our research agenda; using their strength of position and insider knowledge to enhance the validity of our interpretations by having them conduct some parts of our research, or having them do complete pieces of research by their own design. Improving children's meta-cognitive abilities (or thinking about thinking) and the teaching of thinking skills are familiar territory now for teachers and it has also been long recognised that it is possible to teach children any subject in a meaningful way at any stage. The view expressed here is that research can and should be 'on the curriculum', and no doubt it already is, implicitly in an array of projects linked to other subjects. Text books are now appearing that address this arena in detail (for example, Kirby 1999; Kellett 2005). Although a full consideration of this development is beyond our current purpose, it may be helpful to tease out some questions relevant to situations of partial involvement and deciding whether or not we should indeed involve children as co-researchers. According to Kirby (1999) there are a number of questions we should ask ourselves in deciding whether or not it is appropriate to involve young researchers. The main questions are essential in any good practitioner-research design and you should involve children if you can answer as below:

- Is the topic worthwhile?   *Yes*
- What type of information is required (experiences, perceptions, knowledge)?   *Yes*
- Has a needs assessment identified an unmet need?   *Yes*
- Does the topic offer an evaluation of policy or service delivery, identify good or bad practice?   *Yes*

- How will the information be used? *To empower the young researchers*
- Would other methods of obtaining data be more appropriate? *No*

An appropriate decision to involve children as co–researchers may bring certain benefits: for example, less of a power issue between child researchers and child participants; better insider knowledge for obtaining and interpreting data; and positive role modelling for peers. On the other hand, a lack of maturity may mean discomfort with sensitive issues and a lack of confidence in negotiating with agencies; less monitoring of well known confounders such as biased replies, social desirability; and low or poor responses to questionnaires and in interviews.

PRACTICAL 5.1   THE 'I'VE GOT A HUNCH' EXERCISE.

This practical is to demonstrate further that you already possess a basic aptitude for posing research questions and hypotheses and designing approaches.

You may do the practical alone or your tutor will allocate you into relevant groups/pairs sharing an interest (e.g. education, health/nursing, social work). In these groups, discuss the following series of research 'hunches' in terms of:

- the type of study (qualitative, exploratory, experimental, etc.);
- defining the problem to be researched;
- the importance of the question and practical applications of the answers;
- possible research questions or hypotheses;
- who the participants should be and their characteristics;
- possible assessments, materials and equipment;
- problems anticipated in doing the research;
- whether there is a researcher role for the children involved.

Research hunches

1   You are curious about the self-esteem of poor readers.
2   You are concerned about the body image of children receiving surgery.
3   You wonder how the birth of a new baby affects the behaviour of pre-schoolers.
4   You are interested in the experiences of children who are bullies.
5   You wonder how children feel about their parents' divorce and subsequent contact arrangements.
6   You are interested in the child-rearing practices of different British cultures.
7   You wonder how children who are in the care of the authority feel about their experiences of being looked after.

Designing and doing quantitative research with children

The aims of this chapter are:

- To provide an overview of key concepts in quantitative research.
- To introduce common statistical procedures for data analysis.
- To discuss the key issues in interpreting children's test scores.
- To outline the main methods used in quantitative research designs.

1   Two primary school teachers in the same school both have a class of children at the same stage. One says, 'I have a terrible class this year. They have very negative attitudes to school and to their work, they are constantly niggling each other in the classroom and they are lazy and unmotivated.' The other says, 'Mine are the very opposite – they're a great class, really cooperative, hard-working and with positive attitudes.' To see how valid their feelings are they decide to put it to the test, to plan for some positive changes and to see if the changes have resulted in improvements. How would they go about it?

2   A social worker says, 'Far more of my caseload is now made up of really difficult child protection cases and emergency referrals. Three or four years ago I had a far wider spread, with a lot of cases that weren't so serious.' She decides to do some research on referrals of children to her department to see if referral patterns are changing, so that working practices can be adapted to meet the changed demands. How would she set about this exercise?

3   A nurse in a children's hospital says, 'I think Ward A is a better place to be than Ward B. The children there seem to be better adjusted and to make faster progress. I think it's because Ward A is a lot brighter – it faces the sun most of the day.' A colleague replies, 'Is it not just that Ward B tends to have the more serious ones who have to be in longer?' A third colleague interjects, 'But you have to remember that the main catchment area for Ward A is

the posh houses up at Fairways, but for Ward B it's the Blackview housing scheme where you get a lot of problems.' For their quality improvement plan of making the wards a better place to be they decide to start by investigating these hypotheses. How do they tackle it?

Questions of this kind can be reduplicated in every setting where people work with children. They are part and parcel of the interest practitioners have in finding out more about what is really happening on their patch, and of the requirements everyone faces in improving the quality of services and provision. They are all essentially *quantitative research* issues. Ultimately they are questions that are best answered with reference to *quantities* or *numbers*. They refer constantly to comparisons of amounts and levels, to concepts of 'more' and 'less'. They call for traditional research approaches such as experimental methods, hypothesis testing and assessment of probability.

Quantitative research methods are a veritable snake pit to the inexperienced and uninitiated (and often to experienced researchers as well!). This chapter cannot attempt to be a manual of such methods, but what it can do is to point to the key questions that must be asked, particularly in relation to work with children and young people, to outline some of the most useful strategies for dealing with these questions and to provide practical examples and illustrations. It offers an overview of the quantitative approach, introduces the subject of data analysis, covers the important area of understanding and interpreting children's test scores and discusses key methods such as observation, interviews, questionnaires and surveys. At the end of the book some key texts for this chapter are recommended as further reading.

For those who wish to carry out quantitative research the best advice is to *get advice*. It is best from the beginning of a project to have some guidance from someone who is steeped in the quantitative approach, and who can comment on technical issues such as your proposed sample size and your methods of data collection and analysis. This does not just apply to novice researchers. It is very common for experienced researchers in university departments to go and check with someone about how they intend to handle their data – usually the person who lies in bed reading about multivariate statistical analysis for pleasure (there's one in every department!). For those who do not have ready access to academic departments there are similar sources of advice in many of the settings where people work with children. For example, all health boards have statisticians or researchers whose job includes tasks like advising the ethics committee on research proposals, dealing with service audits and preparing annual statistical reports. Likewise local authority departments such as social services, education or the chief executive's office have people who compile results of national testing of children or analyses of population changes. These personnel are generally able to advise employees on appropriate methods.

Quantitative methods: an overview of key concepts

The three examples given at the beginning of this chapter cannot be answered without reference to a number of key concepts that are fundamental to the quantitative approach: probability and significance, levels of measurement, sampling methods, types of research design and the core statistical concepts of measures of central tendency, the standard deviation, the percentile, the effect size and the normal distribution. These will be familiar concepts to those who already have research experience.

Probability and significance

Any hypothesis we generate about the difference between two groups of children, or the comparative effectiveness of two different methods of intervention, will not be proved but rather supported or rejected at a certain level of *probability*. We want to avoid making either a *Type I error* – believing there is a difference when there actually is not – or a *Type II error* – failing to spot a difference when there actually is one. The accepted criterion is to go for at least a 95% level of confidence before deciding that there is a difference. This still leaves a 5% margin of probable error in our conclusion. This 5% (5 in 100, or 0.05) probability of error is expressed as p – in this case, $p = 0.05$, or the '5% significance level'. Similarly, we would be more confident with a probability of error of less than 1% (1 in 100, or 0.01), or less than 0.1% (1 in 1,000 or 0.001). These values would be expressed respectively as $p < 0.01$, or the '1% significance level', and $p < 0.001$, or the '0.1% significance level'. These three levels of significance – 5%, 1% and 0.1% – are the ones most commonly used in research publications, and as a form of shorthand they are often indicated by just putting one, two or three asterisks beside figures shown in results tables. For example, 16.54** would indicate that this score was significant at the 1% level.

Levels of measurement

Before we can decide how to test the significance of our findings we need to know the *level of measurement* that applies to our data. This term tells us the relationship between what is being measured and the numbers used on any scale to record our measurements. Four of these levels are used: *nominal, ordinal, interval* and *ratio*. The nominal level refers to data where the numbers used to describe them do not have any numerical meaning but are simply codes for categories. For example, we might investigate how children come to school and code them as number 1 for those who walk, 2 for those who come by car, 3 for those who cycle, 4 for those who come on the school bus, and so on. These codes have no numerical relationship to each other. They are just categories, and represent nominal data.

Ordinal data tells us that the numbers used are related, but only at the level of the order in which they occurred. If 10 children sit a test or run a race they can be placed in rank order with the numbers 1 to 10, telling us who came first, second, tenth. This is a higher and more informative level of data than nominal, but it still gives limited information about how the numbers 1 to 10 are related to each other. We know that 5 was better or faster than 7, and 7 than 10. All children might have scored high or run fast, or perhaps none of them did. The child who was 2nd might have performed twice as well as the child who was 3rd, while the 3rd might have been only a tiny fraction ahead of the 4th. In other words, ordinal data tell us only about the rank order, but not about the magnitude of the differences between one rank and another.

Interval data are much more informative for researchers, and many statistical tests rely on having this level of data. An interval scale is one that is continuous, that has an arbitrary zero point and that has equal intervals on the scale to represent equal quantities of what is being measured. For example, in physical measurements, a Fahrenheit or Celsius temperature scale is an interval scale. It does not have a true zero, and therefore a reading of 50 degrees is not 'twice as much' as one of 25. Nevertheless, the intervals are equal. A rise in the reading from 8 to 9 degrees is the same interval as a rise from 78 to 79. Many test scores we encounter in working with children, such as IQ tests, are based on interval scales. The test does not have a true zero, so it would be meaningless to say that an IQ of 140 is 'twice' an IQ of 70, but it is nevertheless constructed with a view to having equal intervals all the way along the scale.

Ratio data arise from interval scales with an absolute zero. To test how well pre-school children can identify colours we might flash a range of colours on to a computer screen and test how quickly the right colour is selected when its name is given. This test of reaction time would provide ratio data. If we measure the response in seconds, a speed of 2 seconds would be twice as fast as 4 seconds, and 20 seconds would be twice as slow as 10 seconds.

Sampling methods

Having robust data to analyse using statistical tests does not depend only on level of measurement but also on the nature of our sample. An important question is 'How many?'. If we only have a handful of children in our sample it is unlikely that we will get very far with quantitative analysis unless, for example, we are looking at many measures taken for each child at several stages over a period of time. Small numbers are too prone to being unrepresentative, and an extreme score will distort the data because it has a bigger proportional impact than it would in a large sample. So, in general it is a good idea when using quantitative methods to aim for including a good number of children in our sample if this is feasible. Even with experimental research designs it is possible to work with small samples. However, very small samples in quantitative research are subject to fairly brutal statistics, and large differences between groups tend to be required in order to show significant results. It is helpful to seek advice beforehand about what size of sample will be needed for the type of study you are planning.

In *random sampling* everyone in the population being studied has an equal chance of being selected. This could be done by having a computer generate random numbers, by using the random number tables found in many statistics books or, if the numbers in the population are relatively small – like all the children in a nursery – by putting their names in a hat. Much the same result can be achieved by taking a *systematic sample,* where every *n*th child in a list is selected, and where *n* is just any suitable number. For example, if you want to study a teenage club with 120 members you could get a sample of 30 by taking every 4th name on the list. However, these methods might still fail to give appropriate representation of different groups within your population, such as number of males and females. This can be tackled by *stratified sampling*, in which there is random selection of the right numbers from each group. This could either be *proportionate*, if you want a group with the same proportion of males to females as there is in the entire club, or *disproportionate*, if you perhaps want to study male/female differences by having two equal groups, no matter how many of each there are in the club.

Often researchers do not get the opportunity to be quite as representative as this, and they may therefore use other forms of sampling. If you are interested in studying the characteristics of children who smoke you might opt for a *cluster sample* made up of all the smokers in a particular school or year group, on the assumption that they are likely to be fairly typical of smokers in general. Very frequently the children in your sample may simply be an *opportunity sample.* In other words, you happen to be working with a group of children and you ask each of them, 'Would you like to take part in a research project?'. A final popular method is *snowball sampling* in which, having interviewed your first child you say, 'Have you any friends who might like to take part in this research?'. The issue with these methods is to ensure that the sample turns out to be sufficiently representative. What if the smokers in your cluster sample or opportunity sample all come from a school that is in a very poor or very wealthy area? It may be that this is an important factor affecting the issue being studied. Or what if you are studying children's interests and your snowball sample ends up comprising the entire population of the school chess club? The aim has to be to try for a sample that is large enough to make the study viable and representative enough to reduce bias.

Types of research design

In quantitative research *experimental* designs are popular – that is, designs which manipulate one *variable* to see what effect it has on another. A variable is any factor that can change or vary. For example, if we want to test whether children's behaviour improves when we make more positive statements to them we can manipulate the variable of 'number of positive statements' to see if it affects the outcome 'better behaviour'. The 'purest' form of experimental design is the *randomised controlled trial (RCT)*, which requires a *control group* and one or more *experimental groups*. The control group is treated exactly the same as before, while the experimental group receives whatever form the manipulation of the variable takes, such as an intervention, treatment or change in approach. In the above example the experimental group would receive a larger number of positive statements than previously, while the controls would be just as before. For it to be an RCT, children would need to be allocated to the two groups randomly. This can be done in simple ways in real world child settings. For example, if you are a group worker and have a new programme to build citizenship skills in young people referred for committing offences, you might select 16 possible cases from which you will choose a group of 8. You can then match them in pairs on important characteristics, such as sex, age and type of offences committed. Then you can put their names in envelopes and get a colleague who is not involved in the study to select one envelope from each pair to make up the experimental group.

However, it is often the case that the luxury of being able to make a random selection of children for different groups is not available to us. If you are a practitioner in common child contexts like education, social services, health care or a voluntary organisation you may find a variety of practical or ethical reasons to stop you randomly selecting the children who are to experience or not experience your new practice. In these cases a *quasi-experimental design* can be used. This differs from a randomised control trial in that the allocation to the groups is not random. Nevertheless, every possible step is taken to ensure that the groups are well matched. In one of the five child research studies covered in MacKay (2006) the plan was to see whether secondary school children with reading difficulties would make better progress using a special teaching method. The learning support staff involved did not have the liberty of randomly assigning the referred pupils to different groups because of timetabling and other constraints. Instead, 12 pupils assigned to the group receiving the special method were matched closely with 12 pupils assigned to receive the normal package of learning support. The matching involved both finding pupils with comparable reading ages at the start of the project and taking account of the views of teaching staff about the reading abilities of the two groups.

For many people who are doing research with children neither a randomised controlled trial nor a quasi-experimental design will be possible, since it may not be feasible to have a control group at all, whether randomly allocated or otherwise. For example, there may be access to the study of only one group of children, and all of these children may require to have the same treatment or approach. Suppose, for instance, you are a health visitor and you want to evaluate the effect of a new intervention or an enhanced level of service delivery on the most vulnerable children on your case load. Ethical considerations may prevent you from dividing your case load into those who get the new treatment and those who are left without it, as it will tend to be assumed that it is going to be beneficial and that everyone should have access to it. You can still carry out quantitative research by doing an *outcome evaluation*. This is based on the idea of 'gain scores': you assess the children on a range of relevant factors before they receive the new treatment, and you assess them again afterwards, perhaps at various stages.

Outcome evaluations of this kind are not as robust research designs as experimental and quasi-experimental ones. They raise some obvious questions. Would the children have shown these improvements anyway? Have the changes come about because of the developmental maturity they have experienced through the duration of the pre-post period? Without a control group it is hard to answer questions like these. Nevertheless, outcome studies are very popular and frequently they are the only method available. There are also ways of getting good results from them. First, the general rule is: the larger the gain, the shorter the time and the more direct the measure, the more likely it is to be the effect of the intervention. Children who in a short period have shown a sudden spurt in their scores on the very factors you are trying to change make a good argument for the case that your intervention was successful. Second, if you are using standardised measures, examples of which are described later, you can look at changes in standard scores using basic statistics like the effect size (see below). These can help to tell whether the changes that have been observed were to be expected.

One advantage of using an outcome evaluation is that you can apply it to a *single case design*. There are many child practitioners who may not have access to large or even small groups of children, but who have the opportunity to work intensively with an individual. This includes various counsellors, therapists and support workers. Even though only one child is being studied it is still possible to use traditional quantitative methods, by looking at changes in a range of pre-post scores. An example of a single case design studying the effects of a cognitive behaviour therapy programme on a boy with Asperger's syndrome (Greig and MacKay 2005) is shown in Box 6.1.

Box 6.1   Using quantitative measures in a single case design

Greig and MacKay designed an innovative application, *The Homunculi,* for using cognitive behaviour therapy with young people with Asperger's syndrome, and piloted it with a 13 year old boy. The programme was designed primarily to address mood disorders, such as depression, but also to address other features such as social impairments. The boy was assessed on a range of standardised measures before and after the intervention, allowing a comparison of pre–post scores for evaluating the effects of the programme.

(Continued)

Emotional state outcomes (Brière Trauma Scales)

	Pre	Post	Mean	Effect size
Anxiety	19	5	6	3.7
Depression	21	6	7	3.8
Anger	15	10	9	1.0
Stress	25	8	8	3.2

Social competence outcomes (Spence questionnaires)

	Pre	Post	Mean	Effect size
Parent report	0	5	15	1.60
Pupil report	0	4	16	1.26

Source: Greig, A. and MacKay, T. (2005) 'Asperger's syndrome and cognitive behaviour therapy: new applications for educational psychologists.' *Educational and Child Psychology*, 22 (4): 4–15

All of the above research designs involve the deliberate manipulation of one variable, such as number of positive statements made (the *independent variable*), in order to bring about change in another variable, such as behaviour (the *dependent variable*). Some quantitative designs do not involve the attempt to change anything but instead look at how groups differ from or relate to each other. There is no generally agreed name for these designs, but they are often called *correlational* studies. They investigate whether there is a relationship between different variables. For example, we may study whether children who do well in school have higher levels of motivation than children who do not. Discovering that this is the case tells us nothing about whether one variable causes the other one. All we can comment on is the extent to which these variables are correlated.

Core statistical concepts

Those who are not already experienced researchers are less likely to be familiar with a few core statistical concepts that are introduced here. All of these are essential to the interpretation of children's test scores, a subject that is covered separately later in this chapter.

Measures of central tendency   The first concept is *measures of central tendency*. When we see a range of scores children have achieved on a test we are interested to know what would be a typical or average score for the group. This will tell us something both about the group and also about any individual child's score – is it high or low? The most widely used and certainly the most useful measure of central tendency is the *mean (M)* or average score. This is found by adding all the scores together and dividing them by the number of children. The advantage of the mean is that it is the most sensitive and accurate measure of central tendency, it is the basis of the most powerful statistical tests for analysing data and it is easy to work out on a calculator. It also has one main disadvantage. It can easily be distorted by extreme or 'rogue' scores that are unrepresentative. For example, suppose we are interested in finding out how long seven children take to work out a simple puzzle. If the number of seconds they take are 4, 5, 7, 10, 10, 11 and 135 then the mean will tell us nothing of value about the group. It would be 26 seconds but that would not in any way be a typical score, as there is one rogue score or 'outlier' that distorts the whole picture.

The two other measures of central tendency will not be distorted in this way. The *median* is the middle value in the range of scores. In the above example it would be 10 seconds, a more representative score for the group. However, for most purposes the median is less useful than the mean, as it does not take account of any of the other values in the data set. It is an appropriate measure for data at ordinal level – that is, data that can be ranked but are not at interval level.

The *mode* is the most common score in a data set – the one that occurs most frequently. In the example above the mode would be 10. As such it can be useful in giving a very typical picture, and it is not distorted by extreme values. It can also make more sense than the mean if we want to refer to real situations. The mean number of children in a family may be 2.4, but it is certainly not typical! However, it is not a very useful measure if there is a small number of scores, and it can be affected by even one change in a score. For example, if the first two values in the above puzzle test were both 4 seconds then there would be two modes, 4 and 10, which would not tell us very much. Like the median, the mode does not make use of the other scores in the data set, but if data are at nominal level then only the mode can be used. If most of the children referred to earlier walk to school, and the minority come by car or by other means, then the modal value is the score given to the group who walk.

The standard deviation   Knowing the mean or some other measure of central tendency allows us to put an individual score in context as being 'higher' or 'lower' than the average for the group, but it still leaves important gaps in our understanding of what a score really means. If we measure the blood temperature of 100 children we will probably find a mean of approximately 37 degrees Celsius, with somewhat more than two-thirds of them in the range 36.5 to 37.5 degrees. If we found one with a temperature at 33 and another at 40 we would probably be going for a hot water bottle and ice pack respectively and thinking of calling a doctor. On the other hand, if we measured how long these 100 children could stand on one foot without falling over we might again find a mean of 37 (in this case, seconds) but the range of scores covering two-thirds of them might extend from 6 seconds to over a minute. Therefore, even though the mean is the same at 37, a score of 6 could mean either that the subject is perfectly normal or that the subject is dead, depending on what is being measured.

It is here that measures of how scores are distributed around the mean are crucial, and neglect of these measures can lead to fatal miscalculations about the meaning of data. For example, it is meaningless to say that an 11 year old child is doing badly with a reading age of 10 years. If almost every child at exactly age 11 is scoring between 10 years 9 months and 11 years 3 months, then a score of 10 years is not looking good. However, if about two-thirds of children at age 11 have a reading age somewhere between 9½ and 12½ (and this in fact is the case with reading scores) then a score of 10 years is a totally normal one. The best measure for interpreting what scores mean is the *standard deviation (SD)*.

It is not within the scope of this book to discuss the underlying statistical rationale for these measures or the formulas for calculating them, all of which is fully covered in basic texts such as the book by Coolican (2004). It is important, however, to know what measures like the standard deviation signify. Where scores are normally distributed (that is, where they are not *skewed* or distorted by having a lot more lower or higher values), the standard deviation tells us how many of our children's scores fall in a given range. Most usefully, they tell us that around two-thirds of scores will be within one standard deviation of the mean. Specifically, it is expected that:

68% of cases will fall within one SD of the mean (34.13% on either side)
95% of cases will fall within two SD of the mean (47.72% on either side)
97% of cases will fall within three SD of the mean (49.87% on either side)

For example, an IQ test is usually constructed in a standard way to give a mean of 100 and a standard deviation of 15. Therefore around two-thirds of the population will have scores between 85 and 115, but only 5% altogether will have scores that are either below 70 or above 130. In the case of body temperature the standard deviation is very low, at around 0.4 degrees Celsius, so the scale does not have to rise very much before we decide that someone has a 'temperature' – that is, the score is sufficiently far away from the mean to suggest that it is abnormal. This is very important when interpreting test scores and is covered in more detail later.

The percentile Another extremely useful measure is the *percentile*, or *percentile rank*. It tells us how many of our children score at or below a particular point in a scale. A score at the 10th percentile means that only 10% of our population would have a score at this level or lower. At the other end, a score at the 90th percentile means that 90% would have a score at this level or lower. In other words, the 90th percentile takes us into the highest 10% of scores.

The effect size If our research involves carrying out any intervention in order to bring about change then we are ultimately interested in the question, 'Has there been an effect?'. As noted above, in quantitative research we approach this question on the basis of probability and significance, by asking how likely it is that a change was due to our intervention and not just to chance variation. However, we may at times find that there has been an effect which we can demonstrate at the traditional 5% level of significance, but that the effect is nevertheless not important. Significance levels tell us that there is a statistical difference in the scores, but they do not tell us the size of the difference. We are therefore left with the question asked by all practitioners, 'Did our project bring about a difference that was meaningful and worthwhile?'. We are not just asking 'could we measure a difference' but rather did it '*make a difference?*'. For example, it is possible with large samples to find that a very small change is statistically significant, but not really very important.

It is here that the idea of the *effect size (EF)* is invaluable. It is a standard measure of the magnitude of change. Several different measures of effect size have been proposed but the most common is the amount of change measured in standard deviations. For example, if you carried out a programme to raise children's test scores on a test with a mean of 100 and a standard deviation of 10, and the change in scores was a rise of 5 points, the effect size would be 0.5 – that is, half of one standard deviation. If you raised it by 10 points it would be 1.0. The effect sizes given in Box 6.1 above are an example of how one young person's scores changed in terms of the standard deviations published for the tests shown. We owe this measure of effect size to Cohen (1988), who has given helpful guidance on how to interpret the magnitude of change: 0.2 = small, 0.5 = medium and 0.8 = large.

The normal distribution

If we have scores for a large number of children on almost any test or measure, whether it is height, weight, intelligence, reading ability, school attendance or time spent watching TV each day, we will be able to show these scores graphically. In many cases, including all of the examples cited, the resulting graph will approximate to the *normal distribution curve*, which is bell-shaped. This curve is symmetrical, and the mean, median and mode fall in the central line. Figure 6.1 shows the

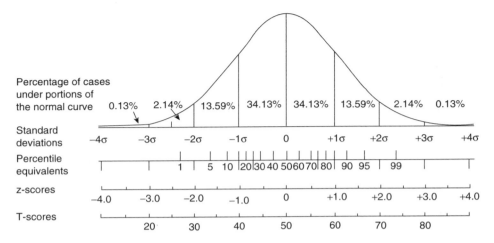

Figure 6.1   The normal distribution

normal distribution curve marked off in standard deviations, percentiles and other scores that are mentioned in the section on interpreting test scores.

Analysing the data

When you collect raw data in a quantitative study they need to be analysed using standard statistical procedures. As this book is not a statistical manual it does not attempt to cover the methodology required for data analysis. There are many basic texts, such as the recommended book by Coolican, that deal with this subject. While it is important to understand the statistical theory required for this task (one of the good reasons for asking advice from experts), it is no longer necessary for researchers to be able to work out the formulas and calculations themselves, as these are all now done for us by statistical software such as SPSS. For people who do not have access to SPSS, the Microsoft Office Excel software, which frequently now comes as part of the package provided with a computer, has a data analysis facility. (If you have Excel and the data analysis facility is not on your Tools menu it can be loaded there by going into the Help menu.) This facility will generate random numbers, do correlations and perform common statistical tests like *t* tests and analysis of variance. There are also formulas on Excel for calculating means and standard deviations and for non-parametric tests like chi-square.

By way of introduction, three types of statistical procedure are referred to here. They provide a starting point for analysing data from many different kinds of research project, but again they should be supported by advice for those who are not experienced in statistical procedures. These are correlation, the *t* test and the chi-square test.

Figure 6.2 Hypothetical correlation between air quality and emergency hospital admissions of child asthma sufferers

Correlation

In everyday language when we say that two things 'correlate' we mean that they 'go together' and are related in a systematic way. If you have been following crime reports in the newspapers in which young children are involved whilst also taking note of the truancy rate at the school in which you work, you may notice a correlation between these two observations. Perhaps as the truancy rate rises, so also do the number of reported crimes committed locally by children. This would be a positive correlation. On the other hand, you may observe that as the truancy rate increases, the crime rate decreases. This would be a negative correlation. Of course it could easily be that there is no correlation, in that sometimes truancy and crime go together and sometimes they do not.

The relationship can be depicted as in Figure 6.2. In this way the direct linear relationship between the two observations can be seen. If there were a perfect correlation between them it would be possible to draw a perfect straight line across the graph.

The symbol for correlation is *r*. It is measured on a scale of 1, with 1 being a perfect positive correlation, 0 no correlation and −1 a perfect negative correlation. Figure 6.3 depicts various degrees of correlation and their *r* coefficient or score.

Correlation is worth mentioning here because of its usefulness in analysing observational data and in establishing the reliability or validity of observational schemes and codes (see also Chapter 5). It tests whether a

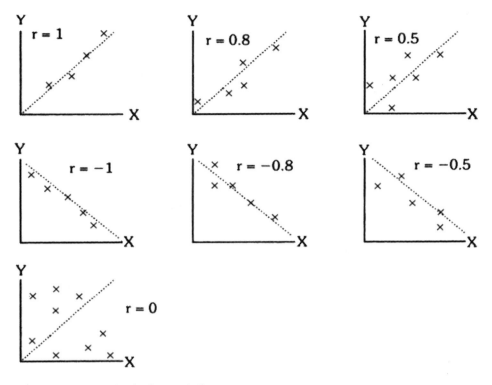

Figure 6.3   Hypothetical correlations

systematic relationship exists between two or more variables. What can a correlation score or coefficient tell us and what can it not tell us? First, because there is likely to be a number of factors covarying we cannot say that X causes Y or Y causes X. A positive correlation between truancy rates and child crime in a particular town cannot be expressed as 'truancy *causes* crime'. Similarly, a positive correlation between children watching violent television and aggressive behaviour cannot be expressed as 'watching violent television *causes* children to behave aggressively', because it may also be said that 'aggressive children prefer violent television'.

The X–Y relationship may also be related in a systematic way to a third, unobserved variable: a positive correlation between attainment and head size in primary school children is likely to be *confounded* by age. Finally, variables can be systematically related, such as the relationship between memory and age, but not show up as being related using linear correlation. This is because the data are 'curvilinear' – that is, they form a curve rather than a straight line, since many aspects of memory increase with age in childhood but decrease again later in life.

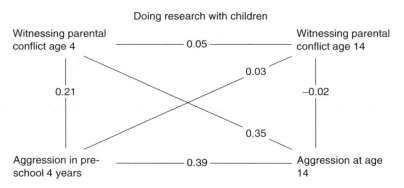

Figure 6.4   Hypothetical cross-lagged correlation data

Some correlational studies attempt to improve internal validity by looking at patterns of correlation in longitudinal designs. The underlying assumption is that if one variable causes another, the first (say witnessing parental conflict) should be more strongly related to the second (say aggression) later in time than when the aggression was measured in the first place. In a sense, it is saying that causes should take some time to produce their effects. However, as correlation is only a method of agreement, it can only enhance the possibility of an explanation. Figure 6.4 shows an imaginary longitudinal (cross–lagged) correlation study. The important data are on the diagonals.

The 't' test

The *t* test is one of the most straightforward ways of comparing the results from two groups to see if they differ. We could take the example of the pre-school children mentioned earlier whose reaction time in identifying colours was measured. We might set up a programme in which an experimental group had a special programme to teach them colour recognition, while a control group did not receive the programme. Both groups would be tested pre–post. The scores could then be analysed using a '*t* test for unrelated data'. In this case the scores of the two groups are independent or unrelated. Alternatively, we could test all the children first, and then give them all the programme and test them again. This would call for a '*t* test for related data', because the two data sets would be made up of related pairs of scores.

The *t* test can be performed on Excel using the '*t* test – paired two sample' option on the data analysis tools for related data, or the '*t* test two sample' for unrelated data. The latter gives a choice of two tests, one 'assuming equal variances' and the other 'assuming unequal variances'. It is this choice that points us in the direction of the requirements that our data must fulfil for the test to be appropriate, so we must ask, 'What are the data assumptions for *t* tests?'.

The *t* test, in common with the other most powerful statistical tests, assumes that the samples have been drawn from a normally distributed population. A simple check on the scores will indicate whether there are obvious quirks in them, such as being very much skewed towards high or low scores. For example, if a test is too hard then too many of our children will score very low or zero (a *floor effect*) whereas if it is too easy too many of them will have the top score (a *ceiling effect*), and this will distort the distribution. Also, the data should be at interval level or above. Finally, in the unrelated *t* test, if the sample size of the two groups is very different, the *variances* of the two sets of scores must not be significantly different. Variance is a measure of how much the scores vary – how widely they are dispersed (technically, it is the square of the standard deviation).

It is these technicalities that highlight the need for advice or sound statistical knowledge. However, the *t* test is very 'robust'. This means that it is very forgiving, and the assumptions can be violated to quite a substantial degree while still getting quite accurate outcomes.

The chi-square test

No matter how robust the powerful analysis tools like the *t* test may be, often the data collected by practitioners doing research with children will not meet the required assumptions. Many useful data sets produce data at nominal level, the lowest level of measurement. For example, we might want to investigate the views of children on whether pupils should be required to wear school uniform, on whether they want to go to university or on whether they believe the voting age should be reduced to 16. For a simple test of whether the numbers vary from what we would predict if the choices were random we can use the *chi-square test* (χ^2). This is based on comparing the observed frequencies of any choice with the expected frequencies.

In the example of school uniform, if 20 out of 50 pupils are for it and 30 against, these are the observed frequencies. The expected frequencies, based on random choices, would be 25 for and 25 against. This would make a table with four *cells* as follows:

	For school uniform	Against school uniform
Observed frequency	20	30
Expected frequency	25	25

A more common example is when we are comparing the views of two different groups. Thus, we could ask the same questions of children of high versus low socioeconomic status (SES) and see if the responses differ. This is referred to as a *2 × 2 chi-square test*, and the table might now look like this:

	High SES (Observed)	Low SES (Observed)
For school uniform	15	5
Against school uniform	10	20

	High SES (Expected)	Low SES (Expected)
For school uniform	10	10
Against school uniform	15	15

In the above example there are 25 children in the high and 25 in the low SES group. Since a total of 20 were in favour of school uniform we would expect that these would randomly have had equal representation from each group, that is, 10 in each. Since 30 were against school uniform we would randomly have expected 15 in each group.

Although we are not concerned here with either the formula or the rationale for a test like this, it is relatively easy to find the results on Excel by putting in the chi–square formula. This can be found by typing in 'chi square' in the Help menu and selecting the CHITEST option, where there is a worked example. If the formula is entered correctly it will be seen that the figures in the first table are not significant ($p = 0.157$) but when the data are broken down by socioeconomic status more high SES children in the hypothetical example want school uniform than low SES children ($p = 0.004$, or we would more probably just say $p < 0.01$).

Despite its appeal as a very flexible test that can use a nominal level of data and that is simple and effective, the chi–square test has some important limitations. It can only be used with frequencies (actual raw numbers in each category), and not with percentages, means, ratios or proportions. Also, it is not appropriate when there are very low frequencies in some of the categories. The general rule of thumb is that the numbers should not fall below 5 in more than 20% of the cells. So, if it is a simple chi–square with four cells, as in the first of the above examples, the lowest cell should have at least 5 in it.

There are, of course, many more sophisticated procedures for analysis of quantitative data, and the general rule is that it is best to use, or to be advised in the use of, the most powerful test that your data set will justify.

Understanding children's test scores

The above overview of quantitative concepts provides the essential basis for understanding and interpreting children's test scores. Many people who are doing research with children gather background information that includes the results of standardised tests, such as tests of intelligence or educational attainments. There may also be tests that the researcher wishes to carry out with children to obtain certain information direct. Test construction is based on a number of key principles and these apply to every type of test that gives some kind of score or quotient, whether it is of intelligence, personality, anxiety, depression, aptitude, attainment or height and weight. Standardised testing is on the whole a specialist area, and many of the tests are only available from the publishers to professionals who have recognised qualifications or experience in the use of the type of test in question. Nevertheless, the results of many of these tests will be available to a wide range of other practitioners, including people who are conducting research, so it is important to understand what they mean.

Understanding test scores can most easily be illustrated with reference to intelligence tests. These tests in general produce scores with which most people are familiar, as the concept of the IQ or intelligence quotient is well established in the public domain. Because they have often been misused, intelligence tests have generated considerable controversy. They also provide rather limited information on most of the population, except where scores are more extreme, such as very low test scores. At the same time they can provide useful background data for people doing research with groups of children in cases where general ability might be a variable that affects the research outcomes. For instance, MacKay (1999) screened children for intelligence before selecting them for three groups of eight in a randomised controlled trial investigating attitudes to reading. The test used was one of the two tests of ability illustrated in Box 6.2, Raven's Coloured Progressive Matrices. Children with extreme scores were excluded since the purpose was to study children of ordinary intelligence who were experiencing reading failure, rather than those where the difficulty might have related directly to a factor associated with intelligence, such as a general learning disability.

The intelligence quotient, as with similar standard scores, is based on the idea that raw score measures do not give as meaningful information about ability. For example, a very bright child aged 4 and a young person aged 15 with a severe learning disability might both have a 'mental age' of 6 years, and therefore achieve similar raw scores on a test. While this gives a description of current performance it does not give an accurate picture of ability. This is done by finding the spread of scores in the population at every age range and converting these into a standard score which can be interpreted the same way for any age. As noted earlier, in the case of intelligence this standard score usually has a mean of 100 and a standard deviation of 15.

It is these standard scores that allow us to interpret what an individual score means. This may be done easily by looking back to Figure 6.1 and relating it to the information given about the two tests that are illustrated in Box 6.2. A score of 70 (on tests with M = 100 and SD = 15) falls two standard deviations below the mean, and is between the 2nd and 3rd percentile. Sometimes you will see this expressed as a z score of -2.0 (a z score is simply the number of standard deviations above or below the mean). A few tests, including some extensively used ones like the British Ability Scales, use 'T' scores, so it is useful to have a reference point for this scale also. You will see from Figure 6.1 that a T score is one which converts the raw scores into a scale with a mean of 50 and a standard deviation of 10. Any T score can therefore be compared directly with any other score. It might seem somewhat arbitrary to have a scale like this, but it is based on a clear logic. It assumes for practical purposes that the normal distribution can be viewed as extending from 5 standard deviations below to 5 above the mean. The T score therefore represents the percentage of the total distance along the normal distribution from 0 to 100. It is for this reason that the mean is 50; that is, it is 50% of the distance along the distribution.

Interpreting low test scores

Referring to an intelligence test score of 70 draws attention to a further important point regarding interpreting test scores. A score that lies two standard deviations below the mean, approaching the lowest 2% of all scores, is regarded frequently as a 'cut-off' point where we may wish to look more closely at its implications. In IQ terms it has traditionally defined the level often described as 'mental retardation'. The main international classification systems for mental and behavioural disorders (which include things like autistic spectrum disorders and ADHD), often refer to a 'clinically significant' impairment in such things as cognitive function, or early language development. 'Clinical significance' is normally understood to refer to the point that falls two standard deviations below the mean. (Equally, if the area of concern was marked by high scores, such as high levels of anxiety or depression, the significant scores to look at more closely would be two standard deviations *above* the mean.) You will see from Box 6.2 that the current version of the Wechsler Scale now uses the description 'extremely low' rather than 'mentally retarded', in recognition of the fact that an IQ score falling under 70 does not in itself define that a child has a learning disability, although it is an important pointer towards fuller investigation.

The descriptions given in Box 6.2 for the Wechsler Scale, ranging from 'very superior' to 'extremely low', are generally useful for interpreting the meaning of any test score. Where you do not have a figure expressed in a standard scale you should find the information that allows you to relate it to the various standard-ised scores we have discussed here. It is meaningless in and of itself to say that a child has a reading test score of 27, and only partially more helpful to be told that this is a reading age of 8 years. This tells you almost nothing about how well the child is doing, other than that if the child is age 6, 7 or 8 the score certainly looks fine. Only the data that will relate it to the normal distribution, such as the mean and standard deviation appropriate to the child's age, will allow the score to be properly interpreted.

Box 6.2 Interpreting children's intelligence test scores

The following are two of the most widely used tests throughout the world for children.

The Wechsler Intelligence Scale for Children, Fourth Revision (WISC-IV) (Wechsler 2004)

This is a general intelligence test measuring the abilities of children across four domains, each comprising several subtests: verbal comprehension (e.g. vocabulary, word reasoning), perceptual reasoning (e.g. block design, picture completion), working memory (e.g. digit span) and processing speed (e.g. coding). These domains can each be given a standard score and can be combined to give a composite Full Scale IQ (in all cases M = 100, SD = 15).

Interpretation The following table shows the official descriptions of the various bands of scores on the WISC-IV – but they are equally useful descriptions for interpreting any tests using standard scores of this type (or their equivalent point on the normal distribution curve).

130 or above	very superior
120–129	superior
110–119	high average
90–109	average
80–89	low average
70–79	borderline
69 or below	extremely low

Raven's Coloured Progressive Matrices (CPM) (Raven et al. 1998)

Raven's CPM is a non-verbal intelligence test measuring capacity for productive thinking in children aged about 5–12 years (and for older less able children and adults). It normally comes in book form and comprises 36 items in three sets of 12, in which the child must make the correct choice from several pieces shown beneath a larger design with one piece missing. These items progress through the stages of intellectual development, starting with distinguishing identical from different figures. For older children and adults there is a higher level of the test, the *Standard Progressive Matrices* (Raven et al. 2000). Each can be combined with a separate vocabulary test.

Interpretation The official descriptions of scores on the CPM are shown below. The standard measure used is the percentile, so again the scores can be related to all other standard scores in terms of the normal distribution.

GRADE I	95th percentile or above–'intellectually superior'
GRADE II	75th percentile or above–'definitely above average'
	(Grade II+ if 90th percentile or above)
GRADE III	between 25th and 75th percentile–'intellectually average'
	(Grade III+ if above 50th percentile; Grade III– if below)
GRADE IV	25th percentile or below–'definitely below average'
GRADE V	5th percentile or below–'intellectually impaired'

Figure 6.5

The following section covers some key methods used in quantitative research: observation, interviews, questionnaires and survey methods. Observation and interviews are also used extensively in qualitative research.

Observation

In a sense, all research involves observation. If the purpose of research is to improve our understanding of an individual, a relationship, a particular social group or culture, then that knowledge begins with observation. Observation means watching children individually, in relationships, in contexts and asking: what do they see, what do they feel, what do they think, what do they do? As a basic technique, observation underpins a variety of approaches to research. There are also a variety of observational techniques to consider, and these vary according to the age of the child, their conceptual abilities, their relationship with the observer and, of course, the purpose of the research. These divide mainly into *participant* and *non-participant observation*. In participant observation the observer becomes part of the group being studied. This could include observation in adult settings in order to obtain data relevant to child studies, such as a social worker working in a social services agency to discover how child referrals to such agencies are handled or an undergraduate working in a school to discover how teachers define quality of curriculum. When observers participate but do not inform other participants of their role, it is called *undisclosed observation*. In *non-participant* observation the observer only watches. This could be a psychologist behind a two-way mirror watching the free play interactions between a mother and her infant and coding the behaviours that are observed.

Observational techniques are particularly helpful for doing research with young children who may be unable to communicate any other way. There are other sound reasons why it is desirable to research children in their natural environments, such as the home, school or neighbourhood rather than subject them to experimental manipulations. For one thing children are particularly reactive to strange people and strange situations. Another reason is their vulnerable position regarding informed consent (see Chapter 9).

A key decision in observation is sampling method – what to observe and how to record it. There are many possibilities. For example, in relation to any behaviour we are studying we can use:

- predominant activity sampling: only the behaviour that best describes what has happened in the interval is sampled;
- unit sampling (or one-zero sampling): the behaviour is recorded only once if it occurs in a given time interval;
- instantaneous sampling: recording takes place at a predetermined moment at regular intervals;
- natural sampling: all relevant occurrences and their length are recorded for a given time interval.

Figure 6.6 shows what observation sheets would look like for each of these procedures. You can devise your own shorthand coding system or use an established method. A useful range of methods is given by Robson (2002). The codes used here draw from Sylva, Roy and Painter's (1980) adaptation of the ethological 'follow individual animals' method, used for following individual children. Shorthand codes are used for the target child (TC), any other child (C), any adult (A), for the social context (e.g. SOL = solitary, SG = small group, LG = large group) and for the event taking place (e.g. PA = physical aggression, HA = hostile aggression, VA = verbal aggression).

Time	On task involved	On task uninvolved	Off task quiet	Off task disruptive
10.00	✓			
10.01	✓			
10.02	✓			
10.03		✓		
10.04		✓		
10.05				✓

(a)

Sheridan's (1975) norms of child development (4.5 years)	Yes	No	Comments
1. Affectionate, confiding	✓		Holds friend's hand and whispers
2. Likes to help domestic chores	✓		Readily argrees to help wash up and took interest in how clean cups were
3. Tries to keep environment tidy		✓	Messed toys and ran away when asked to tidy up
4. Symbolic play	✓		Imaginary friends to tea
5. Joins in symbolic play	✓		Playing weddings with friends each with a role.
6. Shares toys	✓		

(b)

Time	Activity	Language	Social
9.00	TC joins friend at climbling frame	TC → C I can go higher than you, C → TC can't	PAIR
9.01	TC pushes C off frame	TC (laughs)	PAIR
9.02	C Pushes TC off frame	C → TC I was here first, but you can stay	PAIR

(c)

Time Onset	Time Offset	Event (coded) (note, where possible, events preceding + following aggressive event)	Language	Social
9.15	9.18	(PA) + (HA) TC pulls hair of C viciously and she cries	TC → C I hate you	PAIR
9.19	9.20	(VA) TC sneers at C	TC → C You're an ugly sissy	PAIR
9.21	9.22	(PA) TC pushes C on floor		PAIR

(d)

Figure 6.6   Sampling methods in observation: (a) Predominant activity sampling using a pre-coded checklist; (b) Unit sampling using norms of social development scale, for a 4.5 year old; (c) instantaneous sampling; (d) natural sampling

Box 6.3 gives a further example of unit sampling.

Box 6.3   An observational instrument from a study on the comparison of anxiety-reducing potential of two techniques of bathing

Child identification code:
Date:

Behavioural cues:
while observing patient/child indicate the category of behaviour as follows:

Body activation (circle one)

severe anxiety	– continual non-purposeful activity or inactivity
mild anxiety	– some motions not purposeful, activity increase on mentioning pain/operation
no anxiety	– gestures purposeful and appropriate

Facial expressions (circle one)

severe anxiety	– frowning, down-turned mouth continually
mild anxiety	– occasional facial expression of anxiety
no anxiety	– content and pleasant facial expression

Vocalisations (circle one)

severe anxiety	– sighing, inappropriate laughter, 'I don't know', desperate, panicky, terrified
mild anxiety	– angry, depressed, uncomfortable, nervous, frightened
no anxiety	– use of non-anxiety words: happy, optimistic, secure

Conversation (circle one)

severe anxiety	– expresses numerous concerns, worries, complaints, inability to focus on interview
mild anxiety	– occasional expression of worries, complaints
no anxiety	– no expression of dissatisfaction and/or expressions of contentment

Source: Adapted from Barsevick, A. and Llewellyn, J. (1982), 'A comparison of the anxiety-reducing potential of two bathing techniques.' *Nursing Research*, 31 (1): 2–7. Reproduced with permission

Observing a child in the natural environment will give research a 'real world' edge to it. Data collection needs to be unintrusive and slick and can be aided in some situations by the use of concealed or discreet video cameras or tape recorders, well-designed, economic recording sheets and stopwatches. A well-designed observational study will also enable the researcher to record these real life events as they occur. This direct experience facilitates the researchers' ability to understand complex individuals and situations and to build upon theories. Observation methods, however, often do not adapt well from single individuals or simple settings to large groups or complex settings and this limits the possibility of making comparisons and contrasts.

Interviews

Interviews are a very widely used method of conducting research, whether directly with the children and young people themselves or with adults. As a method of obtaining children's own perspectives, it has much to offer, and this subject is developed further in Chapter 8. A significant amount of what we know about children is gained by well-designed and conducted interviews of adults who know them well – parents, teachers, carers, case workers, health visitors and peers being a few examples. Important issues which potentially influence children via policies and practices can also be examined using interviews. Willing participants like being interviewed and the interactive nature of the procedure allows the researcher access to dimensions of information not otherwise available, such as non-verbal cues on feelings. The relatively free-flow interaction enables the researcher to pick up on important and emotive issues by gentle probing and to discover what matters most to the participants from the topics they raise themselves.

It is in their level of *structure* that interviews mainly vary. The extent to which they do or do not have predetermined questions leads to their being described as *structured, semi-structured* or *unstructured*. A structured interview is much like an interactive questionnaire, where the researcher reads out set questions and records the responses. At the other end of the scale an unstructured interview gives maximum scope to the ideas generated by the interviewee and develops according to the topics that arise. In this situation the interviewer takes on the role of an informed prompter, giving sufficient guidance to keep the interview on track but not controlling the way it develops. The most commonly encountered format in research is the semi-structured interview, which has questions or prompts covering set topics, but within that framework allows a lot of scope for the interviewee's own ideas to develop.

Choices about the level of structure for an interviews should be guided by the purpose they are designed to serve. Interviews that aim mainly to obtain facts, or that look for views on a number of predetermined topics, will have more

Table 6.1   Guidelines for designing and doing an interview

Designing it	Doing it
• Get ideas on paper, arrange into themes and list in order of intrusiveness • Turn into open-ended questions: what? when? how? • Ensure questions are clear, unambiguous and short • Put in a logical order starting with easy questions, ending with hard ones • Avoid leading questions, technical terms, emotive language, negatives • End with positive issues/questions • Pilot interview • Re-write	• State purpose, ensure confidentiality and right not to answer and stop at any time, especially if distressed • Choose setting carefully for privacy and intimacy • Make yourself useful, help in a field setting • Be interested and non-judgemental • Tape interview, stick to agenda but allow interviewee some freedom • Techniques to help: expectant pause/glance; encouraging vocalisations; reflection and returning words used by interviewee; skilful probing

structure. Interviews that aim to tap into topics that are meaningful and important to the interviewee, and that will reflect the interviewee's authentic experience, will have less structure. Also, unstructured interviewing can be useful for an exploratory study in a new area. It can be used to generate the background information that will guide subsequent more structured approaches. Bailley et al. (1995) give the example of an investigation into what young people know about illegal drugs. The study begins with three long unstructured interviews to provide background on the kind of language young people used about drugs and the issues that were important to them. On this basis a better informed structured interview is prepared for use with a further 20 young people.

Each form of interview has its advantages and disadvantages. More structured interviews allow each person to be asked the same questions in the same way. This allows for more direct comparisons and is more amenable to quantitative methodology. However, they are less flexible than unstructured interviews and make assumptions that the researcher already knows what the relevant questions are and only has to ask for the answers. In many ways the semi-structured interview can capture the advantages of both approaches.

Interviews take time and require detailed analysis, but a well-done interview is well worth it. Table 6.1 offers some general guidelines for designing and doing an interview.

Questionnaires

Questionnaires are a popular research tool because they can be quickly designed, administered – even by post – to large numbers, and easily analysed.

They are an excellent way of obtaining both factual data, such as attendance rates at school or hospital admissions, and also opinions. Perhaps it is the beguiling simplicity of the questionnaire that makes it so universally used by researchers – but beguiling it is, and there are many attempts at research that have ended up with unanalysable data and meaningless results because of flawed questionnaire design. Box 6.4 provides some salutary advice about compiling your own questionnaire.

Box 6.4   Getting questionnaires right

Questionnaires are among the most common methods used by researchers – and the worst carried out. Bad questionnaires will effectively torpedo the whole project, no matter how much labour is expended on it. They usually end up with an item that says something like, 'If there are any other questions I should have thought of but didn't, please answer them here'. Many of these questionnaires seem to have been sent out when, for all practical purposes, they were still at their first draft. There is only one place for the first draft of any questionnaire – the bin. If you ignore this advice, your project will probably end up there instead. Here are some ground rules for those who are compiling questionnaires.

- Avoid any possibility of ambiguity. Assume that the person answering your questionnaire knows *nothing*. Explain and define your terms exactly.
- State precisely and comprehensively the information you require. Questions that ask me if I have dealt with many school refusers recently will tell nobody anything. Specify all you want to know – times, ages, dates. Does 'last year' mean last calendar year or last session? Your questionnaire is not a rehearsal: you don't get a second chance.
- Put the questions in a suitable form for quantifying the data afterwards. It may not be true to say that if it can't be counted it doesn't exist, but for questionnaire data it is *mostly* true.
- Do not throw in every question you can think of and then wait to see if anything interesting turns up. This is the wrong way round. Decide the variables you are interested in studying and frame the questions to provide the type of information you want.
- Do not present the respondent with an impossible task. For example, I do not know and could not tell you how many primary age children in my service were referred to a psychiatrist in the past 5 years compared with the previous 5.
- Don't ask for pieces of personal information you don't need. You will receive a lower return if you ask for children's names or other personal data if these are not essential.
- Try a 'dry run' first, even if only with a handful of colleagues. You will soon pick up the major flaws.

(Continued)

- Consider beforehand what steps you will take to maximise your return rate. For example, always state the date by which you wish to receive the reply, a few days after that send a friendly reminder and later make a phone call if possible. For the type of questionnaire that is sent to colleagues and other professionals, *a low return is always the fault of the researcher – not of the respondent.*

Source: Adapted from MacKay, T. (1987) 'Planning research in child guidance'. *SALGEP Quarterly,* 6 (1): 3–11.

Researching children's attitudes

Questionnaires can be a good way of finding out about children's attitudes, and they can be designed to cover exactly the areas you are interested in. One such questionnaire, 'What You Think About School', is shown later in Figure 6.7. It was designed to assess attitudes to school and schoolwork on the part of the child, as well as the child's perceptions of parental attitudes. Three questions related specifically to attitudes towards reading and perceived ability in that subject. All but two of the questions were judged to have directionality (that is, to suggest either positive or negative attitudes or perceptions regarding school and education). The remaining two were considered to be neutral ('My favourite time is playtime' and 'I haven't got a best subject at school'). A simple scoring system was devised to give a score of 0, 1 or 2 on each of the 14 relevant items.

However, testing attitudes with young children, especially using questionnaires, can present some major problems, as MacKay and Watson (1999) found to their cost. They tried to adapt the above questionnaire into 'What You Think About School for Younger Children'. Instead of questions of the type, 'I like coming to school', all the questions were replaced with the type, 'Freddie the Fish likes coming to school. Are you like Freddie the Fish – do *you* like coming to school?' The questions were read out to the children, who were 5 years old, in small groups by their teacher. For every question each had a picture (in this case, Freddie the Fish). They were told, 'This side says YES and this side says NO'. They then had to put a circle round their choice.

The result was a disaster! As with any new questionnaire or method, the researchers went to do a quality check to see how it was being carried out. They entered the room at the point where a teacher was saying, 'Minnie the Mouse wishes she didn't have to come to school. Are you like Minnie the Mouse – do *you* wish you didn't have to come to school?' As she asked the question she was unconsciously shaking her head in a disapproving fashion, and with one voice the

---

WHAT YOU THINK ABOUT SCHOOL
(Briggs and MacKay 1993)
We want to find out more about what children think of school.
Please put a tick in one box for each question. There are no 'good' or 'bad' answers. We just want to know what you think.

		TRUE	IN BETWEEN	FALSE
1	I like coming to school	TRUE	IN BETWEEN	FALSE
2	My favourite time is playtime	TRUE	IN BETWEEN	FALSE
3	I think school is important	TRUE	IN BETWEEN	FALSE
4	I am often in trouble at school	TRUE	IN BETWEEN	FALSE
5	My parents think teachers are usually right	TRUE	IN BETWEEN	FALSE
6	It's a good thing to have lots of books at home	TRUE	IN BETWEEN	FALSE
7	I'm not very good at reading	TRUE	IN BETWEEN	FALSE
8	Homework is important	TRUE	IN BETWEEN	FALSE
9	My school is a good school	TRUE	IN BETWEEN	FALSE
10	I'm not very good at working with other children	TRUE	IN BETWEEN	FALSE
11	My friends think school is a waste of time	TRUE	IN BETWEEN	FALSE
12	My parents think school is important	TRUE	IN BETWEEN	FALSE
13	I wish I didn't have to come to school	TRUE	IN BETWEEN	FALSE
14	If I'm in trouble at school my parents usually take my side	TRUE	IN BETWEEN	FALSE
15	I haven't got a 'best' subject at school	TRUE	IN BETWEEN	FALSE
16	I do not like reading very much	TRUE	IN BETWEEN	FALSE

Figure 6.7   A simple attitudes questionnaire used with children

Source: MacKay, T. (1995) 'Reading failure in an area of multiple social disadvantage: response of a psychological service to a school's priorities. In: The Scottish Office Education Department, *Matching Service Delivery to Client Needs: Quality Assurance in Psychological Services.* Edinburgh: The Scottish Office Education Department pp. 210–33.

children responded, 'Nooooo...ooo', and circled the appropriate answer! The write up in the journal article omits the details and just discreetly says, 'The pre- post attitude questionnaires proved unsuitable for meaningful statistical analysis'.

It is very important to avoid the 'social desirability' factor in questionnaires and other methods – in this case pleasing the teacher and being the same as the rest of the group. The above fiasco led MacKay (2006) to develop an innovative and successful method for testing young children's attitudes – but not using a questionnaire. Instead some remarkably low-tech and readily available technical equipment was used (three jam jars!) as described in Box 6.5.

Box 6.5   Testing young children's attitudes: the jam jar technique

How do you assess the attitudes of children as young as 4 or 5 without getting just the socially desirable response – the one the child thinks will be approved by the person asking the question? In this study the aim was to see if the early literacy skills of young children and their attitudes and beliefs about reading would be enhanced by getting them to make three bold declarations every day about becoming good readers.

The children had three glass jars (jam jars) set before them. Each jar contained a large and similar number of small white cards, designed to represent the responses made by other children to the same questions. Every question was presented to each child in the following manner:

- *These children don't like reading very much* (pointing to jar 1)
- *These children think it's OK* (jar 2)
- *These children like reading a lot* (jar 3).

What do you think about reading?

The child was then invited to post a card into the chosen jar, and the choice was recorded. The direction of the questions was varied to avoid response set (for example, always choosing the first jar, or the last one). Posting the cards in this way made the exercise appear more anonymous, and since children have high levels of group conformity it was clear from all the cards already in the three jars that the answers could safely be deposited wherever the children liked.

A score of 1 was assigned to the most positive response for each question, 2 to the middle response and 3 to the negative response. Before the intervention there was no difference in attitudes between experimentals and controls. After the intervention all children were tested again. All of the scores that had changed upwards from less to more positive and downwards from more to less positive were analysed by comparing actual changes with possible changes. This therefore took account of the fact that scores that were already at 1 could not change up, and scores at 3 could not change down. These overall change scores showed that the children who had made the declarations had developed more positive attitudes to reading ($p < 0.01$, chi-square test).

This simple jam jar technique proved highly effective. Of 54 children tested at age 4 – 5 years, only one was unable to engage with the idea of selecting a preferred jar.

Source: MacKay, T. (2006) *The West Dunbartonshire Literacy Initiative: The Design, Implementation and Evaluation of an Intervention Strategy to Raise Achievement and Eradicate Illiteracy.* Dumbarton: West Dunbartonshire Council.

Standardised questionnaires

As well as questionnaires designed specifically for a research project there are also many standardised questionnaires that are useful for researchers working with children. Large numbers of different subject areas have ready-made question-naires available from the catalogues of the main test publishers in the various dis-ciplines of psychology, health and education. For example, the ones designed by Spence (1995) for social skills, social competence and related areas are useful, easy to administer and interpret and very accessible (they come in a photocopiable resource pack). They also have the advantage of providing triangulation by allow-ing comparable information to be collected from different sources – parent, pupil and teacher. The results have been standardised on a mixed age group of children aged 8–17. Each item can be rated as 'not true', 'sometimes true' or 'mostly true'. Examples from the social skills questionnaire for pupils are: 'I listen to other people's points of view during arguments' and 'I control my temper when I lose in a game or competition'.

Survey methods

A commonly used method in education, health and social work research is the *survey*. A broad aim of survey research is to describe what is actually going on in a particular field of practice regarding a particular issue of some importance. An example might be finding out what are the policies, if any, of all pre-school providers on the provision of a core curriculum. Surveys can tell us about stan-dards for comparing existing conditions and help us in determining the relation-ships that exist between specific events (Cohen et al. 2000).

In survey research, a large number of questions are devised into a question-naire, rating scale or structured, interview. The questionnaire can be structured, with fixed, alternative responses, or unstructured, with open–ended questions which allow participants to express their answers in a more personal way. Surveys are designed to be administered to very large numbers of participants who are a representative sample of an even larger population: a survey sent to every social services manager in every local authority in the country represents the views of the entire population of social services managers in the country.

In a classic study, Rutter et al. (1979) combined survey methods, structured interviews and classroom observation. The aim of the study, called *Fifteen Thousand Hours*, was to examine how secondary schools in an Inner London Education Authority area of 6 miles radius differed in terms of academic achievement, atten-dance and delinquency. Variables considered important for differences included sta-tus and sex of pupils and organisation of school environment (size, space, staff, class size, age and sites of buildings). The survey was conducted on how the 12 schools in the area selected measured up in terms of these variables.

A good example of a questionnaire survey is that of Blenkin and Yue (1994) which produced a profile of early years practitioners as an investigation into the quality of educational provision for the early years in England and Wales. This entailed obtaining information concerning both the nature and quality of provision, including quality of setting, resourcing and qualifications of professionals and others working with the children. Qualitative views of practitioners on what is meant by quality of provision were also obtained. Box 6.6 illustrates their objectives in designing the questionnaire. Survey designs like those described enable you to collect a lot of data very quickly and can cover examination of large amounts of variables. They give good descriptions of the way things are and indicate other possible studies and methods.

Box 6.6   Objectives for an education survey questionnaire

Objectives are:

- to elicit information on the nature and qualifications of practitioners;
- to identify key factors/criteria supporting/constraining curriculum development;
- to identify key factors influential in the professional development of practitioners;
- to obtain practitioner definitions of quality curriculum;
- to obtain practitioners' suggestions for improvements in current educational provision;
- to obtain practitioners' suggestions' for improvements in professional training and development.

Source: Adapted from Blenkin, G.M. and Yue, N.Y.L. (1994) 'Profiling early years practitioners: some first impressions from a national survey.' *Early Years*, 15 (1): 13–22. Copyright Trentham Books Limited, 1994. Reproduced with permission

---

Finally, the whole subject of doing quantitative research with children – together with the statistical foundations to support it – involves entering territory that can at times be difficult and exacting for the most experienced of researchers. To conclude this chapter on the lighter side, Box 6.7 takes a tongue-in-cheek look at some of the telling statements found in student dissertations and research reports.

Box 6.7   Reporting quantitative research: the art of dodging

'The results obtained from three of the participants were selected for detailed study' *(The results of the others didn't make sense and were therefore ignored)*

'Results suggest that ...' *(The results were not significant)*

'It is well known that ...' *(No evidence available)*

'A representative sample of Scottish psychologists' *(Me and three friends)*

'This aspect requires further research' *(I can't make head or tail of it myself)*

'A content analysis of 43 items identified 8 distinguishable categories' *(I looked at the cards and put them into 8 piles)*

'Some of the scores from this group were extrapolated' *(I lost the envelope I wrote this group's scores on)*

'Because of complicating factors this group was omitted from the analysis' *(I couldn't sort out the mess so I scrapped the lot)*

'Full details of the statistical procedure will be found in Guilford's "Psychometric Methods"' *(I found the stats utterly incomprehensible)*

'This was a pilot study' *(I messed up the whole project)*

Source: MacKay, T. (1987) 'Planning research in child guidance.' *SALGEP Quarterly,* 6 (1): 3–11. Originally adapted from Nisbet, J. and Entwistle, N. (1970) *Educational Research Methods.* London: London University.

PRACTICAL 6.1   DESIGNING QUANTITATIVE RESEARCH PROJECTS

The aim of this practical is to explore some ways of answering research questions using the information given in this chapter.

Look back to the three examples with which this chapter opens. How would you set about planning a research project to answer each of the questions raised?

What kind of data would you need? From what potential sources might you get it? What methods might be included (for example, documentary sources of information such as referral records, observation, questionnaires, interviews)? What factors would you need to consider in analysing and interpreting your data?

Would all of your data be quantitative, or would you also be able to enrich your projects with qualitative information (see Chapter 7) – rich descriptions from individual children or staff that convey the flavour of what is happening and what it means in their real experience?

PRACTICAL 6.2   INTERPRETING TEST SCORES

The aim of this practical is to give you some experience of interpreting scores on standardised tests.

You are doing a research project with a group of children who are all 9 years old. Six of the children come from one school class. Some of the background information you have includes reading ages. The teacher says, 'This group of children range from those whose reading ages are so high they are at genius level, to those who are so low they clearly have major problems.' Do you agree with her?

The reading test in question has the following properties for children age 9 years: M = 53; SD = 16. Here are the scores for your six children:

	Score	Reading age			Score	Reading age	
Alan	41	7y	11m	Karen	71	11y	0m
Anwar	53	9y	0m	Natalie	50	8y	9m
Benjy	35	7y	3m	Tasha	68	10y	7m

Here is one approach, using the descriptions in the WISC-IV as a guideline.

1   For each of the six scores work out where it lies in standard deviations away from the mean. (For example: Alan's score of 41 is 12 below the mean. The SD is 16 so he is ¾ of a standard deviation below, or –0.75 SD.)

2   Look at the descriptions of the WISC-IV scores given in Box 6.2. For each band work out where it falls in standard deviations away from the mean. (For example, as the mean is 100 and the SD is 15, the 'borderline' band of 70–79 extends from –2 SD to –1.4 SD. (Remember, you would need to get down to this level of score before it became low enough to look like it might be a bit of a problem.)

3   You can now compare your reading test scores with the WISC-IV bands, because they are both expressed in the same measurement of number of SDs away from the mean.

4   What description would you now give to the six reading scores? (For example, Alan's reading age of 7y 11m at age 9 years falls in the 'low average' band, and indeed is just marginally below the middle range of 'average' scores.)

Did you find any apparent 'geniuses' or 'major problems'?

(As a matter of interest, the data here are taken from one of the major standard reading tests, and in common with almost all tests, its results are frequently misinterpreted.)

PRACTICAL 6.3   CHILD OBSERVATION

The aim of this practical is to give you some experience of doing and scoring child observation.

This practical is best done with real children or a good quality video of children interacting. Figure 6.8 shows an observation sheet, designed for sampling of predetermined categories in a checklist format. You are required to indicate each incident of each behaviour by entering a tick alongside the observed category. First, examine the coding scheme and ask yourself what you think it is trying to do. Is it a reliable and valid system? How can we find out? Do you anticipate problems? Conduct the observation.

BEHAVIOUR	FREQUENCY	TOTAL
Social: interactive solitary parallel		
Emotion: laughs cries smiles hits comforts		
Cognition: questions argues instructs fantasy play		

Figure 6.8   Observation sheet

Once you have conducted the observation, ask yourself/discuss with others the following issues:

- What is it trying to do and does it succeed?
- Problems of format/layout.
- What crucial things are missing from the proforma?
- Problems of conducting the observation.
- Can the procedure be improved?
- Problems concerning selection and categories of behaviours.
- Possible improvements in knowing which behaviours to select.

PRACTICAL 6.4   DESIGNING YOUR OWN OBSERVATION SHEET

The aim of this practical is to promote critical thinking in designing your own observation sheet.

Design your own observation sheet for studying target child bullies. In designing it, ask yourself:

- What kind of sampling and recording is best?
- What do I mean by bullying?
- Are there different forms of bullying and if so what are they?
- Who else matters in bullying?
- Do their responses matter and can they be defined and categorised?
- Does it matter how the episode starts and finishes?

PRACTICAL 6.5   QUESTIONNAIRE DESIGN

The aim of this practical is to give you some experience of the issues involved in questionnaire design.

Think of a child research study that would be of interest to you and that could use questionnaires as a method. For example, you might want to find out how many children in a school or group are being bullied, what form it takes and how they deal with it. Or you might be interested in how children spend their leisure time, or what they spend their pocket money on. Or again, you might want to know whether parents of children with autistic spectrum disorders manage to organise family holidays, and if so, where they go, how they travel, what kind of accommodation they use, whether they eat out and whether they manage to get time to themselves.

All of these questions lend themselves to questionnaires, some of which might be completed by the children themselves and others by adults.

1   Construct a questionnaire that will answer your key questions. In doing so, follow the advice given in this chapter, such as the bullet points in Box 6.4.
2   In your questionnaire include the following types of question:

- YES/NO questions;
- multiple choice questions (e.g. selecting which box answers how often people go away on a family holiday, ranging from 'never' through to 'more than 3 times a year');
- scalar questions (e.g. questions where the choice of answer is recorded on a scale, such as one of 3 points or one of 5 points);
- open-ended questions (questions where people write in their own comments).

3   Look at your first draft and refine it through better drafts by asking key questions. For example: is YES/NO unambiguous, or will people be saying 'it's sometimes yes and sometimes no'? Does your questionnaire include enough questions to get all the key data you require from it? Are there any questions that won't really contribute to your analysis and understanding? If you have used a 3-point scale does it have enough range to allow you to capture a variety of viewpoints? Or, if you have used a 5-point scale will you just end up combining the first two points (e.g. 'little' and 'very little') and the last two points ('much' and 'very much')? Do your open-ended questions give enough scope to people to say other important things? Or are they so open-ended that they will just give information that you can't do much with?

4   Once you have a good draft, pilot it on a few children or colleagues – you'll soon find where the flaws are!

7

Designing and doing qualitative research with children

The aims of this chapter are:

- To discuss the nature of qualitative research and its benefits and limitations.
- To outline some of the main methods used in qualitative research designs.
- To give practical illustrations of how research with children may utilise mixed quantitative and qualitative designs.

If something exists, it exists in some quantity. If it exists in some quantity it can be measured. (Thorndike 1905)

If you can measure something, that ain't it. (Kaplan, 1964, cited in Berg 2004: 2)

These two quotations caricature the essential difference between the quantitative and the qualitative approaches to research. The notion of *quantity* refers to the amount of something – to questions of how much, how often and to what extent. *Quality* on the other hand refers to the essence of something – to questions about its nature and how it is experienced and described. However, the two approaches are not as opposed or even as distinct as these quotations suggest. Very many quantitative studies are supported and enriched by qualitative data, and many qualitative studies include some data that can be counted and analysed using traditional quantitative methods.

In some respects the dichotomy between quantitative and qualitative methods is an artefact that is not entirely helpful. Most people who wish to do research with children are practitioners whose concern is with *action research* rather than with 'pure' scientific research conducted in the university laboratory or other contrived settings. Action research, sometimes referred to as 'participatory action research' (Reason 1994), is a process by which the researcher constructs 'knowledge of specific issues through planning, evaluating, refining and learning from the experience' (Koshy 2005). It is a continuous learning process in which new knowledge is both learned and also shared with those who may benefit from it. Action research is viewed as being so central to qualitative approaches that it is given a key place in many qualitative texts (for example, Berg 2004; Holloway 1997). It enshrouds many of the basic principles of qualitative research in that it is carried out in natural, real world settings, is participatory, constructs theory from practice, involves dynamic processes of change as it progresses and aims for understanding of meaning and experience. Nevertheless, many action research projects use traditional quantitative methods.

It is most likely that in your research with children you will use both quantitative and qualitative methods, so although this chapter focuses on qualitative designs it has examples of the mix of approaches that typifies most action research in the real world settings of childhood.

The nature of qualitative enquiry

Qualitative research strives for depth of understanding in natural settings. Unlike the positivist, quantitative tradition it does not focus on a world in which reality is fixed and measurable but one in which the experiences and perspectives of individuals are socially constructed. It is 'a form of social inquiry that focuses on the way people interpret and make sense of their experiences and the world in which they live' (Holloway 1997: 1). It grew out of a concern on the part of many researchers that 'research activities structured through the logic of quantification leave out lots of interesting and potentially consequential things' (Freebody 2003: 35), not just in terms of research aims and content but also in terms of missing the richness of accounts of experience.

The roots of qualitative research are to be found in the social anthropology and sociology of the early twentieth century. Anthropologists such as Bronislaw Malinowski (1922) and Margaret Mead (1928) carried out their classic cross-cultural studies in Melanesia and Samoa respectively, and in doing so used methods of enquiry that aimed to develop deep understandings and provide rich descriptions of the lives and experiences of people in non-Western cultures. The 1960s saw the more formal development of qualitative methods and theories. A key contribution was the publication of *The Discovery of Grounded Theory* by two sociologists, Barney Glaser and Anselm Strauss (Glaser and Strauss 1967). It was their work that began to bridge the gap between theory and practice, to make qualitative research more systematic and rigorous and to establish qualitative methods in their own right rather than merely as exploratory tools for quantitative work (Charmaz 1995; Merriam 2002). By 1978 there was a separate journal devoted to qualitative methods, *Qualitative Sociology*. Later the methods would become fully embedded in most of the professions working with children, including education (Sherman and Webb 1988), nursing (Morse 1991) and psychology (Banister et al. 1994).

Qualitative research is a complex and varied field of enquiry, and the term should not be used so loosely as to refer to almost any research project that does not depend on analysis of numerical data, or that has not been conducted rigorously enough to produce such data. Richardson (1996) issues a number of 'health warnings' for those who would embark on these methods. They include the observations that qualitative research is a specialist area of expertise with its own language, that it is not to be taken as meaning 'easy research' and that it merits proper training and supervision. As a specialist field it has a number of defining features, the most commonly accepted of which are shown in Figure 3.6

There have been many debates about what properly constitutes qualitative research. Kidder and Fine (1987, cited by Willig 2001) distinguish between 'big Q' and 'little q' approaches. 'Big Q' refers to strict qualitative methodologies that are inductive, that are concerned with the exploration of meanings and that seek to generate theory from data rather than starting with a hypothesis. 'Little q' refers to a wider range of less pure methodologies in which various types of non-numerical data are collected, often within the context of more traditional approaches.

This book cannot serve as a manual of either 'big Q' or 'little q' methods of research. There are many comprehensive texts covering both general qualitative methods and specific methodologies. This chapter includes an account of a range of methods that characterise strict qualitative research. However, it also takes a practical approach in recognising that most researchers are more interested in maximum flexibility in choosing methods best suited to their needs rather than in debates about the purity of the research paradigm they adopt. In doing research with children you are likely to find a variety of less pure approaches more useful.

Qualitative research designs: the benefits and limitations

Qualitative approaches are particularly suitable for doing research with children. This applies especially to those whose job is to work with children as opposed to researchers working in academic institutions who choose to do a child study. First, people who work with children are already operating in a real life, naturalistic setting. Indeed, they are much less likely to have ready access to the more contrived settings that often characterise traditional experimental methodologies. Natural environments such as the classroom or the playgroup are ideal arenas for research. Some of the rather 'unnatural' environments, such as the children's hospital ward, are also among the naturalistic settings in which qualitative approaches may be used. They are real life situations which are naturally occurring, as opposed to artificial or contrived ones. Second, many people working with children do so in individual or small group settings. They often do not have access to the larger samples typical of quantitative research, but on the other hand they frequently do have access to small groups at a detailed and intensive level.

Third, children represent an excellent source of the kind of data that are at the heart of qualitative research – rich descriptions in words and pictures that capture children's experiences and understandings, rather than the cold, abstract findings that often derive from numerical analysis. Many research reports, including those that are largely quantitative, are enlivened by qualitative commentary of this kind, particularly when enriched by the actual words used by children and young people themselves. Sometimes a single comment from a child's perspective will convey much more meaning about the impact of research than a whole array of figures. The following extract comes from possibly the largest quantitative literacy study reported in the world, with around 50,000 children participating, but one that was enriched by qualitative data. It is the final part of a statement made by a young person who was not only a research participant but also a contributor to and communicator of the research, by providing an account of her experience of the research process at a dissemination conference:

> When all this started I couldn't read. I was a failure. Now I have a cupboardful of books at home. My favourite authors are Roald Dahl and J.K. Rowling. Now I am a success. (MacKay 2006: 185)

A fourth advantage of qualitative approaches lies in the fact that a very large number of research projects with children are carried out by people who are not ultimately reporting to the major research funding bodies. These major funders have traditionally been concerned with large quantitative studies based on inferential statistics. On the other hand, child practitioners are often giving an account of their work to managers who themselves work in the caring professions – heads of establishments or services in education, health or social services. It is in these settings that most value is often placed on project reports that are enlivened by rich descriptions that highlight the participation and experiences of children. Even some of the large funders, including those with a primary interest in research with children, have in recent times moved towards funding a large number of small scale research projects which in their nature are likely to be qualitative. For example, Koshy (2005) refers to the fact that in the past decade the important role of small scale action research projects has been highlighted in the number of small research grants made available in England and Wales by the Teacher Training Agency and the Department of Education and Skills. She also refers to a similar trend in the United States.

A fifth benefit of doing qualitative research with children arises from its very nature as participative research. A number of research journals, such as those of the British Psychological Society, no longer describe those who take part in research as 'subjects' but as 'participants'. However, while this policy gives out a good signal of respect and partnership it is often the case in quantitative work, as shown in Table 6.1, that people are the subject of study rather than participants in a meaningful sense. Participation is more than involvement. 'Authentic participation means immersing people in the focus of the enquiry and the research method, and involving them in data collection and analysis' (Gray 2004: 374). A theme of this book is partnership with children and young people, and encouraging research that involves true participation. In seeking to promote partnership and authentic participation of children in the literacy study cited above MacKay utilised the five *context variables* of vision, profile, commitment, ownership and declaration (see Chapter 2).

> The entire project was predicated on a context in which everyone was fully committed to it and ownership was enjoyed at every level from researcher to the youngest pupil in nursery. Declarations were constantly made that this project was going to succeed, that nothing would stand in its way. (MacKay 2006: 87)

A final advantage of espousing qualitative approaches is that they have moved from the fringes of science, where they were once treated with suspicion as being less than scientific, to a position in which they are increasingly valued. There is evidence that qualitative research will become still more important and central in society in the future. A survey of the views of over 800 UK psychologists regarding future trends in research pointed to two developments (Haste et al. 2001). First, there would be an increased research emphasis on everyday life, quality of life and the whole person. Second, research would move increasingly from the laboratory to real world settings. These holistic interests in well-being and in research conducted in natural settings are central features of qualitative approaches, and suggest that these approaches will become increasingly important.

Difficulties with qualitative research

At the same time qualitative research also has its difficulties and limitations. Conducting real world research requires a recognition that work must be done in 'complex, messy, poorly controlled "field" settings' (Robson 2002), and those of us who do a lot of it know that real world research with children is usually even messier. MacKay and Watson (1999) characterised their group work intervention for early literacy – a mixed quantitative/qualitative study – as 'an excellent example of such messiness':

> The planned group work intervention for the experimental subgroup could not proceed because the group worker took ill; the home link teacher met with discouragement in her home support plan; the peer tutoring by older pupils in the Easter holidays did not get off the ground because of lack of response; one of the two researchers made a career change in the middle of the study; no sooner had the intervention begun than the school had to prepare for a merger with another school

in the area; and in the middle of it all local government reorganisation took place, resulting among other things in the termination of funding and the necessity for a new grant application. (MacKay and Watson 1999: 34)

These are the real issues that face practitioners seeking to do research with children in the natural environments that dictate the need for qualitative approaches. They are seldom mentioned in published studies, since authors tend to smooth over the wrinkles as much as possible and not to highlight apparent flaws. However, these 'flaws' reflect the unavoidable challenges in this kind of research and they should not be a seen as a discouragement. MacKay and Watson went on to note regarding the above study, 'Nevertheless, the intervention was successful'.

Qualitative approaches are sometimes seen as a less rigorous alternative to quantitative research. This should never be the case, and much of what passes as qualitative is simply sloppy. It should not be a matter of saying, 'We couldn't get the numbers so we turned it into a qualitative study'. Qualitative, as noted in the 'health warning' from Richardson, does not equate with 'easy', and indeed some methods of qualitative analysis are in various respects more difficult and more laborious than quantitative methods.

It is also the case that sometimes the data gathered for a project are left at the level of qualitative descriptions when they could more usefully have been categorised, counted and presented as quantitative data. It is a good maxim that if something can be counted it probably should be. Meaning, significance and trends can easily be lost in the midst of descriptions, and while rich descriptions will always enhance research findings they should not obscure straightforward facts and figures when these will present a clearer account of research results. Finally, qualitative data are prone to being seen as weak and inconclusive, and never advancing beyond the exploratory level. It is here that the principle of triangulation is of particular importance (see Chapter 5). Triangulating the findings from several different perspectives, such as using multiple data sources for the same finding, can strengthen data that would be weak if presented singly but are robust if reinforced from different strands of enquiry. An example of triangulation is shown in the case study by Briggs, MacKay and Miller later in this chapter.

In summary it may be said that qualitative research offers many persuasive benefits for those who are doing research with children. So long as its difficulties and limitations are recognised it is a powerful approach that is likely to prove indispensable for everyone who is working in this field.

Qualitative approaches: an overview

Although we have been able to define key features and themes in qualitative research, it must be acknowledged that this is a complex area marked by few clear definitions, a variety of viewpoints on what constitutes qualitative enquiry, a lack of agreed terminology and a range of approaches which at times show considerable overlap. 'Qualitative is a slippery term, put to a variety of uses, and carrying a variety of conceptual associations' (Freebody 2003: 35).

Four approaches are introduced here, selected on the basis that they are the ones most frequently referred to in basic texts on qualitative research methods, and they are the only ones to be covered in all five of the following widely used key texts: Berg 2004; Crabtree and Miller 1999; Cresswell 1998; Merriam 2002; Richardson 1996. These are: grounded theory, ethnography, narrative analysis and the case study.

Grounded theory

Glaser and Strauss (1967) coined the term 'grounded theory' to convey the idea that theory emerges from or is grounded in the data. (The fact that by the 1990s these two founders of this approach fundamentally disagreed as to what constitutes grounded theory highlights some of the difficulties and complexities associated with the still emerging field of qualitative research.) The starting point is the selection of a real life situation as an area of study, and what is relevant to illuminating that area is allowed to emerge from the data that are collected. These data may be in a vast variety of forms, and are likely to include interviews and observation, with considerable emphasis placed on participants' own accounts of their experience. In addition use may be made of many documentary sources, such as letters or diaries. Grounded theory is especially useful in situations 'where little is known about a particular topic or problem area, or where a new and exciting outlook is needed in familiar settings' (Holloway 1997: 81). It is therefore likely to appeal to practitioners working in the constantly changing world of children, where often researchers come up with interesting and innovative ideas.

Data analysis in grounded theory goes on throughout the research, and progresses by means of *coding* and *categorising*. Coding is the key process, by which data are broken down into component parts. Each separate idea is given a label, often using the words or phrases used by the participants themselves. The transcripts of interviews and observations, and the words used in documents, can be coded line by line, and large numbers of labels generated, so that the ideas are truly grounded in the data and not superimposed on it by pre-existing theories. For example, coding labels in a study of children who have moved to a new area or a new school might include descriptions such as 'missing friends' or 'feeling unsure'. As analysis progresses these codes are collapsed into categories containing similar ideas. These might include 'socialisation' or 'anxiety'. Ideally the process of coding and categorising proceeds until the point of *saturation* is reached, in which no further categories are emerging. The resulting categories are used to generate theory. For example, the data might illuminate particular stages through which children pass when they move home or school. A grounded theory practical is provided at the end of this chapter.

Ethnography

Ethnography has a long history as the research method of anthropology. An ethnography is a description of a cultural or social group or system. Ethnographers conduct research, usually by participant observation, into all aspects of a culture and have been studying child development in varying cultural and social settings for some time (e.g. Mead and Wolfenstein 1955; Whiting and Whiting 1975; Whiting and Edwards 1988). One study involved research teams in different countries asking similar questions about child–rearing practices and using similar methods across social settings (Whiting 1963). In a sociological study, Leavitt (1996) examined the emotional culture in day care settings. Methods included participant observation, field notes and a form of analysis which depended on interaction and telling stories in interpreting events observed and experienced.

The emotional culture of settings was experienced through daily practices, regulative norms (such as rules on crying), caregiver beliefs regarding involvement and professional distance, alienation from the child's emotions, and the construction of the anti–self (in that children's emotions and selves were not given meaning through recognition and response, which leads to a loss of self for the child). As this example illustrates, ethnography is a qualitative research approach which gives importance to the interpretation of actions and the contexts in which they occur. Theory plays an important role in ethnographic research. Existing themes can inform and be tested in this kind of research. Leavitt's research was conducted within a symbolic interactionist framework and interpreted in terms of Marxist theory. Nevertheless, new theory can often emerge from ethnographic field notes, observations and interviews (see Practical 7.3). Box 7.1 lists some of the ethnographic methods used for doing research with children of various ages.

Box 7.1   Some ethnographic methods used for doing research with pre-schoolers

- The **transmission of cultural values**: passive participant observation + informal interviews + formal interviews.
- **Spontaneous use of English at home** as practice play for peer play at school: narrative play – tape recordings of play sessions of a bilingual child + field notes by the mother.
- The **social and creative behaviour** of four 'highly original' children: observation + video + interviews.
- **Peers constructing their own culture**: participant observation of access rituals and friendship and description of field entry strategies.

(Continued)

- **Pretend play**: ethnographic interviewing + non-participant observation + analysis of children's writings.
- **Excellence of practitioners working with children**: life stories and narrative accounts of several excellent practitioners in different contexts; stories constructed from interviews, participant observation, written correspondence and autobiographical reflection.

Source: Adapted from Hatch, J.A. (ed.) (1995) *Qualitative Research in Early Childhood Settings.* Copyright J. Amos Hatch, Praeger Publishers, 1995. Reproduced with permission

Narrative analysis

Narrative analysis uses stories as data. It focuses on first-hand accounts of experience, and recognises that people normally construe their lives in terms of continuity and process, and that 'attempts to understand social life that are not attuned to this feature neglect the perspective of those being studied' (Bryman 2001: 401). A narrative can take many forms. For example, answers to questions in qualitative interviews can in themselves constitute narrative accounts that focus on episodes in personal experience. A popular form of narrative analysis is life history research, and this term and others such as biography, autobiography, life narratives and oral history are often used as being synonymous with the narrative analysis approach.

What can be learned by listening to one person retell the story of their life? It tells us a lot about that person, about the childhood experiences which have influenced them, and the historical events and cultural contexts which have further shaped what this person has become over the years. Suppose what this person has actually become is a first class case worker with a unique talent for helping to maintain unity of families involving child abuse. Now the life history gives us so much more. For example *what* exactly does she *do* in her daily practice and *why*, where does the skill and motivation come from to be as good at her job as she is? This kind of research opens yet another door through which to enter the world of the child. This one person can enlighten us on how to make the world a better place for children to be in. The stories of such individuals who work with children can inform practice by way of example. They can also make powerful statements about troublesome social, educational or health issues such as multicultural education or maintaining the unity of families involved in child abuse. Research of this kind also recognises and uses the intersubjective nature of naturalistic research. It is worth noting that there are different kinds of stories: a life story is about a life, life history includes information on historical and cultural contexts. A narrative is a way of presenting human actions and events in a meaningful structure. Telling stories is a process of creating meaning from one's past experiences as well as creating meaning for the future. There is also the form of story being told in the report of an interview. The method could be of potential use with children and young people directly.   For example, we might do a life history on a young person who has demonstrated enormous resilience and coping in the face of disability to achieve a particular position in society. Box 7.2 outlines a way of doing life story/history research.

Box 7.2   Life history: a method for entering and understanding the lives and work of others

1   Interview participant several times over a year. Seek interviews with key colleagues and relatives.
2   Ask questions leading to intersubjective understanding:

- What was it like for you to do your job?
- How did you come to do your job?
- Tell me as much as you can about your life up to the present time.
- What is the meaning of what you do for you?
- How do you understand it in your life.

3   Respond with stories from your own life.
4   Describe your role in the process to improve validity.
5   Get feedback from the participant on your written report.

Source: Adapted from Seidman, I. (1998) *Interviewing as Qualitative Research: A Guide for Researchers in Education and the Social Sciences*, 2nd edn. Copyright Teachers College, Columbia University, 1998. Reprinted with permission

---

Other narrative forms of research include narrative reports of behavioural observations and self-descriptions written by practitioners. Life story/history research is demanding in the same way as Tavistock Model observation – a trusting relationship needs to be developed and sustained over a long period of time. Narrative essays can be obtained from children also, and in large quantities if a whole class or school is studied at the same time.

Case study methods

What is a 'case' and how is it studied? Our classic idea of a case study is probably exemplified by the work of Freud. Box 7.3 illustrates an extract from Freud's (1909) case analysis of a phobia in a 5 year old boy, Little Hans. Fortunately there are alternative and more modern approaches to case study. More reliable case studies are often used by health practitioners to, for example, monitor the effectiveness of behavioural or medical therapies.

Box 7.3   Extract from Analysis of a Phobia in a Five Year Old Boy (Freud 1909)

Other observations, also made at the time of the summer holidays, suggest that all sorts of new developments were going on in the little boy.

Hans, four and a quarter. This morning Hans was given his usual daily bath by his mother and afterwards dried and powdered. As his mother was powdering round his penis and taking care not to touch it, Hans said: 'Why don't you put your finger there?'

Mother:	Because that would be piggish
Hans:	What's that? Piggish? Why?
Mother:	Because it's not proper.
Hans:	[*laughing*] But it's great fun.'[1]

1   Another mother ... told me of a similar attempt at seduction on the part of her three and a half year old daughter. She had a pair of drawers made for the little girl and ... to see whether they were not too tight for walking ... passed her hand upwards along the inner surface of the child's thigh. Suddenly the little girl shut her legs together ... saying: 'Oh mummy, do leave your hand there. It feels so lovely.'

Source: Freud, S. (1909) *Analysis of a Phobia in a Five Year Old Boy*, Vol. 8, Case History 1. Copyrights The Institute of Psycho-Analysis and the Hogarth Press. Reprinted with permission of The Random House Group Ltd

---

As a research method, the case study is an investigation of an individual, a family, a group, an institution, a community, or even a resource, programme or intervention. It is a study of any single unit or entity, however large or small, with clear boundaries. Some examples might include: the relationship between a mother and her terminally ill or disabled child; one child's strategies for coping with epilepsy at school; or a study of a child's care experience whilst mother is in hospital. An earlier survey on child care workers, which solicits the practices and views of practitioners on the lack of an adequate practice framework for addressing the needs of the children of the mentally ill, can be enhanced by a case study of a family which nicely illustrates the whole situation. If a new practice policy is set up and interventions implemented by way of a special unit, this could be a case study on the process of change, in which views of managers, workers, parents and children are sought. Classic case studies in child research have included Ball's (1981) study of Beachside Comprehensive School and Lewis's (1961) study of the Sánchez family. The idea is to make up a total picture or a vignette which 'says it all'.

Since it is the unit of analysis rather than the methodology that defines a case study, there are no specific methods that are distinctive to this approach. Case studies employ a variety of methods including observation, questionnaires, standardised assessments, rating scales, in-depth interviews and other data sources such as narratives, documents and reports. They can therefore be combined with the other approaches described in this chapter – grounded theory, ethnography and narrative analysis. Indeed, although the case study is one of the main types of qualitative research, it very frequently includes traditional quantitative approaches. Its lack of a complex technical vocabulary and of any sophisticated or distinctive methodology of its own, its capability of being combined with other methods including classic quantitative ones and its suitability for the real life settings in which most child practitioners work make it a very appropriate and popular choice for doing research with children.

One case study is described here in detail (Box 7.4) – the Edinbarnet Playground Project (Briggs et al. 1995). This study is very relevant to the contexts faced by child researchers for a number of reasons. It is a mixed study that includes a range of quantitative and qualitative methods, and is therefore very typical of a design likely to be useful to most practitioners. While the approach was imaginative and the outcome highly effective, the ideas and methods were all essentially very simple and accessible. Also, it was research in an important area: it addressed a real life problem that had to be tackled in an innovative way. In addition, it was carried out without the need for much by way of additional resources, as the main resource was the work and commitment of the practitioners who were already involved in the situation. Another feature was that it highlighted the importance of some of the 'context variables' discussed in Chapter 2. Finally, it was research that *made a difference*. It not only illuminated a situation that required investigation but it also addressed it in ways that brought about lasting and important change.

Box 7.4   The Edinbarnet Playground Project (Briggs et al. 1995): a worked example of a case study

Background: Briggs and MacKay were approached by the head teacher of a large primary school in a neighbourhood of multiple socio-economic disadvantage where they were working as educational psychologists. They were asked to investigate and find ways of solving a major problem – playground trouble. Every day at intervals and lunch breaks the playground had become a focus of conflict, bullying and aggression, and this was spilling over into disruption when pupils returned to their classrooms. Things had become so bad that the worst troublemakers were eventually confined to a particular area of the playground known as the 'OK Corral' under the supervision of the janitor.

Defining the problem: It was decided that a suitable starting point would be to identify as precisely as possible the extent and nature of the problem. Following a period
of playground observation, teachers were invited to nominate pupils in their classes
who had the greatest difficulties with their playground behaviour. Large numbers were
identified, but most of them clustered within two year groups, the primary 4 and 5
classes (ages 8 and 9).

Planning intervention: To address the problem a range of strategies was planned,
with a central focus on a group work intervention. For this purpose a third colleague
(Miller), a local social worker with experience of group work, was enlisted. The janitor, as the person with most experience of the difficulties at the point of occurrence,
was given a key role in making the final selection of the 12 most troublesome pupils
from the year groups in question. A meeting was held with the parents of the identified children, and regular planning meetings were also held involving school management, the researchers and a class teacher assigned to support the group work.
   Two groups of six were run weekly for 10 weeks, each group lasting about an hour.
The groups had closed membership to enhance group identity, and they aimed to
build self-esteem, to explore issues such as honesty and trust, to promote increased
awareness of the negative effects of current behaviour patterns for everyone, including the group members themselves, and to share in the investigation of alternative
ways of behaving. To ensure that the focus was not exclusively on this group of 'problem children', the whole of primaries 4 and 5 participated in a bullying survey, the
results of which were used as a basis for training sessions with the entire staff.
Workshops were also run for the parents of all pupils in these classes. Weekly targets were identified for each child, and teamwork was encouraged to help children to
support one another in reaching the targets.

Data collection methods: Several methods of data collection were used – questionnaires, ongoing teacher ratings of pupil behaviour, playground incident records,
semi-structured staff feedback forms and staff and pupil interviews. All of these methods yielded qualitative data, but several of them also provided data that could be
analysed by quantitative means. These data provided the basis of the published
report but all of the various sources gave a vast amount of additional qualitative information that was of use in informing the intervention as it proceeded and in ongoing
discussions with school staff and management.

Questionnaires: Before the intervention started all pupils in primaries 4 and 5 (N =
90) took part in a bullying survey designed for the project. This sampled their awareness and personal experience of bullying in the school and in the playground, and
allowed them to give their own descriptions of how it made them feel and what they
had done in response to it. This served to highlight the extent of the problem, its
effects on individual children and the key role the playground played as the main
locus of bullying and aggression. Following completion of the project the same pupils
completed a second questionnaire allowing pre–post changes to be assessed.

(Continued)

Behaviour ratings: Class teachers kept individual ratings of the classroom behaviour of the children attending the groups before, during and two months after the intervention period. This was done daily using a 5-point scale ranging from 'very good' to 'very bad', together with descriptive commentary.

Playground incident records: The head teacher kept a record of all playground incidents reported to her for one month prior to the project. This exercise was repeated exactly a year later, well after the conclusion of the intervention, and allowed for longer term follow-up. These records were a detailed description of the incident that had taken place. To assist in coding them, they were entered under one of three categories – 'niggle', 'serious' and 'very serious'. The researchers then gave each record a weighted score to reflect how major or otherwise the incident was. This therefore provided both quantitative and qualitative data.

Staff feedback forms: Most staff in the school returned semi-structured feedback forms after completion of the intervention. These contained simple prompts to generate their views on the process of change taking place in the children and in the school as a whole as a result of the project. This allowed key themes to emerge from the perspective of staff.

Staff and pupil interviews: These were the data sources that provided the richest qualitative descriptions. Staff interviews were conducted at the end of the project with the head teacher and teachers in primaries 4 and 5. These were taped, so that full transcripts could be analysed. The children in the groups were interviewed in pairs.

Results: These multiple sources of data provided the process of triangulation so helpful in small scale projects. Questionnaire returns from pupils were strengthened by teachers' views on feedback forms and interviews and by their ratings of behaviour, and all of these could be compared with records of playground incidents and with the views expressed by pupils in their interviews. The quantitative analysis of questionnaires, behaviour ratings and incident records was conducted using simple methods such as chi-square tests (see Chapter 5), and showed persuasively that there was less of a bullying culture in the school, that the playground was a better place to play, that classroom behaviour had improved and that playground incidents had decreased. While these results produced the straightforward outcomes in terms of statistical significance, the really meaningful sense of what the project was like and what it had achieved emerged from the qualitative data. For example, one boy stated that what he enjoyed most about the group was 'learning to be good', while another commented that he was now playing team games like football whereas previously he only ever played combat games.

Conclusions: The simple ideas and methods used in this project provided a means of identifying the core elements of a problem situation, establishing an intervention to address it and collecting and analysing data to illustrate the quality of the process and to demonstrate the effectiveness of the outcomes. Following the published study, and two years after completion of the initiative, the head teacher was interviewed once

(Continued)

(Continued)

more. She reported that the project had been a turning point that had transformed the school and its ethos and had turned the focus from controlling behaviour to promoting education and citizenship.

Source: Adapted from Briggs, S., MacKay, T. and Miller, S. (1995) The Edinbarnet Playground Project: Changing aggressive behaviour through structured intervention. *Educational Psychology in Practice*, 11,2, 37–44.

The case study described in Box 7.4 was very much in the tradition of 'participatory action research'. The school and its pupils were not subjects to be studied but collaborators in a process of investigation and change. It was *their* project. It demonstrated the importance of some of the *context variables* described in Chapter 2, particularly ownership. In identifying the factors that were seen as being vital to the success of the project, the authors noted that 'school ownership of the project was crucial'. By involving everyone at every stage, 'it was clear that the school owned the project and had a high level of investment in its success' (Briggs et al.1995: 42). It was given the highest profile at all times, not just with the staff and pupils in the main target classes, but throughout the school. An anecdote from the head teacher illustrates this point. One day in the playground a girl was heard to say to one of the boys in the group, 'You can't do that any more – you're on the playground project.' A process was taking place by which the group members became such collaborators that they turned from being the playground tyrants to being its custodians as a place of peaceful cooperation.

One of the attractive features of this case study for practitioners who may feel daunted by more technical qualitative methodologies is that you can select simple but effective methods to gather and present your data. Indeed, sometimes a simple transcript of key themes from an interview will convey a more meaningful sense of the impact of a project than a series of data tables. Box 7.5 shows a transcript taken from the final interview with the head teacher. It provides insights that quantitative data could never convey. The transcript does not appear in the published study but is taken from the authors' data archives.

Box 7.5   The Edinbarnet Playground Project (Briggs et al. 1995)

Excerpt of transcript: final interview with head teacher:

Before it started I was in despair as there were so many children who were having massive fights at lunchtime, and large gangs attacking each other. In fact, underneath

(Continued)

my office I kept the bricks and stones and bits of wood that they had been battering each other with. It was literally that bad. It didn't seem to matter what we did, working with the parents or getting the parents up. It didn't seem to matter – we just couldn't get these children under control. This was a great worry as it became so bad that the school had what came to be called 'the OK Corral' and all the children who couldn't behave, getting into trouble regularly – and there was a great number of them – they were herded into one area of the playground and the janitor's job was to look after them.

When staff went on in-service courses and said what school they were from people used to laugh and members of staff got quite hurt about the school's reputation. Now it is quite different on courses as other people ask about projects like the playground project and this has been a boost for staff morale. I haven't been under stress such as I have been under previously.

One of the things that has come from the project is that I thought that nothing could be done, but I have a more positive view that children can change, and before I was never positive about this. I now see that there are things we can do, and I can see it going on here for a very long time.

Source: Authors' data archives: transcript not in published report

In summary, qualitative research methods, or mixed methods that include a range of qualitative approaches, have a great deal to offer those who are planning to do research with children. Qualitative findings enrich the data reported in every type of project. Despite the health warnings given above about the fact that this is in many ways a difficult and technical field, even the novice researcher will find techniques, including some of those described in this chapter, that are relatively straightforward to apply with fruitful results. There is no predicting where a simple research project with children will lead, even though carried out with limited resources as part of the day-to-day work of a practitioner, if it is well conducted and relates to an important research question. The case study reported above had no research funding and was carried out in a school by practitioners just getting on with their job of 'making things better'. It led in its own small way to two other research studies opened up by its success – the Edinbarnet Reading Project (MacKay 1999) and the Edinbarnet Early Reading Project (MacKay and Watson 1999). These in turn led directly to the West Dunbartonshire Literacy Initiative (MacKay 2006), a long term study of mammoth proportions, involving a sample of over 50,000 children, with millions of pounds of research funding and bringing enormous benefits to a whole council area.

PRACTICAL 7.1   DESIGNING AN ENQUIRY AND
GATHERING QUALITATIVE DATA

You have been asked to investigate the experience of long term hospital care for five children who are in a hospital ward, and to report on how that experience might be improved.

How would you set about designing this study? What types of question would you ask? From whom would you collect information and what would be the range of information you would be interested in? What methods would you use to collect it, and how would you analyse it and present it?

PRACTICAL 7.2   PROFESSIONAL CARE AS MOTHERING

The aim of this practical is to develop skills in designing instruments and methods introduced earlier in the chapter and in describing the results. It also creates the opportunity to consider relevant theory and consider the application of a qualitative framework.

There are many professional situations where a child is removed or has to be apart from the biological mother: the special care baby unit at a hospital; the foster placement of an abused or neglected child; or pre-school provision for the young children of full time working mothers. Situations like this raise many concerns for practitioners with respect to their abilities to be effective substitute mothers to the children in their care. Indeed, is substitute mothering essential for quality care?

To conduct this practical you will need a partner/colleague who is willing to be your participant. The participant should have had actual or similar experience of one of the situations described above. Alternatively, your participant should be able to *imagine* that they have experience of one of these situations. The objective of this 'study' is to *explore* the theme 'professional substitute mothering' and quality of care. You are required to use three different methods:

- life history
- questionnaire
- semi-structured interview

Consult the main text for a general description of each method. For guidance on interpretation of data, see below.

1 *Life history.* Plan and conduct a life history interview with your participant. Try to explore the theme of his/her definitions of quality care in mothering and in professional practice.

2   *Questionnaire.* Design and have your participant complete a questionnaire. It should offer a description of demographic details of the professional provision. Examples of these might include: years as a carer; training experience and qualifications; number and ages of children in care; professional responsibilities; practice policy; and background details. Attitudes to child care could be discussed on a scale, that is, a series of statements for the participant to agree/disagree with: 'I think my role is to be like a mother' – strongly agree, agree, uncertain, disagree, strongly disagree. Try to develop the theme of defining quality mothering and quality care.

3   *Semi-structured interview.* Issues raised from the life history and questionnaire can help identify the focus of the interviews. Questions need to be open-ended, e.g. 'How do you feel about the children in your care?', 'What do you want to offer them?', 'In what ways do your feelings for the children in your care differ from your feelings for your own children?'. Have topics set that you wish to cover with these questions: the participant's relationship with the children in care and their parents; the impact of this kind of work on the participant's family; sources of stress and satisfaction.

4   Summarise data of questionnaire and transcribe all interview data.

PRACTICAL 7.3   ANALYSING AND INTERPRETING THE CONTENTS OF YOUR WRITTEN NARRATIVES/REPORTS OR TRANSCRIPT

The aim of this practical is to introduce you to basic principles of grounded analysis of transcripts. All transcripts from Practical 7.2 should be analysed as described below.

Any written text arising from interviews, observational field notes and other documentary sources are in a form which can be subjected to a *content analysis.* This type of analysis assumes that the emerging language can reveal meanings, priorities, understandings and ways of organising and perceiving the world. In approaching this written data, you will be guided by your research questions, but Charmaz (1995) also recommends asking the following questions: *What is going on? What are people doing? What is the person saying? What do these actions and statements take for granted? How do structure and context serve to support, maintain, impede or change these actions and statements?*

Table 6.1 and Figure 7.1 provide a summary guide for designing, conducting and coding interviews. These are based on the grounded theory approach of Glaser and Strauss (1967) and content analysis (Babbie 1979).

Interview	Headings
I do see them as my own children, it's one of the reasons I do it but how do I know that's what's best? Nobody shows you how to do it.	• Relationship with child • Motivation • Gap in knowledge • Lack of support, advice and training

Figure 7.1   Organising a transcript into themes

Phase 1 – Total immersion in the data
In addition to interview transcripts, notes made during or after the interview are useful. These and transcripts should be read and re-read, enabling you to enter the world of the participant and give you a real feel for the data and the interviewee. These first readings should enable you to make notes on the emerging frames of reference of the interviewee: e.g. 'there's a lot of talk about own early experiences of separation from the mother; a lack of professional training on relationship management seems to be a major dimension'. Photocopy all transcripts for coding and preserve originals.

Phase 2 – Headlining
In the way that a newspaper headline sums up the contents of an article, your next task is to re-read the interview and headline all important issues emerging whilst ignoring meaningless data. Headlines or headings should be freely selected at this stage. (See Figure 7.1.)

These headlines can then be reduced by collating them under broader *categories*: e.g. lack of support, gap in knowledge, lack of training could all be categorised under Training Policy Issues. Each transcript is coded and data reduced into these broader categories to end up with a final list of categories.

Phase 3 – Quality control check
The aim of this phase is to ensure the validity of your categories. This is done by having at least two other people to generate a list of categories without knowledge of the original list. Discrepancies can be discussed and amendments made as a result of this exercise.

Phase 4 – Coding
As you are about to attack the transcripts it is wise to have several photocopies. The original interview needs to be preserved to provide the context. Coloured highlighter pens can be used to indicate the various categories. Go through the/each transcript and highlight each category. Cut the transcript up and collate all statements together which have been coded in the same category. When collating and interpreting items in each category be sure to refer back to the original transcript and recode to maintain a sense of the whole context. Another important part of the writing phase is using existing literature relevant to the topic being raised. The interview might be reported and illustrated separately from a section which links the findings to existing literature. Or, the literature can be included with the findings to illustrate similarities and differences as the writer goes along.

Part III

Special Issues

8

Consultation and participation with children in research

The aims of this chapter are:

- To provide an overview of recent practical advances for fully including children in research and for obtaining their perspectives.
- To provide a practical guide for designing and conducting reliable and valid participatory research involving the perspectives of children.

In the last 10 years, methodological tools for doing research 'on', 'about' 'collaboratively' and with children have proliferated and evolved. A major task of this chapter is to incorporate a brief, critical review of some of the new techniques for consulting with children as participants. The first edition of Doing Research with Children, published in 1999, was the first of its kind, and at that time researchers were yet to fully realize the implications of the need to consult with children that arose from the Children Act (1989). We called then for more studies that sought to listen to the voices of children, studies in which they participated, voiced their perspectives and which potentially empowered them. As well as a revision of the Children Act itself (2004), and the guidance on children participating in research produced by UNICEF in 2002, the ensuing years have indeed seen the publication of a wealth of textbooks and journal articles devoted to doing research 'on', 'with', 'about' and even as 'co–researchers with' children. Some of the best contributions have come from practitioner-researchers who have always, in the interests of good practice, sought to consult with and enter the worlds of children in their professional practice.

Ben Johnson's quip 'speak that I may see thee' pertains to the philosophical notion that it is language that reveals us most. And the understanding of any speaker is not just a question of *hearing* but of being compelled to *listen* to what is being said. Rodenberg (1993), a voice coach, reflected on the empowering potential of her primary school teacher:

I brought her a yellow flower once. She asked me why I liked the flower.
'Because it's yellow like the sun,' I said.
'How do you know it's yellow?' she asked.
'Because the sun gives it something,' I replied.
'How would you describe that something?'
She went on in this fashion, re-inventing me with the Socratic method: seeking the truth by means of questions and answers. (1993: 27)

Listening to children

The most innovative and informative applications of methods of listening to children that are now being used in research do indeed come from the arts and humanities and sociology in particular. Nevertheless, the same basic methods have been around in the field of psychology for some time. They have been widely used in the everyday practice of applied psychologists, but are not well represented in the developmental psychology literature. In all fields, it is increasingly accepted that children are co-constructors of meaning and do have a valid perspective worthy of inclusion in research, even at very early developmental Stages and despite apparent disabilities. In 2001, the Department for Education and Skills issued guidance by the Children and Young People's Unit entitled *Learning to Listen: Core Principles for the Involvement of Children and Young People*. This document provides an official common framework for departments to develop tailored policies, action plans and effective practice for getting children and young people involved in the design, provision and evaluation of services that affect them (e.g. children using mental health, social and educational services such as residential schools). This is about empowering children and it is likely to have been informed by the results of a major ESRC project, the purpose of which was to throw light upon contemporary childhood (1995–2001) and as reported by Prout (2001, 2002). The research agenda posited here is very much the traditional ground of sociology. However, in taking up the task, researchers immediately realized they had a major methodological task on their hands requiring them to embark on a creative programme of research in which children are assumed to be social actors, both influencing and influenced by their social environment. This meant finding new methods for tackling areas such as children as researchers, the documentation of perspectives, children as strategic actors, exclusion and the voice of the child. Some of the methods commonly used in more recent studies of this nature are now described below.

The Mosaic approach

The Mosaic approach (Clark and Moss 2001) is a multi-method process that can be flexibly used with even the youngest children and adapted as a participatory tool for adolescents. The Mosaic comprises a number of separate tools that can be put together in order to address the puzzle of the research question. These tools are 'listening' tools that are both verbal and visual. These include: photographs taken by the children of places and things of importance to them (in specified contexts such as nurseries or neighbourhoods); guided tours of the

Table 8.1   Pieces of the Mosaic for 'What is it like to be at this nursery?'

Tool	Questions
Observation (narrative accounts of researcher)	What is happening here? What does body language, vocalizations, expressions contribute to narrative?
Child conferencing (short interview schedule)	Why do children go to nursery? What do adults do? What are best/worst activities? What are best/worst people/places? Open question
Cameras (cheap single use) for children to take their own photographs	What are your favourite things to photograph? Why did you choose these things?
Tours (child leads and chooses means to document)	Tell me about/show me all the important places
Mapping (of the site, perhaps using the photos or drawings)	Observe, ask, listen, tape-record, map-making
Role-play (using pre-selected toys depicting nursery world and story-stem techniques)	Tell me what is happening in your story now? Then what happens?
Parent and practitioner perspectives (short interviews)	What do you think your child feels about nursery? What do you think is a good/bad day for your child at home/nursery

setting being studied which are documented in a variety of ways (tape, drawings, maps); mapping; talking about the meaning of documents or materials produced; interviews or conferencing and observation. Applied psychologists may recognize this as a contextual assessment. Thus it is an eclectic use of both traditional and new techniques in a way that acknowledges both the context and the child as a co-constructor of meaning. Table 8.1 provides an overview of the tools of Mosaic and some considerations in their use.

The Mosaic approach is based on participatory rural appraisal methods (PRA) that aims to access the views and empower those who live in impoverished, rural communities. Elements of the approach have been adapted for use with older groups of children in social services research (O'Kane 2000), in health education research (Morrow 2001) and addressing risks and coping in mental health research on adolescents (Punch 2002a, 2002b). Typically, these studies seek to empower young people through research so that they might influence both service delivery and policy developments that affect them. Table 8.2 summarizes a number of research studies in terms of the questions being asked, the tools and procedures.

Table 8.2 Summary of participatory methods used with young people

Study question and study population	Tools	Procedure
Do levels of social support in the community have an important effect on well-being?	Freely written/taped accounts	Answer questions on: Who is important to me and why? What is a friend? What are friends for? Where do I feel I belong?
102 12–15 year olds in two London schools (Morrow 2001)		What happens when I'm not at school? How long have you been friends? How long have you lived here? Future aspirations?
	Photographs	Choice of what is important to photograph. Control of cameras. Explanatory captions of the photos for discussions.
	Maps Group discussions	Drawing local maps. Newspaper articles on antics of young people in their area for discussion.
What are your views on the decision making processes that affect you?	Decision making chart	Areas of concern and degree of decision making perceived (none, some, a lot) along two axes and coded. Large visual poster and stickers.
Young people in the care of the local authority (O'Kane 2000)	Pots and beans activity	Six statements given that are to be rated on a scale of 1–3, e.g. 'how much you like meetings' and six pots given for each statement. The child gives each pot/statement 1, 2, or 3 beans. If it gets 3, they say why. If it gets less they say what needs to happen to get the other beans
	Diamond ranking exercise	Nine statements identified in a focus group discussion are put onto little diamond-shaped cards and arranged in the shape of a diamond, the top representing most important and the bottom least important.
How do children aged 8–14 negotiate independence as they grow up?	Drawings	Freely done for engagement and later used in discussion and for information.

Table 8.2   *(Continued)*

Study question and study population	Tools	Procedure
Children in schools in rural Bolivia (Punch 2002a)	Photographs	As above
	Spider diagrams	This is a larger circle with key question in it (e.g. places I go), which is given several 'legs' along which the name of a place is written, and a 'foot' at the bottom of each leg. In the foot, the child puts the number of times that place is visited
	Diaries	Capture every day activity and routine aspects to life
What are the coping behaviours for mental health problems?	Worksheets	Ability-appropriate, based on life in the community, places, likes/dislikes, school work and chores
86 young people in mainstream and residential schools (Punch 2002b)	Interviews: Individual	More private sensitive topics, completing tasks.
	Group	More general themes and perspectives
	Secret box	Overcoming inhibition by having problems written and posted into a sealed and shuffled box, so respondent remains anonymous on secrets that have never been told to anyone
	Themed discussions on mental health topics	Video clips from soaps; problem page letters, common phrases
	Ranking of worries task	Identify 20 worries and put them into big worry, middle worry, and little worry piles
	Coping spider diagrams	The big worry circle and coping legs (see also above)

Those researchers conducting participatory interviews with children have found that both individual and group formats can be helpful. In order to explore this topic further, we turn to a study by Hill et al. (1996), which was one of the first to address the glaring gap in research addressing the voices of primary school aged children.

Group interviewing: listening to the voices of 5–12 year olds

The general oversight of the usefulness of qualitative methods for doing research with children applies particularly to the 5–12 year old age group. Typically, researchers have focused on pre-schoolers and adolescents because they are presumed critical phases in child development. To this end, Hill et al. (1996) explored qualitative methods which can be used to hear the voices of primary school children. The children's perspectives on their emotions and well-being were explored by adapting qualitative strategies used by practitioners such as social workers and teachers. The result of this research provides an excellent and flexible framework for those who wish to interview children. The paper recommends two principal methods of engaging with children: focus group discussion and individual interviews.

The optimal focus group size is five or six with a small age range, and for some purposes same sex groups may be a viable option. Children should receive clear explanations of the group's purpose and format with a limited number of themes planned for exploration. Questions should be put in a straightforward open-ended manner, with the provision of a discussion overview from time to time. An important role of the interviewer is to facilitate productive peer interaction for all group members. The discussion agenda set by Hill and co-workers had the following limited themes: purpose of the research; listing of feelings children have; explaining emotions; the relative importance of different feelings; persistent negative feelings and responses; children's problems and worries; responses by others to children's concerns; adult's feelings and what could promote children's well-being. These group discussions were conducted in the children's schools and individual interviews either at home or in school. The individual interviews used some of the same techniques and emerging themes of the group discussion but were able to explore particular emotions in greater depth with individual children. In this case, the researchers felt the children were more relaxed in the school setting than at home. Table 8.3 summarises the variety of methods used to engage the children in both group and individual contexts. The preferred modes vary according to the age, context and individual child.

For consulting with children about the strength of their thoughts or feelings, there needs to be a conceptual understanding of the notion of a scale such as 1–5 or 1–10. Researchers often use visual versions of this, such as a feelings thermometer (0 = no anger; 10 = very angry) or a series of faces showing increasing levels of happiness (e.g., a smile getting bigger on each successive face) and the child can then point to which face they think is like them.

Critique of methods for participation and consultation

The studies briefly reviewed here demonstrate that, with appropriately designed tools, children and young people can be keen, constructive commentators on their perspectives of every day life at home, school and beyond. In addition, they can collaborate in data production, contribute to research design and its implementation (Prout 2001). These researchers have also demonstrated the importance of critical reflection on the effectiveness of these tools and have responsibly disseminated both the advantages and disadvantages of use in each case. Clark and Moss (1999) found that their Mosaic method informed service evaluation, promoted a climate of

Table 8.3   Methods for obtaining 5-12 year olds' perspectives on their emotions and well-being

Group interviews

Introductions	Researcher and children make name labels and say a bit on self
Brainstorming	Naming and noting all feelings thought of for discussion focus
Visual prompts	• Outline faces showing different emotional expressions • Mr Numb the Alien with no feelings for children to explain meanings of feelings named • Pictorial vignettes: four pictures showing two friends fighting and making up (discuss likely cause and resolutions). Picture of a couple rowing while washing and drying up (discuss family tensions)
Role-play	Act out situations where a child is unhappy/fearful/worried and an adult is sought to help. Gives information on typical adult interventions. Needs careful preparation and debriefing
Self completion (work sheet) questionnaires	Gives quantifiable data. Provide help for less verbally articulate children Sentence completion: 'I am sad when ____' Fantasy wishes: 'List 3 things that would make you happier' Simple chart: indicates who the child would ask for help with worries mentioned
Drawing	Entitled 'This is a child who is feeling _____ because _____'

Individual interviews

Introduction	About myself sheet. Likes/dislikes (food, pop stars)
Ecomap	Important people: 'Easiest to talk to', 'best helpers', 'most fun' also used in later discussion on specific emotions noted
Outline faces	As in group
Sentence completion cards	On intense feelings 'I feel really safe when _____', 'the saddest I ever felt was _____'
Role-plays	Researcher pretends to be a child seeking help from a friend: situations extracted from group prior discussion
Questionnaire	As in group

Source: Adapted from Hill, M., 'Laybourn, A. and Borland, M. (1996) 'Engaging with primary-aged children about their emotions and well-being: methodological considerations.' *Children and Society*, 10: 129–44. Copyright John Wiley and Sons, Ltd, 1996. Reproduced with permission

change, dialogue and the development of participatory skills. It was less clear, however, that the agenda was not resource driven by adults, or that the children had sufficient privacy, or that any given culture would be in a state of readiness to promote 'listening'. This will take time, training and will compete with curriculum agendas. Classic participatory tools of tours, maps, photos etc. do generate useful data, but without the support of other methods, may not be truly emancipatory. There can be practical problems with camera use ranging from the ethics of introducing a gadget in a poor community that will not be available after the research, to children taking shots of the wrong things or them not turning out at all, and finally to sabotage. Drawings, worksheets, diaries are all easily obtained by individuals and larger groups and mostly enjoyed. However, these tools most depend on the quality of adaptation of concepts being explored to match the abilities of the participants. Not all children like drawing and some just cannot do it. When there is a mismatch between the task and actual abilities in literacy and other academic skills, there will also be missing and incomplete data. Participants and their parents may feel burdened by tasks that go home, eating into other work and leisure tasks. Well-designed worksheets and diaries are very useful for generating data and insights, but it will take time to get the design right (Punch 2002b). Figure 8.1 illustrates a tongue–in–cheek attempt of the first author to give a lot of freedom in the collation of the perspectives of two children, Claire aged 12 years and Gemma aged 6 years. The girls were given a digital camera and asked to photograph the things that were important to them when they had a sleepover at their aunt's house. Once the photographs had been taken, the girls were asked to say why they chose to take the photographs they did. It is not difficult to guess what the pitfalls of this type of research might be involving children and young people. It is also possible to see the potential for powerful statements, and if we can manage the pitfalls and plan carefully, some lasting data that make a real impact could be obtained.

Getting started
Claire: 'I asked my aunt to take pictures of me trying to get Gemma to choose things to photograph but all she was interested in was her dolls and taking pictures of Barbie, yuk! Then she went into a huff when I tried to show her how to take pictures with it. I decided to do it myself, but she did join in by following me around and annoying me!'

Favourite views

Claire: 'These are not very clear pictures but there are lovely horses at the stables that can be seen from the garden, out exercising. I love to watch them. And from my bedroom window I can see the farms, the sea and the lights across the sea on the land at the other side. My house is in a busy street.'

My bedroom

Claire: 'I like to sleep in this room because this was Granny's room when she stayed too. I miss Granny so much since she died last year, she really loved me very much and was kind. Mum and Dad have made my own room at home a lot like this one because I liked it so much, I even have the same bed, only its bigger!'

Bed time

Claire: 'I took this picture of fairy stories because at night my aunts would come into my room and we would read some of the stories in Scottish dialect. I like scary stories and my favourite one is *The Strange Visitor*. My aunts know a version of this by heart because Granny taught it to them when they were little girls. It's scary and really good fun. I especially like the bit that goes '"muckle muckle"!'

Breakfast time

Claire: 'A special breakfast treat just for me when I stay at my aunt's is fresh baked bread with melted butter and honey toasted into it. It tastes really nice. My aunts gave me the nickname Honey Child because I liked it so much. It makes me feel special.'

Figure 8.1 'What it's like living with my aunt'

With respect to participatory interview techniques, the focus group method is good for giving confidence to individuals within the group and allowing the children to set part of the agenda. The individual interview context is, of course, both more private and intimate. It is not difficult to imagine the many research situations in which this approach is vital. Furthermore, used in conjunction with a prior focus group the discussion could go a long way on establishing a rapport with an anxious child via group support, acceptance and an emerging structure of issues to be explored in greater depth with individuals. While group interviews have proved very useful for obtaining perspectives, they do have some drawbacks. They are difficult to tape-record and transcribe (who is saying what?) and impossible to record in note form whether you are leading the group or merely observing. Group activity also leads to group effects, with some voices being heard more than others (Hill et al. 1996).

Conclusions

The studies reviewed above could be described as those which take a standard research tool such as questionnaires and interviews (see Chapters 6 and 7), adapt them creatively to address the research purpose and to ensure appropriate levels of task demands on participants, and which have the specific aim of obtaining valid perspectives. It is not, therefore, the tool in itself which is innovative, but the way in which it is used. In the cases reported, tools have been used in a qualitative, inductive and participatory manner in the search of understanding and empowerment of voice. Psychologists use these basic tools too, and in creative ways, especially in developmental social psychology on topics such as bullying. Nevertheless, research in developmental psychology generally intends to uncover developmental progression, and in its most creative and rigorous investigations, it will help to inform other researchers about what type of questioning and presentation of materials are actually appropriate for the type of children or young people being included in the research. A cognitive-developmental approach to consultation and participation in research with children is very important (see also Lewis and Lindsay 2000) and is also addressed in Chapter 5. In Chapter 9 ethical considerations are explored in more detail with respect to reasonable expectation when collaborating with child research participants.

Although there are increasingly many ways of assessing children and creatively using such assessments as part of research, it is still important to consider their original theoretical basis. Some research questions will remain irrelevant to perspectives. In such cases we need to return to the business of basic research questions (see Chapter 5). Is the assessment compatible with what you wish to do both theoretically or practically? Do you think it is a reliable and valid way of making the assessments? Is the task or method of engagement designed at an appropriate level and in an engaging way for your particular participant or group of participants? Do you require specialist knowledge, training or supervision in the use of a particular method?

PRACTICAL 8.1   THE MOSAIC APPROACH

This practical aims to provide you with experience of designing and conducting a study using a participative research approach to consulting with children and young people.

Choose one of the following research questions and plan methods of data collection and analysis:

1   What do secondary school pupils think of the ways they are supported with mental health issues at school?
2   What are the views of children and/or young people who regularly attend reviews (e.g. children with special educational needs or disabilities; children who are fostered or looked after by a local authority)?
3   How do young homeless teenagers taking part in housing projects feel about the project and its impact on their lives?

Remember to use a range of age and interest-appropriate techniques that empower the participants in terms of expressing their views and facilitating an impact.

Recording interview data will require permission from individuals and their carers.

9

Ethics of doing research with children

The aims of this chapter are:

- To explore the basis of contemporary ethical thinking in relation to research with children.
- To examine regulation of research activity with children.
- To discuss the importance of informed consent in research with child participants.
- To examine the process of gaining access to child participants.
- To provide a practical guide to assessing ethical versus non-ethical research.

Professionals who work with children learn many skills as part of their initial training, through working alongside more experienced practitioners, by reflecting upon each new situation they encounter and in many other different and diverse ways. The difficulty for the would-be researcher who wishes to learn research skills is that opportunities for observing experienced researchers in practice are few and far between. Research in itself can be a time–consuming and lengthy process. A great deal of the development of research design involves cognitive rather than overt behaviours, and the very nature of the researcher–participant relationship often makes it undesirable, if not impossible, to have an outsider present. Such intrusion can influence the research milieu, can be restrictive and can potentially have an effect on the internal validity of the research.

Ensuring that the process of undertaking research adheres to sound ethical principles is part of the general repertoire of skills which the novice researcher will find it difficult to observe or indeed practise. Inexperienced researchers can practise designing interview schedules or questionnaires, they can rehearse their questioning techniques and enhance their powers of observation, but equipping themselves with a repertoire of skills which will prepare them for the ethical dilemmas they might meet when undertaking research with children and their families is much more challenging. It can be argued that ethics is the one part of the research process that should *never* be learned in practice and that the would-be researcher should have ensured that all the potential ethical dilemmas have been considered prior to embarking upon the research. This is true to some extent but careful planning can fail, particularly when human participants are involved. When those human participants happen to be children the unpredictability factor rises steeply!

This chapter will therefore explore how researchers, and in particular the novice researcher, can be prepared for those ethical challenges which might occur during the process of undertaking research in practice. As we have said previously this is a practical text, and we will endeavour to explore how the researcher can best be prepared for the unexpected, giving examples from our own experiences and the experiences of others. Before we embark on this exploration, however, it is important that we examine the ethical principles which should underpin the preparation of our research. This examination inevitably includes looking at the foundation of contemporary ethical principles in research and at the differences which exist between professional groups, particularly in relation to the direct involvement of children in research. We consider that regardless of these differences all professionals undertaking research work with children should embrace and adhere to the strictest of ethical codes even though they may disagree about methods. The practical at the end of this chapter asks you to consider this point in relation to your own profession so that you can make up your own mind.

Basis of contemporary ethics in research with children

The study of ethics in relation to research with children involves an underlying knowledge of both general ethics theory and exploration of the general principles of undertaking research on human participants. This is necessary because the study of ethics in research involving children has only recently (in relative terms) been the subject of debate and discussion in the literature, leaving us to draw upon more general theory which can be applied to children. This apparent lack of specific application to children is, without doubt, partially attributed to the place which children have held in society (see Chapter 1). As we have discussed previously, it is only within the past few decades that societies have come to appreciate and recognise that children have rights which are specific and which dictate that they should be consulted in matters that affect them.

A useful starting point in this discussion on the ethics of research involving children is perhaps to focus more broadly on the general value of research to the human race. It is all too easy to focus on the grave errors of the past and not to dwell, albeit briefly, on the positive. Beauchamp and Childress (2001) remind us, for example, that all of us who are alive today owe that life or the quality of that life to our ancestors who were prepared to participate in research. The wide use of antibiotics and other medication, the successes of surgical intervention and organ transplantation, and the development of modern cancer treatments are evidence of earlier participation in research by human participants.

Several ethical principles are defined by Beauchamp and Childress (2001): autonomy, which is *self-rule that is free from both controlling interference by others and from limitations, such as inadequate understanding, that prevent meaningful choice* (p. 58); beneficence, which requires that as professionals we do no harm and that we make judgments about the *comparisons and relative weights of costs, risks and benefits* (p. 194), with probable overall benefits outweighing the risk to participants; and justice, which is according the participant *what is fair, equitable, and appropriate treatment in light of what is due or owed* (p. 226). These are principles which, it could be argued, have relevance to our behaviour as moral human beings in all aspects of our personal and professional lives. In terms of undertaking research involving human participants, clearly we should act with morality and should not suppose that putting on a label which calls us *researchers* gives us licence to act in any way which is not moral. So why then did it become necessary to develop ethical codes which govern the way in which we undertake research? The simple answer is that abuse of the principles which guided research necessitated its regulation so that there should no longer be any room for subjective interpretation of what is or is not moral. Much of this abuse occurred in Nazi Germany during the Second World War and was brought to the attention of the world during the Nuremberg Trials. The messages which emerged were clear, according to Müller-Hill (1992: 48) when writing about the ethical implications of Nazi experimentation:

> The attempt of science to provide acceptable values and ethics has failed. Medicine and science should never again be trusted when they promise to deliver their own ethical values; these values have to come from other sources.

The view that scientists should not self-regulate in relation to ethics and research involving human participants was founded on the notion that the so-called scientists involved in experimentation during the war were not *monsters or madmen* (Vigorito 1992: 11) but were, according to Katz (1992), part of a regime where obedience was paramount, and where the superiority of the Aryan race was not questioned. Experimentation was aimed at advancing knowledge for the benefit of the Aryan community (a kind of warped and misguided beneficence) but at the expense of adults and children who were considered inferior. It is proffered, for example, that Mengele, who undertook experiments on 1,500 sets of twins (including many children), was interested in discovering the secrets of multiple births (Vigorito 1992) so that what was thought of as the superior race could be multiplied at twice the natural rate, and that he was also interested in discovering the hereditary basis of behaviour and physical characteristics (Segal 1992). His methods were torturous, inhumane and frequently resulted in the deaths of the twins.

The value of such research must be questioned, and debate continues as to what should be done with data from these and other experiments. Kor (1992), a survivor of the twin experiments who was liberated from Auschwitz–Birkenau in January 1945, suggests that because the experiments were unethical the use of the data is also unethical. She also warns doctors and scientists in a way which is far more direct than any of the ethical codes in existence, by urging them to take the following pledge:

1   To take a moral commitment never to violate anyone's human rights and human dignity.
2   To promote a universal idea that says: 'Treat the subject of your experiments in a manner that you would want to be treated if you were in their place.'
3   To do your scientific work, but please, never stop being a human being. The moment you do, you are becoming a scientist for the sake of science alone, and you are becoming the Mengele of today. (Kor 1992: 7)

Regulation of research activity

Following the Second World War and the Nuremberg Trials there was shock at what had happened under the guise of this umbrella term called research as well as determination that such atrocities should not occur in the future, resulting in various forms of governance and regulation which are briefly discussed below. While children do not form a discrete group within this governance they are clearly part of the overall concern. From the Nuremberg Trials conducted following the war, between October 1946 and April 1949 emerged the *Nuremberg Code*, which stated certain moral, ethical and legal principles relating to research involving human participants. The Code includes details relating to the necessity for voluntary consent of research participants, the need to ensure that the research is for the good of society, that designs should have been previously tried out on animals and that unnecessary physical and mental suffering should be avoided. It also refers to the need to assess risk and the rights of research participants to withdraw from the experiment if they wish, as well as stating that the researcher should be scientifically qualified to undertake the experimentation.

The *Geneva Conventions* of 12 August 1949, and in particular the fourth Geneva Convention, formed an addition to international law in relation to civilians. The original convention of 1864 only applied to combatants, as did the Regulations concerning the Laws and Customs of War on Land, annexed to the *Fourth Hague Convention* of 1907. The general provisions of the *Geneva*

Convention Relating to the Protection of Civilian Persons in Time of War make important statements both about research and about children. Article 14 necessitates
the setting up of safety zones, during hostilities, to protect children under the age
of 15 and mothers of children under the age of 7 years, and Article 82 states that
during internment children and their families should be lodged together to
enable them to lead *a proper family life* (International Committee of the Red
Cross 1949: 184), whereas Article 147 prohibits '*wilful killing, torture or inhumane
treatment, including biological experiments*' (p. 211) (see also Boyden (2000) for a
contemporary discussion about conducting research with war-affected children).

Some 15 years following the publication of the Geneva Convention and the
Nuremberg Code, the *Declaration of Helsinki* (the most recent version of which
was published by the World Medical Association in 2004) outlined recommendations to guide physicians in biomedical research involving human participants.
This was adopted by the World Medical Assembly in Helsinki in June 1964, and
has been amended and clarified in a number of subsequent World Medical
Assemblies. The Declaration of Helsinki provides a standard of international
ethics in research involving human participants and, while it reinforces the details
contained within the Nuremberg Code and indeed elaborates and clarifies, it
also examines the issue of children as research participants in relation to
informed consent. The Declaration discusses that not only should the informed
consent of the child's legal guardian be sought but that where a minor child is
able, the informed consent of the child should be sought *in addition* to that of
the legal guardian. The issue of informed consent is discussed in more detail in
the following section.

The *United Nations* was set up and had its charter adopted in 1945, following
the collapse of its predecessor, the League of Nations, at the beginning of the
war. It made provision for the establishment of a Commission on Human
Rights, which set out to prepare an International Bill of Rights (later called the
Universal Declaration of Human Rights) following the General Assembly of the
United Nations in 1948. Within the United Nations family are a number of specialised agencies which have relevance to research involving children, including
the *United Nations Educational, Scientific and Cultural Organization* (UNESCO)
and the *United Nations International Children's Emergency Fund (UNICEF)*. The
Universal Declaration of the Rights of the Child, first declared in 1959 and con-
firmed in the *Convention on the Rights of the Child* in 1989, sets out the fundamental human rights to which every child is entitled (see Taylor 2005 and
Chapter 1 of this book). Taking guidance from the Convention, UNICEF (2002)
has provided useful recommendations for researchers undertaking studies with
children.

In addition to the charters and conventions mentioned above, a number of
professional groups have established their own international and national codes
which aim to regulate research within professions, for example, the British

Psychological Society (2006) and the National Children's Bureau (2003). Clearly there are too many to mention within the confines of this chapter, but professionals and students hoping to enter the professions should be conversant with their own particular international codes as well as those which directly provide governance within their own countries.

Clearly the unethical experiments carried out during the Second World War are extreme examples and we could argue that they have little bearing on our behaviour today. The point which is important and which is alluded to above by Kor (1992) is, however, that all researchers are potentially in a position of power and that power carries the potential for abuse. The relative power of adults to children makes this a double-edged sword when involving children as research participants. Whilst there are varying extremes to which this abuse can exist it is always important for researchers to consider the potential ethical implications of their work and to ensure that they are guided by the ethical principles we have referred to above. This applies not only to those who are carrying out medical research, but to all researchers. There are rules, although they are not always particularly clear, relating to medical research, but researchers from other professional groups do not all have such widely established regulation. The difference is largely around the issue of power and the level of participation. UNICEF (2002) cites Hart's eight-degree scale of participation which provides a gradient of participation from 'manipulation' of the child in research to full participation with the research being child-initiated. In medical research participation is likely to be generally at the least participative end of the range (see Figure 9.1) whereas in social research the trend over the past decade has been towards much fuller participation so that the voices of children are heard (see also Chapters 6 and 7; France 2004; Hill 2005). Whatever the level of participation, researchers have responsibilities to ensure that they protect children's best interests. UNICEF (2002) have produced a useful adaptation of questions for managers of research, monitoring and evaluation activities, based on the work on children, ethics and social research undertaken for Barnardo's by Alderson (1995).

The debate about the extent to which children should be directly involved in research is one we wish to highlight rather than continue. Suffice it to say that there has been a sea-change over the past two decades and the majority view in most circles is that children have a right to participate, just as they also have a right to refuse to participate and that research about children should be *with* children and not something that is done *to* children. Regardless of differences in professional stances there are also commonalities between the professions in terms of the need to gain access to children (either by *proxy* or directly), that informed assent and consent should be sought (from children as well as from significant adults) and that the ethical principles of autonomy, beneficence and justice should be adhered to. A useful way of ensuring that you have considered all the ethical implications of an investigation is to identify *all* those who are

Level of participation	Research examples
Child initiated, shared decisions with adults	
Child initiated and child directed projects	Research about the experience of *being* a child and of childhood.
Adult initiated, sharing decisions with children	
Participation in which children are consulted and informed	Research about services designed *for* children
Assigned but informed participation Tokenism – children are given a voice but have little choice about the subject, the style of communicating it or any say in organizing the occasion	
Decoration – children are asked to take part in an event but are not given any explanation of the issues or the reason for their involvement	Research about the effects of a drug *on* a child participant
Manipulation	

Figure 9.1   Levels of participation in research

involved in the study, including controls and those who are not directly being studied (such as, for example, the siblings of children who are the actual research participants) and to go through each ethical principle with each person to ensure that all risk has been identified. It is useful during this process to collaborate with a more experienced researcher who is not involved in the particular study but who has some expertise in the area of investigation. This will facilitate your reaching an objective viewpoint before you attempt to gain access. We will discuss this further later on. See Figure 9.1 and Table 9.1 for summaries on levels of participation and research and good practice guidelines.

Informed consent

As we mentioned above, one of the common factors in all ethical considerations, including regulatory frameworks, is the need to gain informed consent from research participants. According to the Declaration of Helsinki (World Medical Association 2004), even though a child may not be legally competent, to give consent researchers should gain informed *assent*. UNICEF (2002), in its guidance on child participation, also makes it clear that parental consent is 'not an adequate standard in light of the rights of the child' (p. 5). The *child* as well as the parent must be aware of the implications of the research, and the child if able should give assent in addition to the consent of the adult with parental responsibility. This means ensuring that, if they are capable of doing so, they *know* they have a choice as to whether to participate in the research (in other words that they are true volunteers), that they *know* that they have the right to withdraw

Table 9.1   Summary of good practice guidelines for research standards in general and in relation to children

Standards for *all* participants	Additional standards for consideration for *children* as participants
Careful choice of participants related to purpose of research and likely costs and benefits	Which children stand to benefit from the research? How much of their time can we take up? How much intrusion is justified? What are the implications of failure?
Selection criteria	Is it ever justified to exclude children with learning or physical disabilities?
Engagement (respect, rapport, openness, listening)	Requires extra time with children? Requires creation of innovative techniques
Privacy, confidentiality, consent, choice of participation	Adults in the child's life usually need to be consulted regarding permissions as well as the child, and this includes resulting publications
	Do young participants know and understand their right to decline or withdraw participation?
	Is there an element of coercion? What is too much responsibility for the child? Can older children still participate if they wish even if a parent declines?
Presentation of information on the purpose, processes and expectation of involvement for the child in the research	Is the information available and accessible to the child, parents, carers and professionals involved?
Control of research materials	How much responsibility is it reasonable to give the child? How much should adults intervene?
Review, revision and dissemination of research	Are the child and carers consulted on the research design, and can they contribute to the plan? Will they receive reports and do they have any control over the final reports? Can they reflect critically in terms of research evaluation?
Appropriate sources of funding	Should funding be accepted from an organization that does not always work in the interests of children?
Use of participatory methods	Are they sufficiently engaging and fun for children? Are they productive as well as fun? Are they well designed to address individual or group abilities or preferences? Is the language use appropriate?

(Continued)

Appreciation and reward	Will children be thanked and rewarded for their efforts?
Careful choice of context	Is the setting comfortable, safe and predictable for the child? Is it managed in terms of power relations and impression management?
Participant's perspective	How possible is it to overcome the power relations in research with children and to avoid adult interpretation of child views?

Sources: Alderson 1995; Roberts 2000; Punch 2002; BPS Code of Conduct 2006

from the research at any time if they so wish without detriment to their care, that they *know* exactly what their role in the research is (that is, what they must do if they choose to participate), and that they *know* what will happen to the data that are generated from the research.

This should involve appropriate advice which is relevant to the individual's understanding of the consequences of their participation. For example, if participation involves taking a new drug participants should be informed of the potential side effects. They should be told in a way that leaves no uncertainty about what will happen to the results of the research. They need to be aware that it may be published and who will ultimately have access to it. We have seen a few examples in student dissertations of where written consent has been obtained on a form which promises that participants' names will not be used and confidentiality and anonymity will be upheld, but because of our local knowledge and involvement in early years practice we have been able easily to identify participants, particularly in some of the qualitative studies that are popular among sociology and health care students. In some cases it has been necessary, because of the potential harmful effects of placing certain information in the public domain (such as the library or through publication), to restrict access to the final product. Since, in the words of one of the great educational researchers, Lawrence Stenhouse, 'research is systematic enquiry made public' (Skilbeck 1983), it is clearly essential to conduct all aspects of our enquiry in ways that will be compatible with appropriate dissemination of the results.

Researchers must be particularly aware that age alone is not a foolproof indicator of a child's ability to understand or to give either consent or assent. There are different legislative frameworks governing this subject both within the UK and in other countries.

In relation to England and Wales, while the Family Law Reform Act 1969 gives the right to consent to *treatment* to young people age 16 and 17, and to younger children if they are mature enough to understand what is proposed, the legal position is less clear in relation to consent to *research*. Young people age 16 and 17 with sufficient understanding may consent to 'therapeutic research', that is, research which aims to be of direct benefit to them. Children under 16 are able to given their full consent for therapeutic research provided they satisfy the Gillick criteria of competence, namely, that they have been counselled and do not wish to involve their parents and that they have sufficient maturity to understand the nature, purposes and likely outcome of the proposed research. The position in relation to 'non-therapeutic research', that is, research which does not aim to offer direct benefits to the child, is less clear. (For a discussion of some of the legal issues involving children and consent see Dimond 2005.) In practical terms, the best advice to researchers is to seek at all times to have the full cooperation of both children and parents in participating in the research.

Gaining access

It might perhaps seem strange to discuss gaining access after our discussion about informed consent, rather than before. However, our reasons for doing this are because issues of informed consent should be considered prior to gaining access, mainly because those people whom you will approach to gain access will wish themselves to be informed as to how you intend to gain consent from either the child, the parents (or those with parental responsibility) or both. They will also wish to see copies of letters or forms which you intend to send or issue to participants to gain their written consent.

Gaining access to research participants or research sites normally requires approaching what are known colloquially as *gatekeepers*, meaning basically those people who attempt to safeguard the interests of others and who can give formal or informal permission for research to proceed. In different countries and for different departments the procedures vary, so it is important to find what procedures apply to your own particular context. Sometimes the arrangements will be quite informal and at the discretion of managers of local establishments, while at other times they will be governed by very formal frameworks. For example, in the UK, in relation to research in the field of health, while there are separate Research Governance Frameworks for England, Northern Ireland, Scotland and Wales, the Central Office for Research Ethics Committees (COREC) in England works closely with its counterparts throughout the country. This system of Research Ethics Committees (REC) is very important in setting standards and in enforcing policy and legislation, and no research within the NHS involving individuals, their organs, tissues or data may proceed without their prior approval (see Department of Health 2005).

The process of gaining consent from a local REC should not be underestimated. Our own experiences show that committees operate in very different ways and to different time scales. The proposal forms are quite daunting to complete and not totally appropriate if you are intending to undertake a qualitative study, using for example a focused interview as your data collection method. Our experience has shown, however, that it is possible to work with NHS RECs and indeed they can be extremely positive. One chairman we know admits that his personal experience of qualitative methods is limited but acknowledges the importance of all approaches to research. It is almost always useful to have informal discussion with the committee chair person prior to submitting a written proposal, particularly if your intended study does not fit the mould of traditional, positivistic research. Other important gatekeepers are those people who manage the research site or access to those people who are your intended participants. Again these people can be extremely helpful and good communication with them is a prerequisite to success. For example, Ersser (1996) discussed the helpful relationship he established with the ward sisters and doctors who were the gatekeepers in his ethnographic study. On the other hand, Hood et al. (1996) experienced difficulties with their gatekeepers, necessitating a change in approach. Their description shows a similar frustration felt by many:

> We originally planned to obtain the majority of our sample via a local health centre, where staff identified many families with children of the appropriate ages on the practice lists. However, the general practitioners (GPs) and the practice manager were clear that they would need to obtain parents' consent 'prior' to being contacted by us. The practice staff sent out letters explaining the study with tear-off slips to be marked 'I agree' or 'I do not agree' to being contacted; these were returned to the practice. Thus we were positioned at the end of a long chain of negotiation. Most potential participants did not reply and we were able to make contact with only a small number of patients. (Hood et al. 1996: 120)

Hood et al. also discuss similar problems when accessing schools and nurseries, although our own experiences show that on the whole they are more willing than health care practitioners to act as indirect rather than direct gatekeepers. For example, one of our students wished to replicate a study relating to safer sex among older school children, and after making some minor alterations to the proposed questionnaire, the head teacher allowed the researcher to give consent forms to children to give to their parents, and to the children themselves. In this way the researcher, in liaison with the school, was able to give the information she wanted in the way she wanted, rather than yet another letter from the school arriving along with the consent form for the next school outing!

Gatekeepers to children themselves, particularly when research is taking place with younger children or if it involves visiting the home environment or if it requires that children visit a special site, are the parents. If research involving children is to be successful then it is of prime importance that the relationship with parents is good. Fundamental to this process is gaining trust, which requires that you are honest and reliable and communicate well. Obvious features to maintaining a good relationship include such things as good manners – remembering to say a simple thank you may help to ensure that the parents turn up the next time.

Practical ethics involving children

It is not our intention to provide a prescriptive or restrictive approach to ethics in research involving children. Indeed it would be very difficult in any case because of the varied research approaches taken and the almost infinite research problems which could be studied. Ethics should be placed within the context of both the problem and the approach and should not be seen as an 'add-on'. It can appear sometimes in student dissertations that the same rather repetitive statements are made about informed consent, anonymity and confidentiality. The statements are without context and therefore fail to convince the reader that the researcher has thought through the ethical implications of *this* study as opposed to any other study. That is not to say that informed consent, anonymity and confidentiality are not important, because clearly they are. It is about ensuring that ethical principles are applied, which means examining the ethical implications of *your* study and ensuring that ethical principles are upheld in the context of *your* particular piece of research.

   Practically, to this end, there are a number of questions which you can ask yourself as a researcher and which you can prepare answers to. There are many benefits of doing this, particularly, for example, if you are asked to attend an ethics committee hearing. The list of questions below, which we have divided into sections relating to the research process, is not finite but is designed to help you to focus on what can be a difficult task. It is also designed to reinforce the notion that ethics is not something the researcher should pay lip service to, but is of the utmost importance in any research study.

Problem
Have any ethical difficulties been raised in any of the literature relating to the research problem? If so, what were these difficulties and how were they addressed? In your opinion were they addressed in a satisfactory way? If so, why? If not, why not and what could you do to provide a satisfactory solution?

Research questions
Are your research questions necessary and of substance? Have the questions been answered before? If so, why are you doing the research? Do the questions require the involvement of child participants? Is the involvement direct or indirect (indirect might, for example, be when research is being undertaken with another family member, or in a school)? If you are involving children have you considered issues such as informed assent? If you are not involving

children are you certain that your research questions can be answered accurately by *proxy?*

Sampling

Why have you selected the particular sampling strategy? Will your participants understand the strategy (children can be hurt by virtue of being excluded!)? When do you intend to approach your sample? What gatekeepers do you need to contact to gain permission? Have you got permission? Do you have relevant information about your study in an appropriate format to give to your sample (such as information appropriate to the first language of the child or pictorial information)? How will you document their informed consent? Whom do you need to gain informed consent from? Have you done so? If the research is being done with children, how will you demonstrate that their assent was based on understanding?

Data collection instruments

What do your participants need to do in order to provide you with your data? Are there any potential physical, psychological, social or emotional risks to the participants or those close to them? If so are these negligible or more than negligible? How have you defined negligible? If they are more than negligible how can they be justified? Have you explored every possible avenue to reduce risk? If not, why not? Have you checked this out with an objective third party?

Data analysis and afterwards

How have you ensured the ethical processing of data? Where will you store data? Would you be happy for such data about yourself to be stored in this way? If no, what will you do to address this? Are you breaking any data protection laws? If yes, how will you change things to ensure that you are not breaking the law? Do you break any promises or assurances made to your participants? If yes, why? What will happen to your data after your study has been completed? Do you have a plan for sharing results with those who participated? If your research involves children's drawings or diagrams are there issues of ownership of the research 'data', and if so have you considered how you will return these 'data' to the rightful owners?

Finally, can you categorically state that, after answering all of these questions, you will do no harm to your participants?

A concluding note

We hope that by now you will have gained an understanding that ethics is not a part of the research process that can be dismissed without thought. The ethical implications of a particular study constitute an essential consideration which is of the utmost importance. Any researcher who does not give due consideration to ethics is not only doing potential harm to the research participants but is also potentially damaging his or her chosen profession and fellow professionals. We know of an example where one practitioner undertook research in an NHS primary care setting without adhering to ethical principles and without gaining consent from the appropriate gatekeepers. Not only were some of the research participants extremely distressed about information given to them, all research activity (including that which had been through the appropriate access processes) was stopped, leading to a great deal of distress for colleagues.

Giving appropriate thought to potential ethical dilemmas and approaching and gaining permission from relevant gatekeepers is essential before you start to collect data. Your responsibility as an ethical researcher does not, however, cease when all permissions have been granted and consent forms signed. It continues throughout the study and extends beyond. If you are party to information which is confidential at the time of its being given it must remain confidential, and if you have made promises to destroy data you must do so.

Ethics is a very serious business, and ignoring ethics can harm your participants, your colleagues and ultimately your own reputation as a professional and a researcher.

PRACTICAL 9.1   APPLYING ETHICAL CODES

1   Find out (for example, from the library, the Internet or your professional association) what national and international codes exist which relate directly to your own actual or potential professional grouping.
2   Write down what the code or codes say about autonomy, beneficence and justice. Does the code make specific reference to research involving children?
3   Next find a piece of research undertaken by a professional from your field which involves children. Using the code or codes you have found, and the list of questions found in the section under 'Practical ethics involving children', write down the strengths and weaknesses of the piece of research from an ethical perspective.

10

Themes and perspectives

The aims of this chapter are:

- To draw together, and examine, the main common themes that emerge from doing research with children.

This book has brought together research knowledge intended to support the professional working with children in using research intelligently and to help prepare the would-be researcher by focusing on the special nature of children and doing research with children. We came to feel that this book was necessary partly through our own observation when working with students preparing to work with children and partly through our own experiences of doing research. Research texts that are generic tend to pay very little attention to the differences between undertaking research involving children and undertaking research with adults; there may perhaps be a couple of lines or a paragraph given over to the special nature of children, but generally there is little or nothing at all. So the idea of this book was originally born. We are delighted that in preparing this second edition we have been able to refer to other research texts that are specifically about children, which we were not able to do when the first edition was written. There has been a real impetus to make sure that doing research with children is seen as a discipline in its own right and we are glad to have contributed to this emergent discipline.

What we have attempted to do in our book is, on the one hand, to draw out those aspects of undertaking research involving children that are different, such as special techniques and ethical implications. In other chapters we have taken generic aspects and applied them to children's settings so that the reader can grasp that all research must be contextualised. We will consider this more fully later on.

What has become apparent, however, through the writing of the book, is that there are a number of common themes and perspectives which recur within each chapter and which are worthy of emphasis as we draw together what we hope you will find an exciting and meaningful text.

Children are different

At the very beginning of this book we discussed the special place children hold in our society. They are not little adults but are developing and growing beings who have their own specific characteristics. The growing number of professional programmes focusing specifically on children emphasises the fact that working with children requires a different and distinct set of skills. This is also true of research involving children. The techniques required to gather data, the ethical considerations and the underpinning theories are different from those involved in researching with adult subjects. Children perceive and understand the world in a different way from adults and while the adult researcher cannot, for very obvious reasons, see the world from the child's perspective, acknowledging that children's worlds are different is a sound starting point.

It is important to realise too that children do not represent an homogeneous group. Within the overarching phase of childhood there exist a multitude of differences – differences which can be as a result of age, gender, ethnicity and culture, education, social class, upbringing and so on. The list is indeed endless. We hope that after reading our book you have an understanding of the importance of the differences which exist between child and adult and between child and child, and some of the factors which contribute to those differences.

Knowledge is the key to success

Our second theme, which clearly relates strongly to the first, is that the successful researcher undertaking research involving children must not only be aware that children are different but must also have an underlying knowledge of the child from a number of perspectives. These include knowledge of theories of emotion and cognition, of learning and personality, of physical growth and development, and of children's relationships. Apart from these basic skills the would-be researcher will also need to develop special skills which relate to the particular problem being studied. These can be achieved through wide reading and through critical analysis of previous research undertaken in a particular field. This is important if the researcher is to develop research protocols which are sensitive and appropriate. Embracing theory is fundamental to the research process, and time taken to enhance your knowledge base is time well spent.

Knowledge is also something we can absorb through a variety of activities, not least through our everyday practice and through the observation of others who are more skilled than ourselves. The professions have traditionally relied in part upon this type of apprenticeship system whereby the student professional will work alongside those who have more experience. The amount of knowledge and how meaningful that knowledge is to us is a very individual thing. We are certainly not sponges who will absorb knowledge purely by being in a certain environment – unfortunately! We have to observe what is going on around us, ask questions and seek clarification from the literature when we do not get satisfactory answers. We must learn to be reflective practitioners so that each new experience is thought about, compared with our past experiences and made sense of.

Special techniques

Imagine for a moment the ridiculous thought of a researcher entering a neonatal unit in a hospital and attempting to interview the babies (see Figure 10.1). We have discussed above that children are different and that the researcher should hold a knowledge base which will enable greater understanding of the differences. Hand in hand with this knowledge is the repertoire of research skills which can capture the world of the child. Interviewing babies is an extreme example of incompetence but there are many grey areas between total incompetence and total competence. In the second section of the book we have placed strong focus upon the special skills and techniques which can be used when undertaking research involving children. As with all research techniques these require practice and careful consideration. We hope that this book will help you to become both discerning and discriminating when designing research. It is not enough to 'pick off the shelf' a tool designed for adult subjects. Undertaking research with children requires special tools just as it requires special skills. We do not pretend to have all the answers by any means, but the important point to make here is that you should use your knowledge of child development, and your experiences of working with children, to inform your choices. Too often students compartmentalise their knowledge into rigid boxes which disallow the integration of their knowledge. Research involves you in utilising all your skills and learning about children, because it draws upon so many theories either directly or indirectly.

Approaching research from different perspectives

Linked to the need to employ special techniques when undertaking research with children is the fourth theme that has permeated our discussion. This is the consideration of the place of both qualitative and quantitative methods within research involving children. There is room for both paradigms. The researcher needs to identify the most appropriate approach based on previous work in the field and the research problem the researcher is seeking to address.

Throughout the book we have referred to both research approaches and have highlighted where one approach may be favoured over another. Both research

Figure 10.1

approaches carry with them a set of discrete skills, methods and techniques. We have pointed to the danger that the researcher might 'bend' the approach to match his or her own expertise rather than adopting the approach most appropriate to the research problem. Such decisions should logically flow from the problem rather than the research preferences of the researcher. It is worth acknowledging here that most professional disciplines involving children now acknowledge that both qualitative and quantitative approaches have a place in generating and building our knowledge about children.

Training

Our fifth key theme, which again has clear links to those mentioned above, is training. We are aware of the difficulties of being able to observe researchers directly when they are gathering data, as this may sometimes interfere with the researcher–participant relationship. There are, however, other ways of learning: through simulation, role-play, in the laboratory and so on. It is also useful when learning research skills to engage expert supervision, which is the usual arrangement for students learning research as part of an academic course. There is, we believe, also a role for supervision after you have qualified, when you are undertaking research. Your supervisor might well be a colleague or a peer, rather than someone with vast amounts of experience in undertaking research, but the advantage of this type of mentorship is that it brings a fresh and more objective perspective to what you are doing. In any case, two heads are always better than one, we are told!

There are also other informal ways of gaining training when you are undertaking research. We know from experience that even the most eminent researchers are usually more than willing to discuss their research in depth with novices and students. We have had several students who have engaged in protracted international e-mail exchanges which have enabled them to gain great insight into why a researcher took a particular decision, or why they did not pursue a specific avenue of enquiry. We have also found that, on the whole, researchers are willing to share with you their ideas and even their data collection instruments so long as they have access to your results. Even if you cannot engage on such a scale, if you are undertaking a study around a particular topic which is of interest to an experienced researcher, that person is likely to be interested in what you are doing and why.

Inter-agency working

Another theme we wish to draw out in our conclusions is the professional working relationships of those involved with children. Professionals rarely work in isolation and those involved in working with children will most usually be part of a multi-disciplinary team, working with professionals from different agencies. In terms of research this is an important consideration. Integrated children's services are becoming the norm and research has to acknowledge and work with this assumption in mind. This requires two considerations. First, when undertaking research which looks at service provision the researcher will need to consider the perspectives of the different professionals involved in the particular care pathway. Second, researchers must consider when writing about their research that it will not only be people from a single professional group who will access the work. Other professionals (and indeed parents and children themselves) will access professional journals and the researcher should bear that in mind when writing. Most professional journals are much more willing than previously to consider publication of a broad range of research – rather than being restricted to a particular research 'type'.

The voice of children

On a different note, there have appeared throughout the book a number of perspectives and thoughts on the actual involvement of children in research, which is our penultimate theme. As we have said in the book, there is general agreement that children must have a voice and be able to participate in research; the debate is about the extent to which this should occur. We have referred to various models that can help the researcher to make decisions about participation, which range from a somewhat tokenistic involvement to children taking the role of researcher themselves. Those designing research need to make sure that they consider a whole range of factors when involving children, from undertaking risk assessments of the 'field' in which research takes place, to considering the ethical implications, to giving children the right to be consulted about issues that affect them.

Part of our inability to resolve the debate may stem from our own different academic backgrounds and associated views which stem from our own professionalisation. We are, however, not alone in experiencing some disagreement, and we have referred in the book to the different professional points of view that exist. In practice we should perhaps embrace such differences as these for they make us question the origins of our colleagues' views rather than ignoring them. Certainly in this era of interprofessional research and education we welcome the challenges these different perspectives bring. Our learning is certainly richer because these differences make us reflect upon our own point of view as well as the views of others. What is important is that we should not allow our differences to halt our progress in research terms. A spirit of cooperation, respect and trust will enable healthy collaboration to take place and we must all make sure that, as a minimum, we uphold the rights of the child to be consulted about matters that involve them as upheld by law.

Contextualisation

Our final theme, which we hope has been emphasised again and again, is that research involving children, whether their involvement is direct or indirect, must be placed into a context. The three of us are experienced at supervising research, doing research and reading research and with experience comes an almost intuitive understanding of what is 'good' research and what is not. We believe the answer is contextualisation. That is, the ability of the researcher really to demonstrate that the research problem, the sampling, the choice of tools, the ethics and all other aspects of the research process exist in a meaningful rather than a stagnant way. Children themselves lead complex lives, and we have already referred to the need to understand the developing child. It is also important that the researcher gains an understanding of the social child. Children are not mere recipients of their environment, but they influence what goes on within their worlds and are active in making the environment what it is. Therefore, as a researcher, whatever your professional background and research tradition, it is so important that you take an holistic approach to the study of children. Only then can you understand children and only then can you start to make sense of their worlds through that enigmatic process called research.

References

Adler, A. (1916) *The Neurotic Constitution: Outline of a Comparative Individualistic Psychology and Psychotherapy*. New York: Moffat, Yard.

Ainsworth, M.D.S., Blehar, M.C., Waters, C.C.E. and Wall, S. (1978) *Patterns of Attachment: A Psychological Study of the Strange Situation*. Hillsdale, NJ: Erlbaum.

Alderson, P. (1995) *Listening to Children: Children, Ethics and Social Research*. London: Barnardo's.

Axline, V. (1964) *Dibs: In Search of Self*. Harmondsworth: Penguin.

Babbie, E. (1979) *The Practice of Social Research*, 6th edn. Belmont, CA: Wadsworth.

Bailey, V., Bemrose, G., Goddard, S., Impey, R., Joslyn, E. and Mackness, J. (1995) *Essential Research Skills*. London: Collins Educational.

Ball, S. (1981) *Beachside Comprehensive: A Case Study of Secondary Schooling*. Cambridge: Cambridge University Press.

Bandura, A. (1977) *Social Learning Theory*. Englewood Cliffs, NJ: Prentice Hall.

Bandura, A. (1986) *Social Foundations of Thought and Action*. Englewood Cliffs, NJ: Prentice Hall.

Banister, P., Bruman, E., Parker, I., Taylor, M. and Tindall, C. (1994) *Qualitative Methods in Psychology: A Research Guide*. Milton Keynes: Open University Press.

Baron-Cohen, S., Leslie, A.M. and Frith, U. (1985) 'Does the autistic child have a "theory of mind"?' *Cognition*, 21: 37–46.

Barsevick, A. and Llewellyn, J. (1982) 'A comparison of the anxiety-reducing potential of two bathing techniques.' *Nursing Research*, 31 (1): 2–7.

Bartsch, K. and Wellman, H. (1989) 'Young children's attribution of action to beliefs and desires.' *Child Development*, 60: 946–64.

Beauchamp, T.L. and Childress, J.F. (2001) *Principles of Biomedical Ethics*, 5th edn. New York: Oxford University Press.

Berg, B. (2004) *Qualitative Research Methods for the Social Sciences*, 5th edn. Boston, MA: Pearson.

Blenkin, G.M. and Yue, N.Y.L. (1994) 'Profiling early years practitioners: some first impressions from a national survey.' *Early Years*, 8 (1): 13–22.

Bowlby, J. (1951) *Maternal Care and Mental Health*. Geneva: World Health Organisation.

Bowlby, J. (1952) *Maternal Care and Mental Health: a report on behalf of The World Health Organisation as a contribution to the United Nations programme for the welfare of homeless children*. (2nd edn). Geneva: World Health Organisation.

Bowlby, J. (1953/1965) *Child Care and the Growth of Love*. Harmondsworth: Penguin.

Bowlby, J. (1979) *The Making and Breaking of Affectional Bonds*. London: Tavistock Publications.

Bowlby, J. (1969/97) *Attachment and Loss: Volume 1, Attachment*. London: Hogarth Press: Institute of Psychoanalysis.

Bowlby, J. (1973/98) *Attachment and Loss: Volume 2, Anxiety and Anger*. London: Hogarth Press: Institute of Psychoanalysis

Bowlby, J. (1980/98) *Attachment and Loss: Volume 3, Loss: sadness and depression*. London: Hogarth Press: Institute of Psychoanalysis.

Boyden J. (2000) 'Conducting research with war-affected and displaced children: ethics and methods'. *Cultural Survival Quarterly*, Summer: 71–3.

Bretherton, I. and Ridgeway, D. (1990) 'Story completion tasks to assess young children's internal working models of child and parent in the attachment relationship.' In M.T. Greenberg, D. Cicchetti and E.M. Cummings (eds), *Attachment in the Preschool Years: Theory, Research and Intervention*. Chicago and London: The University of Chicago Press. pp. 273–308.

Briggs, S., MacKay, T. and Miller, S. (1995) 'The Edinbarnet Playground Project: changing aggressive behaviour through structured intervention.' *Educational Psychology in Practice*, 11 (2): 37–44.

British Psychological Society (2006) *Code of Ethics and Conduct*. Leicester: BPS.

Bronfenbrenner, U. (1979) *The Ecology of Human Development*. Cambridge, MA: Harvard University Press.

Bronfenbrenner, U. (1986) 'Ecology of the family as a context for human development: research perspectives.' *Developmental Psychology*, 22: 723–42.

Bronfenbrenner, U. (1992) 'Ecological systems theory.' In R. Vasta, (ed.), *Six Theories of Child Development: Revised Formulations and Current Issues*. London: Jessica Kingsley. pp 187–249.

Bruce, T. (2004) *Developing Learning in Early Childhood*. London: Paul Chapman.

Bryman, A. (2001) *Social Research Methods*. Oxford: Oxford University Press.

Buchanan, D.R. (1994) 'Reflections on the relationship between theory and practice.' *Health Education Research: Theory and Practice*, 9 (3): 273–83.

Bugental, J. (1964) 'The third force in psychology'. *Journal of Humanistic Psychology*, 4 (1): 19–25.

Carlson, N.R., Martin, G.N. and Buskist, W. (2004) *Psychology*, 2nd edn. Harlow: Pearson.

CEMACH (2005) *Stillbirth, Neonatal and Post Neonatal Mortality 2000–2003*. London: Royal College of Obstetricions and Gynaecologists.

Charmaz, K. (1995) 'Grounded theory'. In J. Smith, R. Harré and L. van Langenhove (eds), *Rethinking Methods in Psychology*. London: Sage. pp. 27–49.

Child, D. (1997) *Psychology and the Teacher*, 6th edn. London: Cassell Education.

Clark, A. and Moss, P (2001) *Listening to Young Children: The Mosaic Approach*. London: National Children's Bureau and Joseph Roundtree Foundation.

Cohen, J. (1988) *Statistical Power Analysis for the Behavioural Sciences,* 2nd edn. New York: Academic Press.

Cohen, L., Manion, L. and Morrison, K. (eds) (2000) *Research Methods in Education*, 5th edn. London: Routledge.

Coolican, H. (2004) *Research Methods and Statistics in Psychology*, 4th edn. London: Hodder–Arnold.

Crabtree, B. and Miller, W. (1999) *Doing Qualitative Research*, 2nd edn. London: Sage.

Cresswell, J. (1998) *Qualitative Inquiry and Research Design: Choosing among Five Traditions*. London: Sage.

Crittenden, P. (1992) 'Quality of attachment in the preschool years.' *Development and Psychopathology*, 4: 209–241.

Dashiff, C. (2001) 'Methodological issues in nursing research: data collection with adolescents.' *Journal of Advanced Nursing*, 33 (3): 343–9.

Davey, G. (ed.) (2004) *Complete Psychology*. London: Hodder Arnold.

Denham, S.A. and Auerbach, S. (1995) 'Mother–child dialogue about emotions and preschoolers' emotional competence.' *Genetic Social and General Psychology Monographs,* 121 (3): 311–37.

Department for Education and Skills (2001) *Learning to Listen: Core Principles for the Involvement of Children and Young People.* London: DfES Children and Young People's Unit.

Department for Education and Skills (2003) *Every Child Matters.* London: The Stationery Office.

Department of Health (1990) *The Care of Children: Principles and Practice in Regulations and Guidance.* London: HMSO.

Department of Health (1993) *Report of the Taskforce on the Strategy for Research in Nursing, Midwifery and Health Visiting.* London: Department of Health. Available at www.dh.gov.uk.

Department of Health (2005) *Research Governance Framework for Health and Social Care,* 2nd edn. London: Department of Health.

Dimond, B. (2005*) Legal Aspects of Nursing,* 4th edn. Harlow: Pearson.

Donaldson, M. (1978) *Children's Minds.* London: Fontana.

Douglas, J.W.B. (1975) 'Early hospital admission and later disturbances of behaviour and learning.' *Developmental Medicine and Child Neurology,* 17: 456–80.

Dunn, J. (1995) 'Children as psychologists: the later correlates of individual differences in understanding of emotions and others' minds.' *Cognition and Emotion,* 9 (2/3): 187–201.

Dunn, J. (1996) 'The Emanuel Miller Memorial Lecture 1995. Children's relationships: bridging the divide between cognitive and social development.' *Journal of Child Psychology and Psychiatry,* 37 (5): 507–18.

Dunn, J. (2004) 'Annotation: Children's relationships with their non-resident fathers.' *Journal of Child Psychology and Psychiatry,* 45 (4): 659–671.

Dunn, J. and Deater-Deckard, K. (2001) *Children's Views of their Changing Families.* York: Joseph Roundtree Foundation.

Eppel, E.M. and Eppel, M. (1966) *Adolescents and Morality: A Study of Some Moral Values and Dilemmas of Working With Adolescents in the Context of a Changing Climate of Opinion.* London: Routledge and Kegan Paul.

Erikson, E.H. (1950/1963) *Childhood and Society,* 2nd edn. New York: Norton.

Ersser, S. (1996) 'Ethnography in clinical situations: an ethical appraisal.' In L. De Raeve (ed.), *Nursing Research: An Ethical and Legal Appraisal.* London: Ballière Tindall.

Eysenck, H.J. (1952) 'The effects of psychotherapy: an evaluation.' *Journal of Consulting Psychology,* 16: 319–24.

Eysenck, H.J. (1964) *Crime and Personality.* London: Paladin.

Flavell, J.H. (1978) 'The development of knowledge about visual perception.' In C.B. Keasey (ed.), *Nebraska Symposium on Motivation,* Vol. 25. Lincoln, NB: University of Nebraska Press.

Flavell, J.H. (1985) *Cognitive Development,* 2nd edn. Englewood Cliffs, NJ: Prentice Hall.

Flavell, J.H. (1988) 'The development of children's knowledge about the mind: from cognitive connections to mental representations.' In J.W. Astington, P.L. Harris and D.R. Olson (eds), *Developing Theory of Mind.* New York: Cambridge University Press. pp. 244–67.

Fonagy, P., Redfern, S. and Charman, T. (1997) 'The relationship between belief–desire reasoning and a projective measure of attachment security (SAT).' *British Journal of Developmental Psychology,* 15: 51–1.

Fook, J. (2002) *Social Work Critical Theory and Practice*. London: Sage.

Fox, D. and Prilleltensky, I. (1997) *Critical Psychology: An Introduction*. London: Sage.

France, A. (2004) 'Young people'. In S. Fraser, V. Lewis, S. Ding, M. Kellet and C. Robinson (eds) *Doing Research with Children and Young People*. London: Sage.

Fraser, A. (1984) *The Weaker Vessel: Woman's Lot in Seventeenth-Century England*. London: Methuen.

Freebody, P. (2003) *Qualitative Research in Education: Interaction and Practice*. London: Sage.

Freud, S. (1901/1976) *The Psychopathology of Everyday Life*. Pelican Freud Library (4). Harmondsworth: Penguin.

Freud, S. (1905/1977) *Three Essays on the Theory of Sexuality*. Pelican Freud Library (7). Harmondsworth: Penguin.

Freud, S. (1909/1977) *Analysis of a Phobia in a Five Year Old Boy*. Pelican Freud Library (8). Harmondsworth: Penguin.

Freud, S. (1923/1984) *The Ego and the Id*. Pelican Freud Library (11). Harmondsworth: Penguin.

Gazzaniga, M., Ivry, R. and Mangun, G. (2002) *Cognitive Neuroscience: The Biology of the Mind*, 2nd edn. New York: Norton.

Glaser, B.G. and Strauss, A.L. (1967) *The Discovery of Grounded Theory*. New York: Aldine.

Goldsmith, D.F. and Rogoff, B. (1995) 'Sensitivity and teaching by dysphoric and nondysphoric women in structured versus unstructured situations.' *Developmental Psychology*, 31: 388–94.

Goodenough, F.L. and Harris, D.B. (1963) *Goodenough–Harris Drawing Test*. San Antonio, TX: PsychCorp/Harcourt Assessment.

Graue, M.E. and Walsh, D.J. (1996) 'Children in context: interpreting the here and now of children's lives.' In J.A. Hatch (ed.), *Qualitative Research in Early Childhood Settings*. Westport, CT and London: Praeger.

Gray, D. (2004) *Doing Research in the Real World*. London: Sage.

Greene, S. and Hill, M. (2005) 'Researching children's experience: methods and methodological issues.' In S. Greene and D. Hogan (eds), *Researching Children's Experiences: Approaches and Methods*. London: Sage.

Greig, A. (2001) 'The educational psychologist as practitioner-researcher: reality or dream?' *Educational and Child Psychology*, 18 (4): 75–88.

Greig, A. (2004) 'Childhood depression – Part 1: Does it need to be dealt with only by health professionals?' *Educational and Child Psychology*, 21 (4): 43–54.

Greig, A. (2005a) 'Personal, social and emotional development'. In J. Taylor, and M. Woods (eds), *Early Childhood Studies: An Holistic Introduction*, 2nd edn. London: Arnold. pp. 57–77.

Greig, A. (2005b) 'Play, language and learning.' In J. Taylor, and M. Woods (eds), *Early Childhood Studies: An Holistic Introduction*, 2nd edn. London: Arnold. pp. 99–116.

Greig, A. and Howe, D. (2001) 'Social understanding, attachment security of preschool children and maternal mental health.' *British Journal of Developmental Psychology*, 19 (3): 381–93.

Greig, A. and MacKay, T. (2005) 'Asperger's syndrome and cognitive behaviour therapy: new applications for educational psychologists.' *Educational and Child Psychology*, 22 (4): 4–15.

Guidubaldi, J., Cleminshaw, H.K., Perry, J.D., Nastasi, B.K. and Lightel, J. (1986) 'The role of selected family environment factors in children's post divorce adjustment.' *Family Relations*, 35: 141–51.

Haste, H., Hogan, A. and Zachariou, Y. (2001) 'Back (again) to the future.' *The Psychologist*, 14 (1): 30–3.

Hatch, J.A. (ed.) (1995) *Qualitative Research in Early Childhood Settings.* Westport, CT and London: Praeger.

Hawthorn, P. (1974) *Nurse, I Want My Mummy!* London: Royal College of Nursing.

Health and Safety Executive (1991) Local Research Ethics Committees: NHS Executive Guidelines. HSG(91)5. London: Department of Health.

Hendriks, T., de Hoog, M., Lequin, M.H., Devos, A.S. and Merkus, P.J.F.M. (2005) 'DNase and atelectasis in non-cystic fibrosis pediatric patients.' *Critical Care*, 9: 351–6. Available online http:ccforom.com/content/9/4/R351

Henwood, K. and Pidgeon, N. (1995) 'Grounded theory and psychological research.' *The Psychologist*, March: 115–18.

Hetherington, E.M. and Stanley-Hagan, M. (1999) 'The adjustment of children with divorced parents: a risk and resiliency perspective.' *Journal of Child Psychology and Psychiatry*, 40 (1): 129–140.

Hetherington, E.M., Cox, M. and Cox, R. (1979) 'Play and social interaction in children following divorce.' *Journal of Social Issues*, 35: 26–49.

Hetherington, E.M., Cox, M. and Cox, R. (1985) 'Long-term effects of divorce and remarriage on the adjustment of the children.' *Journal of the American Academy of Child Psychiatry,* 24: 518–30.

Hill, M. (2005) 'Ethical considerations in researching children's experiences.' In S. Greene and D. Hogan (eds), *Researching Children's Experiences: Approaches and Methods.* London: Sage.

Hill, M., Laybourn, A. and Borland, M. (1996) 'Engaging with primary-aged children about their emotions and well-being: methodological considerations.' *Children and Society*, 10: 129–44.

Hinde, R. (1997) *Relationships: A Dialectical Perspective.* Hove, UK: Psychology Press.

Holloway, I. (1997) *Basic Concepts for Qualitative Research.* Oxford: Blackwell.

Hood, S., Kelley, P. and Mayall, B. (1996) 'Children as research subjects: a risky enterprise.' *Children and Society,* 10: 117–28.

House of Lords (1994) *Report of the Select Committee on Medical Ethics: Volume 1.* London: HMSO.

Husson, R.N., Comeau, A. and Hoff, R. (1990) 'Diagnosis of human immunodeficiency virus in infants and children.' *Pediatrics*, 86 (1): 1–9.

International Committee of the Red Cross (1949) *The Geneva Conventions of 12 August 1949.* Geneva: International Committee of the Red Cross.

James, W. (1899) *Talks to teachers on psychology; and to students on some of life's ideals.* London: Longman's, Green and Co.

Jung, C. (1921) *Psychological Types, or the Psychology of Individuation.* New York: Harcourt and Brace.

Katz, J. (1992) 'Abuse of human beings for the sake of science.' In A.L. Caplan (ed.), *When Medicine Went Mad: Bioethics and the Holocaust.* Totowa, NJ: Humana Press.

Kellett, M. (2005) *How to develop children as researchers: a step by step guide to teaching the research process.* London: Paul Chapman.

Kirby, P. (1999) *Listening to Young Children: The Mosaic Approach*. London: Save the Children.

Kor, E.M. (1992) 'Nazi experiments as viewed by a survivor of Mengele's experiments.' In A.L. Caplan (ed.), *When Medicine Went Mad: Bioethics and the Holocaust*. Totowa, NJ: Humana Press.

Koshy, V. (2005) *Action Research for Improving Practice*. London: Sage.

Kulka, R.A. and Weingarten, H. (1979) 'The long-term effects of parental divorce on adult adjustment.' *Journal of Social Issues*, 35: 50–78.

Leavitt, R.L. (1996) 'The emotional culture of infant–toddler day care.' In J.A. Hatch (ed.), *Qualitative Research in Early Childhood Settings*. Westport, CT and London: Praeger.

Lewis, O. (1961) *The Children of Sánchez*. New York: Vintage.

Lewis, A. and Lindsay, G. (2000) *Researching Children's Perspectives: A Psychological Dimension*. Buckingham: Open University Press.

Lewis, V. and Kellett, M. (2005) Disability. In Fraser S., Lewis V., Ding S., Kellett M. and Robinson C. (eds), *Doing Research with Children and Young People*. London: Sage.

MacKay, T. (1987) 'Planning research in child guidance.' *SALGEP Quarterly*, 6 (1): 3–11.

MacKay, T. (1999) 'Can endemic reading failure in socially disadvantaged children be successfully tackled?' *Educational and Child Psychology*, 16 (1): 22–9.

MacKay, T. (2006) *The West Dunbartonshire Literacy Initiative. The Design, Implementation and Evaluation of an Intervention Strategy to Raise Achievement and Eradicate Illiteracy*. Dumbarton: West Dunbartonshire Council (ISBN 0-906938-12-0).

MacKay, T. and Watson, K. (1999) 'Literacy, social disadvantage and early intervention: enhancing reading achievement in primary school.' *Educational and Child Psychology*, 16 (1): 30–6.

Malinowski, B. (1922) *Argonauts of the Western Pacific: An Account of Native Enterprise and Adventure in the Melanesian New Guinea*. New York: Dutton.

Martin, D., Sweeney, J. and Cooke, J. (2005) 'Views of teenage parents on their support housing needs'. *Community Practitioner,*. 78 (11): 392–6

Maslow, A. (1954) *Motivation and Personality*. New York: Harper and Row.

Mayo, E. (1933) *The Human Problems of an Industrial Civilisation*. New York: Macmillan.

McCall, R.B. (1994) 'Commentary.' *Human Development*, 37: 293–8.

Mead, M. (1928) *Coming of Age in Samoa*. New York: Morrow.

Mead, M. and Wolfenstein, J. (1955) *Childhood in Contemporary Cultures*. Chicago: University of Chicago Press.

Meins, E. and Russell, J. (1997) 'Security and symbolic play: the relation between security of attachment and executive capacity.' *British Journal of Developmental Psychology*, 15: 63–76.

Meins, E., Fernyhough, C. and Russell, L. (1998) 'Security of attachment as a predictor of mentalising abilities: a longitudinal study'. *Social Development*, 7: 1–24.

Merriam, S. (ed.) (2002) *Qualitative Research in Practice: Examples for Discussion and Analysis*. San Francisco, CA: Jossey–Bass.

Miller, M.F., Humphrey, J.H., Iliff, P.J., Malaba, L.C., Mbuya, N.V., the ZVITAMSO Study Group and Stoltzfus, R.J. (2006) 'Neonatal erythropoiesis and subsequent anemia in HIV-positive and HIV-negative Zimbabwean babies during the first year of life: a longitudinal study'. *BMC Infectious Diseases* 6 (1) retrieved from www.biomedcentral.com/1471-2334/6/1 (last accessed 30 August 2006).

Minnis, H., Millward, R., Sinclair, C., Kennedy, E., Greig, A., Towlson, K., Read, W., Hill, J. (2006) 'The Computerised McArthur Story Stem Battery – a pilot study of a novel medium for assessing children's representations of relationships.' *International Journal of Methods in Psychiatric Research*, 15 (4).

Morrow, V. (2001) 'Using qualitative methods to elicit young people's perspectives on their environments: some ideas for community health initiatives.' *Health Education Research: Theory and Practice*, 16, 3, 255–268.

Morse, J. (ed.) (1991) *Qualitative Nursing Research: A Contemporary Dialogue.* Newbury Park, CA: Sage.

Morse, M. (1965) *The Unattached.* Harmondsworth: Penguin.

Muller-Hill, B. (1992) 'Eugenics: the science and religion of the Nazis.' In A.L. Caplan (ed.), *When Medicine Went Mad: Bioethics and the Holocaust.* Totowa, NJ: Humana Press.

National Children's Bureau (2003) *Guidelines for Research.* London: NCB.

National Statistics Online 2003 Census (2001) www.statistics.gov.uk/CCI.bet

Newson, J. and Newson, E. (1963) *Patterns of Infant Care in an Urban Community.* Harmondsworth: Penguin.

Nisbet, J. and Entwhistle, N. (1970) *Educational Research Methods.* London: London University Press.

Ó Dochartaigh, N. (2002) *The Internet Research Handbook.* London: Sage.

O'Kane, C. (2000) 'The development of participatory techniques: facilitating children's views about decisions which affect them.' In P. Christensen and A. James (eds), *Research with Children: Perspectives and Practices.* London: Falmer. pp. 134–59.

Panton, J.H. (1945) *Modern Teaching Practice and Technique.* London: Longmans, Green and Co.

Pavlov, I.P. (1927) *Conditioned Reflexes.* Oxford: Oxford University Press.

Petersen, C. and Seligman, M. (2004) *Character Strengths and Virtues: A Handbook and Classification.* Oxford: Oxford University Press.

Piaget, J. (1929/1952) *The Child's Conception of the World.* New York: International University Press.

Piaget, J. (1937/1954) *The Construction of Reality in the Child.* New York: Basic Books.

Piaget, J. (1945/1962) *Play, Dreams and Imitation in Childhood.* New York: W.W. Norton.

Plomin, R., DeFries, J., Craig, I. and McGuffin, P. (eds) (2002) *Behavioural Genetics in the Postgenomic Era.* Washington, DC: APA Books.

Prilleltensky, I. and Nelson, G. (1997) 'Community psychology: reclaiming social justice.' In D. Fox and I. Prilleltensky (eds), *Critical Psychology: An Introduction.* London: Sage. pp. 166–84.

Prose, N. (1990) 'HIV infection in children.' *Journal of the American Academy of Dermatology*, 22: 1223–31.

Prout, A. (2001) 'Representing children: reflections on the 5–16 programme.' *Children and Society*, 15: 193–201.

Prout, A. (2002) 'Researching children as social actors: an introduction to the children 5–16 programme.' *Children in Society*, 16: 67–76.

Punch, S. (2002a) 'Interviewing strategies with young people: the "Secret Box", stimulus and task-based activities.' *Children in Society*, 16: 45–56.

Punch, S. (2002b) 'Research with children: the same or different from research with adults?' *Childhood,* 9 (3): 321–41.

Raban, B., Ure, C. and Waniganayake, M. (2003) 'Multiple perspectives: acknowledging the virtue of complexity in measuring quality.' *Early Years*, 23 (1): 67-77.

Raven, J., Raven, J.C. and Court, J. (1998) *Coloured Progressive Matrices.* (Manual for Raven's Progressive Matrices and Vocabulary Scales, Section 2.) Oxford: Oxford Psychologists Press.

Raven, J., Raven, J.C. and Court, J. (2000) *Standard Progressive Matrices*. (Manual for Raven's Progressive Matrices and Vocabulary Scales, Section 3.) Oxford: Oxford Psychologists Press.

Reason, P. (ed.) (1994) *Participation in Human Enquiry*. London: Sage.

Reder, P. and Lucey, C. (1995) *Assessment of Parenting*. London: Routledge.

Richardson, J. (ed.) (1996) *Handbook of Qualitative Research Methods for Psychology and the Social Sciences*. Leicester: BPS Books.

Robertson, J. and Robertson, J. (1989) *Separation and the Very Young*. London: Free Association Books.

Robson, C. (2002) *Real World Research: A Resource for Social Scientists and Practitioner-Researchers*, 2nd edn. Oxford: Blackwell.

Rodenberg, P. (1993) *The Need for Words: Voice and the Text*. London: Methuen.

Roethlisberger, F. and Dickson, W. (1939) *Management and the Worker*. Cambridge, MA: Harvard University Press.

Rogers, C. (1951) *Client-Centred Therapy: Its Current Practices, Implications and Theory*. Boston, MA: Houghton–Mifflin.

Rutter, M. (1989) 'Isle of Wight revisited: Twenty-five years of child psychiatric epidemiology.' *Journal of the American Academy of Child and Adolescent Psychiatry*, 28: 633–53.

Rutter, M., Graham, P. and Yule, W. (1970) *A neuropsychiatric study in childhood*. London: Spastics International Medical Publication in association with Williams Heinmann Medical Books.

Rutter, M., Graham, P., Chadwick, O. and Yule, W. (1976) 'Adolescent turmoil: fact or fiction?' *Journal of Child Psychology and Psychiatry*, 17: 35–6.

Rutter, M., Maughan, B., Mortimore, P. and Ousten, J. (1979) *Fifteen Thousand Hours: Secondary Schools and their Effects on Children*. London: Open Books.

Rutter, M., Roy, P. and the English and Romanian Adoptees (ERA) Study Team (2004) 'Are there biological programming effects for psychological development? Findings from a study of Romanian adoptees.' *Developmental Psychology*, 40: 81–94.

Samuel, J. and Bryant, P. (1984) 'Asking only one question in the conversation experiment.' *Journal of Child Psychology and Psychiatry*, 25 (2): 315–18.

Schaffer, H.R. (1998) *Making Decisions about Children: Psychological Questions and Answers*, 2nd edn. Oxford: Blackwell.

Segal, N.L. (1992) 'Twin research at Auschwitz–Birkenau.' In A.L. Caplan (ed.), *When Medicine Went Mad: Bioethics and the Holocaust*. Totowa, NJ: Humana Press.

Seidman, I. (1998) *Interviewing as Qualitative Research: a Guide for Researchers in Education and the Social Services*. New York: Teachers College Press.

Seligman, M. (2002) *Authentic Happiness: Using the New Positive Psychology to Realise your Potential for Lasting Fulfilment*. New York: The Free Press.

Seligman, M. and Csikszentmihalyi, M. (2000) 'Positive psychology: an introduction.' *American Psychologist*, 55 (1): 5–14.

Sherman, R. and Webb, R. (1988) *Qualitative Research in Education: Focus and Methods*. London: Routledge Falmer.

Skilbeck, M. (1988) 'Laurence Stenhouse; research methodology', *British Educational Research Journal*, 9 (1): 11–20.

Skinner, B.F. (1938) *The Behavior of Organisms*. New York: Appleton – Century – Croft.

Spence, S. (1995) *Social Skills Training: Enhancing Social Competence with Children and Adolescents*. Windsor: NFER.

Stern, D. (1977) *The First Relationship: Infant and Mother*. London: Fontana/Open Books.

Stine, G.J. (1997) *AIDS Update 1997: An Annual Overview of Acquired Immune Deficiency Syndrome*. Upper Saddle River, NJ: Prentice Hall.

Storr, A. (1964) *Sexual Deviation*. Harmondsworth: Penguin.

Sylva, K., Roy, C. and Painter, M. (1980) *Childwatching at Playgroup and Nursery School: Oxford Pre-School Project Grant*. London: McIntyre.

Taylor, J. (2003) *Study Skills in Health Care*. London: Nelson Thornes.

Taylor, J. (2005) 'Perspectives on early childhood research.' In J. Taylor and M. Woods (eds), *Early Childhood Studies: An Holistic Introduction,*' 2nd edn. London: Edward Arnold.

Taylor, J. and Müller, D. (1995) *Nursing Adolescents: Research and Psychological Perspectives*. Oxford: Blackwell Science.

Taylor, J. and Thurtle, V. (2005) 'Child health.' In Taylor J. and Woods M. (eds), *Early Childhood Studies: An Holistic Introduction*, 2nd edn. London: Edward Arnold.

Taylor, J. and Woods, M. (eds) (2005) *Early Childhood Studies: An Holistic Introduction*, 2nd edn. London: Hodder Arnold.

Thorndike, E. L. (1905) *The Elements of Psychology*. New York: Seiler.

UNICEF (1959) 'Universal Declaration of the Rights of the Child'. New York: UNICEF.

UNICEF (1989) 'The Convention on the Rights of the child.' www. unicef.org/crc/convention.htm.

UNICEF (2002) Children Participating in Research, Monitoring and Evaluation (M & E) – Ethics and Your Responsibility as a Manager. Geneva: UNICEF.

Vigorito, S.S. (1992) 'A profile of Nazi medicine.' In A.L. Caplan (ed.), *When Medicine Went Mad: Bioethics and the Holocaust*. Totowa, NJ: Humana Press.

Vygotsky, L.S. (1978) *Mind in Society: The Development of Higher Mental Processes*. Cambridge, MA: Harvard University Press.

Watson, J.B. (1913) 'Psychology as the behaviourist views it', *Psychological Review*, 20: 158–177.

Watson, J.B. (1930) *Behaviourism*. New York: W.W. Norton.

Wechsler, D. (2004) *The Wechsler Intelligence Scale for Children, Fourth Revision (WISC IV)*. San Antonlo, TX: The Psychological Corporation.

Wertsch, J.V. and Hickman, M. (1987) 'Problem solving in social interaction: a microgenetic analysis.' In M. Hickman (ed.), *Social and Functional Approaches to Language and Thought*. New York: Academic Press. pp. 251–66.

West, P., Sweeting, H., Der, G., Barton, J., and Lucas, C. (2003) 'Voice-DISC identified DSM-IV disorders among 15 year olds in the West of Scotland', *Journal of the American Academy of Child and Adolescent Psychiatry,* 42 (8): 115–128.

Whiting, B. (1963) *Six Cultures: Studies of Child Rearing*. New York: Wiley.

Whiting, B. and Edwards, C. (1988) *Children of Different Worlds*. Cambridge, MA: Harvard University Press.

Whiting, B. and Whiting, J. (1975) *Children of six Cultures*. Cambridge, MA: Harvard University Press.

Willig, C. (2001) *Introducing Qualitative Research in Psychology: Adventures in Theory and Method*. Buckingham: Open University Press.

Wink, J. (2004) *Critical Pedagogy: Notes from the Real World*. Harlow: Allyn and Bacon.

Woods, M. (2005) 'Early childhood studies: first principles'. In J. Taylor and M. Woods (eds), *Early Childhood Studies: An Holistic Introduction,* 2nd edn. London: Edward Arnold.

World Health Organisation (1951) Expert Committee on Mental Health, Report on the Second Session 1951. *Technical Report Series No. 31*. Geneva: WHO.

World Health Organisation (2004) *World Medical Association 2004 Declaration of Helsinki*.

Yin, R.K. (2003) *Case Study: Design and Methods*, 3rd edn. London: Sage.

Author Index

Subject Index